England's Maritime Heritage from the Air

England's Maritime Heritage from the Air

Peter Waller

 Historic England

Published by Historic England, The Engine House, Fire Fly Avenue, Swindon SN2 2EH
www.HistoricEngland.org.uk

Historic England is a Government service championing England's heritage and giving expert, constructive advice.

Images © Historic England Archive, Aerofilms Collection. The Aerofilms Collection was acquired by English Heritage (now Historic England) in 2007 and has been digitised and made available on the *Britain from Above* website at www.britainfromabove.org.uk/.

First published 2017

ISBN 978-1-84802-298-0

British Library Cataloguing in Publication data
A CIP catalogue record for this book is available from the British Library.

The right of Peter Waller to be identified as author of this work has been asserted by him in accordance with the Copyright, Designs and Patents Act 1988

Historic England holds an unparalleled archive of 12 million photographs, drawings, reports and publications on England's places. It is one of the largest archives in the UK, the biggest dedicated to the historic environment, and a priceless resource for anyone interested in England's buildings, archaeology, landscape and social history. Viewed collectively, its photographic collections document the changing face of England from the 1850s to the present day. It is a treasure trove that helps us understand and interpret the past, informs the present and assists with future management and appreciation of the historic environment.

For more information about images from the Archive, contact Archives Services Team, Historic England, The Engine House, Fire Fly Avenue, Swindon SN2 2EH; telephone (01793) 414600.

Brought to publication by Sarah Enticknap, Publishing, Historic England.

Typeset in Source Sans Pro 9/12pt

Edited by Karen Rigden
Page layout by Hybert Design

Printed in the UK by Gomer Press.

Front cover: EAQ110579 Pool of London
Frontispiece: EAW033408 Eastern Docks, Southampton
Back cover: EPW042128 Morecombe

Contents

Preface

The genesis of this book was the result of a chance conversation that I had with Robin Taylor at the book launch of Steven Brindle's history of Paddington station – held, appropriately, within that superb building in 2013. In many ways, however, its conception can be said to have its roots almost a quarter of a century ago in the ongoing relationship that developed between the Aerofilms company, when it was still a subsidiary of Hunting Group and was still based at its long-term home at Gate Studios in Elstree, and my then employers, Ian Allan Ltd.

Ian Allan's Director of Publishing at the time, Simon Forty, developed with Peter O'Connell of Aerofilms the idea of a series of walking guides based upon original aerial photography converted into linear maps to explore some of Britain's most important long distance walks. Today, such a project through the use of digital photography and computer-based design software would be easy; then it was a case of creating photographic mosaics with physical overlays to add relevant detailing – all resulting in a complex package of film-work (no computer to plate technology available in those days) that had to be dispatched to the printers.

Through the conversations that occurred during the development of these books, it became clear that Aerofilms possessed an archive rich in material to interest those with a variety of specialist interests. This resulted in the publication of a range of books on sport and leisure, most notably the annual *Guide to Football Grounds* that went through 18 editions until publication ceased in 2012. This relationship survived through the changing ownership of Aerofilms, via Simmons and Blom, until the archive was split from the ongoing business of aerial surveying.

In addition to the walking guides and the books on sport, Ian Allan Ltd undertook the publication of a number of books drawing upon Aerofilms' remarkable collection of railway views. Some of these were combined with specially commissioned new photography to provide a 'then and now' approach to the subject. Over more than a decade Ian Allan Ltd produced a number of large-format volumes devoted to the great range of railway scenes available from the archive. Although not carrying my name as author, I undertook the research into the archive and wrote the captions in my role as Publishing Manager and then Publisher (Books) at Ian Allan Ltd.

Over the decade, I spent many days at Elstree and then Potters Bar, where the company was based following its initial move from Elstree, searching through the large collection of albums in which the reference prints were stored. There was often a sense of frustration that the company's photographers would insist, for example, on photographing notable buildings, such as cathedrals, on a virtually annual basis while, had the cameras been turned round 180 degrees, there was much of interest – sadly unrecorded – going on behind the photographers. Lateral thinking – such as the knowledge that a football ground was located close to the city's gas works – sometimes unearthed some gems, as did an almost uncanny ability on the part of those cataloguing the images to misidentify locations. Just as you'd be giving up the search for a specific facet of railway history in the area in which it was supposed to be you'd find it misidentified elsewhere.

Inevitably, during the research involved with these books, I got to know those who worked within the archive at Aerofilms very well; they were all great to work with and had a knowledge and enthusiasm for the archive that made nothing too much trouble. It was during these sessions that ideas for further books would be discussed, often sparked off by what I'd seen during the course of that day's research. It was during one of these discussions that the idea of a volume devoted to the maritime images held by the archive first emerged.

Sadly, with the sale of the company to Simmons initially and then to Blom, it seemed to me as an outsider that with both new owners – with their emphasis on the commercially attractive aerial surveying business – the archive was being neglected. Talking to the staff it became evident that relocation of functions away from Potters Bar had resulted in the archive effectively being the sole occupant of the site and the income being generated was not sufficient to justify its retention. The closure and subsequent disposal of the archive thus came as no surprise; the acquisition of part of the collection by English Heritage and its subsequent transfer to Historic England has allowed this project finally to come to fruition.

Acknowledgements

Over the years, I've been fortunate to work with a number of people from the Aerofilms company; in particular, I'd like to thank Elaine Amos with whom I developed the original concept for this book many years ago. Steven Brindle very kindly invited me to the launch of his history of Paddington station and it was there that the germ of the idea was first discussed with English Heritage. From English Heritage – now Historic England – Publishing I'd like to thank in particular Robin Taylor, who saw the book through the commissioning process and arranged for me to have access to the files of prints now held at Swindon, John Hudson, Head of Publishing, Sarah Enticknap, the project manager, and Clare Blick, the publicity manager. The PR for the book was expertly handled by Rachel Kennedy. The book was copy edited by Karen Rigden, to whom I am grateful for her professionalism in working with my manuscript. I'd also like to thank my good friend Gavin Watson for reading through the proofs and making comment upon them. A book of this nature inevitably draws upon a wide range of sources; the majority of published works used are cited in the bibliography, but there were three websites that proved immensely useful in the validation of dates and of engineers as well as detailing the status of listed buildings; these are www.engineering-timelines.com, www.gracesguide.co.uk and historicengland.org.uk/listing/the-list/. In researching the book, it became evident that in a number of cases contradictory dates could and did exist. I hope that I've exercised due care in trying to be as exact as possible; if there are errors, please write to me c/o of the publisher. Needless to say, in the event of any mistakes, these are entirely my responsibility.

Abbreviations

ABP	Associated British Ports Holdings Ltd
APCM	Associated Portland Cement Manufacturers Ltd
BOAC	British Overseas Airways Corporation
BP	British Petroleum
BTC	British Transport Commission
BTDB	British Transport Docks Board
DFDS	Det Forenede Dampskibs-Selskab (*The United Steamship Company [Danish]*)
EU	European Union
C&WR	Canterbury & Whitstable Railway
CEGB	Central Electricity Generating Board
GCR	Great Central Railway
grt	Gross Registered Tonnage
GWR	Great Western Railway
HMS	His/Her Majesty's Ship
HMY	His/Her Majesty's Yacht
LBSCR	London Brighton & South Coast Railway
LSWR	London & South Western Railway
LT&SR	London, Tilbury & Southend Railway
L&YR	Lancashire & Yorkshire Railway
LB&SCR	London, Brighton & South Coast Railway
LDDC	London Docklands Development Corporation
LMS	London, Midland & Scottish Railway
LNER	London & North Eastern Railway
LNWR	London & North Western Railway
LSWR	London & South Western Railway
MDHB	Mersey Docks & Harbour Board
MR	Midland Railway
MS&LR	Manchester, Sheffield & Lincolnshire Railway
MV	Motor Vessel
P&O	Peninsular & Oriental Steam Navigation Co
PLA	Port of London Authority
PS	Paddle Steamer
RFA	Royal Fleet Auxiliary
RMS	Royal Mail Ship
RN	Royal Navy
RNAS	Royal Naval Air Station
RNLI	Royal National Lifeboat Institution
RNTE	Royal Naval Training Establishment
RNVR	Royal Naval Volunteer Reserve
SER	South Eastern Railway
SNCF	Société Nationale des Chemins de fer Français
SR	Southern Railway
SS	Steam Ship
TS	Training Ship
TSS	Turbine Steam Ship
UDC	Urban District Council
UNESCO	United Nations Educational, Scientific and Cultural Organisation

Introduction

This royal throne of kings, this scepter'd isle,
This earth of majesty, this seat of Mars,
This other Eden, demi-paradise,
This fortress built by Nature for herself
Against infection and the hand of war,
This happy breed of men, this little world,
This precious stone set in the silver sea,
Which serves it in the office of a wall,
Or as a moat defensive to a house,
Against the envy of less happy lands,
This blessed plot, this earth, this realm, this England.

So wrote William Shakespeare in his play *King Richard II* (Act 2 Scene 1). There is perhaps no greater literary tribute to England and its relationship with the sea. Implicit within it is the strength that England has gained from its ability to retreat, when necessary, behind the defensive shield that being an island nation offers.

As an island nation England, and later the United Kingdom, has seen the sea as a natural first line of defence against foreign invasion.

From the loss of the land bridge to continental Europe after the last Ice Age through to the opening of the Channel Tunnel in 1994, the sea represented the only route by which Britain could be reached. Successive waves of invaders, from the Celts onwards, migrated to Britain and many of today's coastal settlements and port towns owe their origins to these early lines of communication. Archaeological evidence – for example, the carefully carved ornamental mace head discovered at Knowth in Ireland believed to have been made in England in *c* 3,000 BCE – suggests that even in the late Stone Age patterns of trade existed. Settlement of Britain's interior followed the river courses and these

rivers provided a connection through to the trading posts on the coast.

Although these early trading settlements were probably largely based around the beaching of ships, there is evidence of the construction of early quays in wood; this became more pronounced following the Roman invasion and settlement. Evidence of quays has been found in the Thames, to supply the military that defended London, and on the Tyne, the route by which the garrison defending Hadrian's Wall was replenished and supplied.

From the Norman conquest until the 18th century, the focus of England's trade was with Europe; until the loss of the last of England's French possessions – most famously Calais in 1558 – the ports of the south coast were part of the essential chain that linked the kingdom of England with its monarchs' possessions in France. The importance of the Cinque Ports – Hastings, Dover, Hythe, Romney and Sandwich, plus the ancient towns of Rye and Winchelsea – was a reflection of this strategic and commercial connection. The role of Lord Warden of the Cinque Ports, still today an important ceremonial position, was an essential one in the defence of the country. The dominance of the Hanseatic League from the 15th century onwards saw the rise in importance of the docks in places such as Boston and King's Lynn.

England's focus shifted from the 16th century, however, and this was to impact on the history of port development in the country. The traditional major harbours, focused on the European trade, declined in relative importance, to be replaced by the expansion of ports such as Bristol and Liverpool. There were several factors behind this shift: the development of

the transatlantic trade following the first sighting of the future Newfoundland at the end of the 15th century; the hostility of much of Catholic Europe to England following Henry VIII's break with Rome and the threat posed to Elizabeth I later in the 16th century; the growth of Britain's colonial empire in North America and the Caribbean; and the development of trade with India and the East Indies. London, however, remained the pre-eminent port; its role as the nation's capital and major mercantile centre ensured that, through the creation of monopolistic companies through Royal Charter (such as the East India Company), the Thames with its riverside wharves and quays was the route through which much of Britain's trade flowed.

Although there had been the construction of quays and wharves earlier, it was not until the end of the 17th century that the first wet docks began to emerge. These, with their locks, permitted a constant water level to be maintained and thus eased the handling of goods to and from the quays. The development of improved facilities continued through the 18th century, but it was the Industrial Revolution and Britain's role as the 'Workshop of the World' from the end of that century and the first half of the 19th that witnessed a massive investment in dock facilities. The needs of industry, through the importation of raw materials such as cotton, and the growing population, with the country increasingly reliant upon imported foodstuffs, meant that new wet docks were constructed the length and breadth of the country. The new wet docks had additional advantages; they could, for example, be made secure, through the construction of surrounding walls, thereby reducing the potential of theft through pilferage that occurred when transhipping goods from larger vessels to lighters for movement upstream.

The process of dock construction continued through the 19th century as the size of ships increased; older wet docks, such as those at Bristol, became less significant as newer – and larger – docks were completed downstream. The inexorable increase in the size of vessels and in the changing nature of the cargo carried have resulted in the development of new facilities over the past 20 years and this trend seems to be unremitting. Felixstowe is a product of this; a port that was relatively insignificant in the early 1960s has grown exponentially to cater for the ever-increasing number and size of container vessels, and the plans for the new London Gateway at Thames Haven – on the site of the former Shell refinery – demonstrate that demand for suitable port facilities seems destined to increase for the foreseeable future.

The evolution in the importance of individual docks and ports has continued through the past century; most conspicuously as the size of vessel has increased and as the trend towards containerisation has continued, the traditional wet docks have declined, resulting in dereliction and high levels of unemployment. The rise of the container began in the early 1960s and it was from this period that, however much investment went into the traditional dock-handling facilities, there was an inexorable decline in trade in the conventional way. The old docks in Liverpool are now but a poor shadow of their historical scale, but trade continues to flow through Liverpool, now handled by the container port at Seaforth. The same is true of London, where Tilbury has come to dominate while the upstream wet docks have now all ceased to handle commercial traffic. Ports like Felixstowe have emerged as major new facilities, while other ports, such as Southampton, continue to expand their container-handling facilities.

The challenge facing society as these old ports declined was how to find new employment for the displaced dockworkers and new uses for the vast estates of land released as the old dock closed. The regeneration of the traditional docklands in London has seen the historic landscape radically altered; wet docks have been infilled and vast new commercial and residential developments have appeared. There are, however, elements of the traditional dockside heritage that survive: the occasional warehouse or lock gate, for example.

The docks – both large and small – were more than simply a means by which goods could be transhipped; there was a whole support industry that grew up around them. In the age of sail, rope, for example, was essential and ropewalks, with their long buildings, were a facet of most harbours. Fishing ports required markets through which the catch could be quickly sold and dispatched to customers. The whaling industry, with ships sailing from ports such as London and Whitby, required plants that could convert the blubber into oil. As these trades ebbed and flowed, so the shore-based infrastructure to serve them also evolved.

Another industry that was to be a feature of many docks and ports was shipbuilding. As the size of wooden vessels increased from the late Middles Ages, specialist facilities grew up. This process accelerated from the late 18th century as the size of the Royal Navy and the growth of Britain's mercantile trade – which was strictly controlled by the various Navigation Acts from the late 17th century until their repeal in 1849 – meant that significant investment went into the construction of graving docks capable of accommodating the construction of ships. With the arrival of iron and steam in the early 19th century, this process was

further accelerated and shipbuilding became a major industry on rivers such as the Tyne and the Wear and at ports such as Birkenhead and Barrow-in-Furness. The modern naval dockyards – Chatham, Plymouth and Portsmouth – were also to build significant numbers of vessels.

Shipbuilding remained a major industry until the 1980s; however, most of the famous yards that once existed, such as Swan Hunter on the Tyne, are now history, the victims of the decline of Britain's mercantile dominance, the reduction in the size of the Royal Navy and the rise of Far Eastern shipbuilders. Even the naval dockyards are no longer building ships. The last – at Portsmouth (controlled by BAE Systems) – closed in 2015 with future surface warship construction destined largely for the remaining shipbuilders on the River Clyde. There are survivors, however, with Barrow-in-Furness receiving major investment to facilitate the next generation of the Royal Navy's nuclear submarines.

Allied to the shipbuilding industry are ship repair yards and ship breakers. Most wet docks constructed included at least one graving – or dry – dock primarily for the purposes of repairing ships and most vessels – both wooden- and metal-hulled – required regular dry docking for maintenance. This process is still an essential – and expensive – feature of modern docks and ports; while the shipbuilding industry may have declined, ship repair work is still a significant employer in many of the country's major ports. Ships can, and if well maintained do, operate for many years; however, the vast majority will reach the end of their economic lives at some stage, and the ship breaking industry has been a feature of many ports over the years. At the end of both world wars, for example, the end of hostilities resulted in a significant number of warships being redundant and thus disposed of. Again, with the exception of a number of specialist yards, this is a trade that has largely been transferred abroad, with ships now heading to breakers yards in Turkey or to the beaches of the Indian subcontinent.

The sea also provided a rich harvest in the form of fish and seafood. There is evidence from early historical graves that fish provided a significant part of the diet. By the time of the Norman conquest and certainly by the 13th century, freshwater fish were being cultivated with manors and monasteries having ponds in which the fish were grown and there are a number of place names – most notably incorporating 'Fishponds' – that reflect this. Saltwater fish, such as herring, and mammals, like porpoises, were also caught but through much of this period fish was predominantly a high-status food, costly to acquire and difficult to transport. For the population, fish also had religious importance: for a predominantly Christian country, as England was, meat was not to be consumed on Fridays and certain holy days but fish was permitted.

By the Middle Ages, fishing ports on the coast were putting ships to sea in significant numbers and new types of fish were being landed. The opening up, for example, of the fisheries around Newfoundland from the end of the 15th century resulted in what Mark Kurlansky in his history of the species called the 'Cod Rush'. Improved methods of salting and better means of transport meant that saltwater fish could be sold more widely but, as with other factors, it was the massive population growth of the late 18th and early 19th centuries that encouraged the considerable expansion of the fishing industry during this period. New fishing docks were established and, with the arrival of the railway and the later development of refrigeration, it was increasingly possible to transport fresh fish over much greater distances.

Until comparatively recently, fish used to be marketed on the slogan that there were plenty more in the sea. Over more recent years, however, the realisation that overfishing and other factors have resulted in a decline in the catch has led to the gradual disappearance of many of the traditional fisheries. The world wars allowed for herring stocks to recover – it was difficult to follow the shoals down the North Sea when it was a war zone – but by the early 1960s the trade had all but disappeared. In the South West the traditional catch was the pilchard, but these stocks were almost exhausted by the middle of the 20th century. North Sea cod was exhausted and the fishing grounds off Iceland were also to become out of bounds as Britain and Iceland squared up over the Cod Wars as the latter sought to extend its territorial waters and exclude fishermen from Britain. The once massive trawler fleets of places such as Grimsby are now much reduced. There is evidence, however, that the adoption of sustainable limits has resulted in the gradual recovery of stocks; while it is unlikely that fishing will ever return to the scale of the 1960s and earlier, it does look as though the trade does have a future. There is plenty of fish in the sea; it just needs to be caught in a sustainable way and the stocks properly managed.

With the growth of air transport from 1945 onwards, allied to the opening of the Channel Tunnel in 1994, the sea is now no longer as essential a link between the UK and the world beyond the British Isles as it once was. But that is a relatively late change in the history of the country; historically, it was by ship that travellers made their way to and from the country and, during the 19th and 20th centuries, considerable investment went into providing the facilities that these travellers required. Ferry terminals became a feature of many of England's most important ports. These were not required solely for international travel; crossings of many of the major rivers – such as the Humber and the Mersey – were, or are, dependent upon ferry services. With the opening of the Channel Tunnel there was a perception that this might mean that the traditional cross-Channel ferries would decline; in fact the reverse has happened. The growth in demand for both private and commercial traffic across the Channel is such that Dover is continuing to expand its ferry facilities to accommodate this growth.

Just as the sea provided England with its route to trade, it also provided the country with its first line of defence against its continental enemies. The first attempts to capitalise on this were before the Norman conquest of 1066 but it was not until the Middle Ages that the concept developed into a more formalised navy and it was the 16th century and the reign of King Henry VIII that saw the Royal Navy – the 'Senior Service' – emerge as a significant force. With the French and then the Dutch being the threat, naval dockyards were established on the River Thames at Deptford and Woolwich – both long closed before the era of aerial photography – as well as on the Medway and at Portsmouth. When the country's strategic focus shifted towards the Empire and the protection of trade worldwide, so the focus of the Royal Navy shifted increasingly to Portsmouth and Plymouth. As the size of the fleet grew during the 19th and early 20th centuries, the naval facilities at dockyards such as Chatham and Sheerness, were also expanded.

Since World War II, however, the Royal Navy has undergone a considerable retrenchment, with the fleet much reduced – replicating, perhaps, the decline of the country as a world power with the gradual retreat from Empire – and thus its requirements for bases. Chatham and Sheerness have both ceased to accommodate the navy, while Portsmouth and Devonport have also been reduced in scale. With their histories, these naval dockyards have some of the most significant maritime heritage extant and the challenge, with the decline of the navy, has been to try and secure the future of this.

Despite the size of the Aerofilms archive, relatively few images, however, actually portray the naval dockyards and other facilities operated by the Royal Navy. For reasons of security, aerial photography was restricted; even in the late 1980s, the staff at Aerofilms was still doctoring images to remove sites of strategic or military importance. The importance of the Royal Navy to England's maritime heritage cannot be overstated, however, and the archive does include a range of images that does portray aspects of the Royal Navy – warships, buildings and other facilities – over more than 90 years.

Through much of history and as reflected in this book, the sea has represented a fundamental element in England's trading relationship both domestically and internationally. From the mid-18th century onwards, however, there was a new strand in the use of the coast: the rise of the leisure industry. The supposed health-giving benefit of sea bathing resulted in the development of seaside resorts, such as Brighton, where, initially, the well-heeled were encouraged to partake of sea bathing.

Industrialisation and urbanisation – the twin consequences of the Industrial Revolution – resulted in the growth of major conurbations, such as the West Riding of Yorkshire and south Lancashire. Historically, there had been the tradition of Wakes holidays linked to festivities associated with the patron saint of the local parish church. With the growth of the industrialised society, these celebrations became adapted into regular summer holidays, with individual towns and cities opting for specific weeks when all the factories and mines closed. These holidays were unpaid and permitted routine maintenance to be undertaken on the factories and mines concerned.

From the mid-19th century, the development of the railway network linking the industrial centres to the developing resorts permitted the vast numbers of workers from these new industrial centres to reach the seaside quickly and cheaply. In 1860, for example, 23,000 people made the journey from Oldham to the coast during that town's Wakes Week.

The concept of regular breaks was further enshrined by the Bank Holidays Act of 1871. This designated four new Bank Holidays in England – Easter Monday, Whit Monday, the first Monday in August and Boxing Day. Good Friday and Christmas Day, being traditional days of rest for religious purposes, were already deemed to be holidays. These additional days were influential in developing the concept of the day trip; the long weekend break was still to come as, for most workers, Saturday was still a working day and Sunday was set aside for religious observation.

The consequence of this was that resorts such as Blackpool and Scarborough grew to cater for this new

trade and means of mass entertainment had to be provided. The 19th century witnessed an explosion in the construction of seaside piers, often with theatres or other entertainment. A further form of entertainment came with the use of steamers, often sailing from the new piers, that offered pleasure cruises along the coast.

It must be borne in mind, however, that the majority of these holidays represented unpaid leave for the workers involved; it was not until the Holidays with Pay Act 1938 that those workers whose minimum rates of wages were fixed by trade boards were given the right to one week's holiday per year. This was the first law on paid leave in the United Kingdom, but it fell short of the two weeks demanded by the trade unions and did not cover all workers. The onset of war in September 1939 meant that many of the benefits of this reform were not felt until the post-war years.

One of the most dramatic aspects of the changing face of England's traditional docks is how far they have come to be dominated by the rise of the leisure industry. Increasing wealth and leisure time, allied to longer life expectancy with good pensions, have resulted in the boom in sailing as a recreational activity and the vast number of marinas constructed over the past 30 years has been remarkable. Many of the once thriving traditional ports now have a buzz that results from yachts and other leisure craft.

If recreational sailing has been a saviour to the economy of many traditional ports, the decline of the seaside holiday, in favour of package tours to guaranteed sunshine abroad, has been a death knell to many seaside resorts and has led to the decline and disappearance of many of the once-proud seaside piers;

the tragedy of Brighton West is not unique – it has been replicated at resorts across the nation.

For the most part Britain's relationship with the sea is relatively harmonious but, even when it's at its most benign, the sea can still be dangerous. Over the years there have been notable storms that have led to major loss of life both among seafarers as well as those on land. On 30 January 1607 a tidal surge – now possibly described as a tsunami – affected the Bristol Channel. Although the Welsh coast was more severely affected, destruction was also inflicted in England, with the Somerset Levels under water and some 30 villages in the county affected. On 7 December 1703, the southern half of England was battered by a great storm. Again the Somerset Levels were severely affected, with hundreds being drowned, while ships were wrecked on the Thames and, at sea, the Goodwin Sands claimed a number of Royal Navy ships and the lives of almost 1,500 sailors. Among other casualties was the first Eddystone Lighthouse, which disappeared in the storm along with its builder Henry Winstanley. Daniel Defoe, author of *Robinson Crusoe*, commented of the storm: 'No pen could describe it, nor tongue express it, nor thought conceive it unless by one in the extremity of it.' In February 1953, a storm surge in the North Sea combined with high spring tides resulted in major destruction along the coast of East Anglia and the Thames estuary.

That the sea remains a potent force was demonstrated again in the spring of 2014 with the serious damage wrought to the railway line along the Dawlish sea wall and, as sea levels rise, the threat of coastal erosion becomes ever greater. Although strenuous efforts are made to protect the coast, particularly where there are major centres of population, the sheer cost of erecting and maintaining these defences now means that it is no longer possible to defend the entire coastline. There is nothing new in this; the coast of the East Riding of Yorkshire has been retreating for millennia, while Spurn Head, the famous spit that forms the northern part of the Humber estuary, has remade itself regularly. The impact of coastal erosion is also evident on the coast of East Anglia, where the village of Happisburgh regularly features in reports as more buildings gradually succumb to the power of the sea while the port and town of Dunwich, once one of the most important in the realm, largely disappeared under the waves in the Middle Ages.

The following 150 images demonstrate various aspects of England's maritime heritage: the history, the buildings, the famous ships and the changing nature of commerce over the past 100 years. The Aerofilms collection represents a fascinating archive of a lost England; through the photographs it is possible to see graphically how the landscape of places such as London and Liverpool came to be dominated by the great ports and how, as commerce has changed, the land use has radically altered.

Royal Harbour, Ramsgate
February 1920

One of the earliest images within the Aerofilms collection to feature a harbour, this scene records the Royal Harbour, Ramsgate, in early 1920. The harbour was granted the right to be called 'Royal' in September 1821 in recognition of the hospitality shown to King George IV by the residents of the town when he used the harbour to depart from and arrive back on a trip to Hanover. Construction of the harbour at Ramsgate was started in 1749, although plans had been formulated earlier in response to the great storm of 1703. Proposals for the development at Ramsgate had been opposed by Sandwich and it was not until 18 February 1749 that an Act permitting construction was passed. Construction was not straightforward, however, as the new harbour became prone to silting and it was only the involvement of the great John Smeaton (1724–92) that resulted in the problem being resolved. Smeaton adopted a method of sluice gates and channels that used the power of the water released to cleanse the silt from the inner harbour.

Completed just after Smeaton's death, but pre-dating the harbours at both Dover and Folkestone, Ramsgate harbour was to play a major role during the French Revolutionary and Napoleonic wars between 1792 and 1815 as the major port of embarkation for British soldiers heading to Europe. During the 19th century, the harbour's importance was largely one linked to the fishing industry, a role that subsisted through to the early decades of the 20th century and evinced in this view of the Royal Harbour.

Taken looking towards the north, the view portrays, on the extreme right, the area adjacent to the Clock House designed by John Shaw (1776–1832) who also designed the obelisk to mark George IV's visit in 1821, the lighthouse and the steps of Jacob's Ladder. In this work, he was assisted by his son, also called John (1803–70). The Clock House, home of the Ramsgate meridian (five minutes 41 seconds ahead of Greenwich), is now a museum; the museum's exhibits include *Sundowner*, one of the little ships that played an essential role in Operation Dynamo – the successful evacuation of the British army from Dunkirk in 1940, an operation that was launched from Ramsgate and which resulted in 40,000 of the rescued soldiers passing through the port (more than 10 per cent of the total).

EPW000091

While the development of the docks at Liverpool, visible across the River Mersey to the north, was predominantly along the bank of the river, in Birkenhead the docks grew up through the conversion of an inlet – the Wallasey Pool. This view sees, in the foreground, the West Float with its graving docks. Beyond is the East Float and, between the East Float and river itself, is Alfred Dock. To the south of Alfred Dock is Vittorio Dock. Also visible, between Alfred Dock and the river, are Wallasey, Egerton and Morpeth docks.

The first phase of the construction of the docks at Birkenhead was at the eastern end of the pool. Work on Egerton Dock commenced in 1844. It was named after Sir Philip de Malpas Grey Egerton, who laid the foundation stone; it opened three years later. Construction of Morpeth Dock was concurrent with Egerton; also opening in 1847, it was named after Lord Morpeth, 7th Earl of Carlisle. Both of these docks were designed by James Meadows Rendel (1799–1856); the latter was modified by John Bernard Hartley (1814–69), the son of Jesse Hartley, in 1868. As can be seen in the view, Morpeth Dock was provided with an entrance to the river. Also served by the East Float was Wallasey Dock; this was completed in 1877 and occupied the site of the earlier Great Low Water Basin.

The development of the East and West floats was also originally planned by Rendel in 1844 but the financial problems of the Birkenhead Dock Co delayed construction until 1851; work was still in progress when, in 1858, ownership of Birkenhead Docks passed to the Mersey Docks & Harbour Board. The new docks opened in 1860. In all, the West and East floats encompassed some 45ha of water and offered 6.5km of quays.

Alfred Dock was completed in 1866 and was opened formally by Prince Alfred, Duke of Edinburgh; originally, it was provided with three locks connecting it to the river and three channels through to East Float. However, these were replaced by the two larger locks visible in the 1980 view in 1929 and by the two channels with their bascule bridges.

The last dock in this view to be constructed was the Vittoria; this was designed by Arthur George Lyster (1852–1920), the second son of George Fosbery Lyster (1821–99) who had done much to expand Liverpool's docks in the late 19th century. The son was appointed Acting Engineer-in-Chief to the MDHB in 1890, and was appointed to the substantive post in 1898, holding it until 1913. During the construction of the new dock, on 6 March 1909, a dam collapsed killing 14 navvies; the completed dock opened later that year. The derivation of the name is uncertain although it is generally believed to have been named after the Battle of Vittorio (21 June 1813).

To the west of the West Float (and out of this view), the final part of the tidal pool was converted into a new dock. Planned in the late 1920s, the new dock – initially known as the West Float extension and later as Bidston Dock – was opened in March 1933. Although it was anticipated that the new dock would comprise a basin plus four branches, only part of the basin was completed. The primary traffic was iron ore for the steelworks at Shotton. Much of the trade through Bidston Dock had ceased by the 1990s and the dock was largely infilled in 2003.

Since 1980, much has changed. At the eastern end, Morpeth Dock has lost its entrance to the river and has been partially infilled. Egerton Dock has lost its connection through to the East Float, effectively rendering it and the remains of Morpeth Dock landlocked. The remains of both are listed as Grade II. Between the two docks is Egerton Bridge; this bascule bridge was constructed between 1928 and 1931 to replace an earlier structure. This was fully restored in 1993. Wallasey Dock was infilled in 2001 to provide additional parking space for the new Twelve Quays roll-on/roll-off ferry terminal.

Situated at the eastern extremity of the East Float, the 1863-built central hydraulic tower and engine house still stands. This was designed by Jesse Hartley and was based upon the Palazzo Vecchio in Florence. The 35m-high tower was damaged during World War II and not completely restored. At the time of writing, the building was in a very poor condition although Peel Holdings has plans for its reuse. Of the two river entrances that once served Alfred Dock, the southern was closed in the 1980s and infilled, leaving the northern one to serve the dock; the bascule bridge still exists over the dock access, although that over the southern entrance has been replaced by a fixed link. To the west, two of the three graving docks were infilled as well (during the 1980s), although the third remains extant. Across from the single-storey warehouses standing between Vittoria Dock and the East Float (which still survive), two of the massive grain warehouses built in the early 20th century (when Birkenhead Docks represented a major milling centre) still exist and have been converted into apartments. Much of the rest of the scene in 1980, particularly in the foreground, is now largely derelict although there remains some commercial traffic.

EAW398267

Bristol, dating back to the 13th century, was one of the most important ports in the country. By the 15th century, ships from Bristol were travelling widely to Iceland, and in 1497 John Cabot (Giovanni Caboto; c 1450–98) sailed from Bristol, leading to the European discovery of Newfoundland and the north-eastern seaboard of North America. In the 18th century Bristol grew rich on the slave trade and the growing trading connections in the Americas and Africa. However, Bristol's docks were situated 10km inland, which severely constrained the size of ship that could reach the docks, allowing Liverpool's docks to gain a competitive edge. In response, in 1802, William Jessop (1745–1814) proposed a scheme to install a dam and lock to create a new wet dock.

Work commenced in May 1804, and included a tidal cut of the River Frome from Netham to Hotwells and the construction of the Cumberland Basin with its two locks on to the River Avon and the Junction Lock at the eastern end into the historic channel of the River Frome. The new facility opened on 1 May 1809.

This view is towards the north-west across the Underfall Yard, with the timber yards of Canada and Baltic wharves in the centre and Cumberland Wharf and Hotwells Dockyard in the distance. In the foreground is the New Cut of the River Frome, completed in 1809 as part of the creation of the Floating Harbour (so named because the water level allows vessels to remain afloat irrespective of the state of tide). The original Junction Lock was replaced in the 1860s by that seen on the north side; the original lock remained but was blocked off at its western end.

To the east of Cumberland Basin, Merchants Dock, the first wet dock to serve Bristol, was built in 1768 by William Champion (1709–89) and sold two years later to the Merchant Venturers, the guild that held a Royal

Charter from Edward VI in 1552, giving it a monopoly on Bristol's sea trade. Seen stored in the dock is the PS *Ravenswood*; built in 1891 by McKnight of Ayr and owned by Campbell Steamers, it was the first vessel to be acquired by a company that was to provide leisure cruises in the Bristol Channel until 1981. PS *Ravenswood* was scrapped in 1955. To the east of Merchants Dock is a graving dock which was opened in 1772 by James Martin Hilhouse (1749–1822) for his shipbuilding business. Hilhouse & Co built both merchant and naval vessels for 73 years; on its demise in 1845, the yard was taken over by Charles Hills & Sons. From 1852 the yard was owned by G K Stothert & Co, established by George Kelson Stothert (1833–1908). Although shipbuilding in the yard had ceased in 1904, repair work continued until the 1930s and the dock was then used for importing coal. The dock's final use, until closure in 1991, was to accommodate the dock's sand dredgers.

The Underfall Yard was named after the sluices designed by Isambard Kingdom Brunel (1806–59) to improve the water flow through the Floating Harbour. Jessop's harbour was suffering from silting and in the 1830s Brunel came up with a solution. The original Brunel sluices were enlarged and modified in the 1880s and remain in use.

Today virtually all the commercial activity and buildings visible on the quayside are gone but the land immediately to the east and west of the Grade II listed Vauxhall swing bridge (across the River Avon in the foreground, constructed in 1900 by John Lysaght & Co and with hydraulic equipment supplied by Armstrong Whitworth) is housing, while much of Baltic Wharf has been converted into the Baltic Wharf Caravan Club park. Across the harbour the graving dock still exists, albeit now without its gates, but Merchants Dock has been infilled.

Beyond, Cumberland Basin remains, as does part of its locks at the eastern end, little used as a lock today but they do form part of the city's flood defences. The westernmost locks serving Cumberland Basin are still used to provide access to the city centre wet docks. The area around the graving dock and Merchants Dock has also been redeveloped for housing, with the Grade II listed Pump House, designed by the Docks Engineer Thomas Howard (1816–96), now a public house. On the island formed by Jessop's original locks at the eastern end of Cumberland Basin to the south and the larger replacements to the north, there are two terraces of houses that survive; these eight Grade II listed properties date to 1831 and were built for the Bristol Docks Co. Also listed Grade II is the surviving parts of Jessop's original South Junction lock of 1804–9.

The Underfall Yard, located to the west of Baltic Wharf is now a scheduled Ancient Monument and contains a number of listed structures relating to ship repair work. Much of the equipment was installed during the 1880s by the then Docks Engineer John Ward Girdlestone (1840–1911). The yard still provides maintenance for the dock's facilities as well as for the leisure craft that use the marina located to the east of this view. Part of the Underfall Yard is occupied by a trust dedicated to encouraging the preservation of traditional boat-building and repair skills.

EPW005470

Queen Square and Floating Harbour, Bristol
14 February 1971

This view, taken slightly to the east of the previous image, records Bristol's Floating Harbour with the New Cut in the foreground. The original course of the River Avon can be seen heading towards the north-east under the Redcliffe bascule bridge (constructed in concrete and steel between 1939 and 1942 with Sir George Oakley [1863–1950] as consulting engineer).

In the foreground is the triangular Bathurst Basin; this was completed as part of Jessop's Floating Harbour and was constructed by enlarging the mill pond of the tidal Trin Mills. The basin was provided with locks into the New Cut and could operate as a half-tidal dock. To the east of the basin, the Bristol General Hospital was constructed in 1858; in order to part fund the work, the hospital was built with basements that acted as additional warehousing. Between 1872 and 1964 the link between Bathurst Basin and the Floating Harbour was crossed by a further bascule bridge; this carried the Bristol Harbour Railway and connected the Floating Harbour and Temple Meads station but had been dismantled by the time the 1971 photograph was taken. Bathurst Wharf (now called Merchants Quay) was developed in the 1860s.

To the west of the Prince Street swing bridge, which was built in 1878 to replace an earlier structure, the transit sheds of Prince's Wharf can be seen; the wharf itself was constructed in the 1860s but remodelled with new sheds in the 1950s following wartime damage. Prior to the construction of the wharf the site had been used for shipbuilding and it was here that Brunel oversaw the construction of one of his trio of steam-powered ships – the *Great Western*.

Across from Prince's Wharf can be seen St Augustine's Reach with its wharves to the east of Canon's Marsh; this represents the confluence of the River Frome with the Avon. The Frome itself passes through the city centre to the north through a culvert (completed between the 1890s and 1930s). St Augustine's Reach represents a man-made trench completed in 1247 to provide better harbour facilities.

By 1971 the Floating Harbour was approaching the end of its career as a commercial port. The construction of the Royal Portbury Dock on the west side of the Avon's estuary between 1972 and 1977 – built to accommodate larger vessels than the existing Floating Harbour could handle and to supplement the earlier Royal Edward Dock at Avonmouth – resulted in the Floating Harbour closing to commercial traffic in 1975. Bathurst Basin is now a marina, while the land immediately to the basin's north has been redeveloped for housing. The long warehouse alongside Prince's Wharf is now a museum; it was the Bristol Industrial Museum until closure in 2006 and is now known as the M Shed (or Museum of Bristol) following reopening in 2011. The Grade II listed General Hospital, which closed in 2010, is the subject of a conversion into residential accommodation. The westernmost section of the Bristol Harbour Railway, from Prince's Wharf to Wapping, forms the preserved Bristol Harbour Railway. The B Bond warehouse, at the western end of Prince's Wharf, now accommodates the Bristol Record Office.

Beyond Redcliffe bridge, a number of quayside warehouses survive, having been converted for residential and commercial use. The southern end of St Augustine's Wharf is now crossed by Pero's bridge; this was completed in 1999 to a design by Eilis O'Connell (b 1953). The Canon's Marsh area has been largely redeveloped although the Watershed Media Centre now occupies the modified E transit shed that was originally completed in 1894 to the design of Edward Gabriel (d 1928). On the east side of St Augustine's Reach a number of historic buildings survive; these include the southernmost structure visible in the 1971 photograph – Bush House. Now the Arnolfini Art Gallery, this Grade II* listed structure was designed as an anchor (later tea) warehouse by Richard Shackleton Pope (c 1793–1884) for the engineering company Acramans and completed in 1831. It was extended to the north during 1835 and 1836. This building was one of the first to be completed in the local Bristol Byzantine architectural style; this was a form of Byzantine Revival architecture that was popular for commercial buildings in the city between 1850 and 1880.

EAW209373

Royal Edward Dock, Avonmouth
31 July 1946

By the middle of the 19th century, Bristol's location 10km upstream was proving a commercial liability as the size of ships increased. There were two options: improve the navigability of the River Avon or construct new docks at the river mouth. The former would have been prohibitively expensive and so the decision was made to construct a new dock at Avonmouth. The first phase of the new dock opened in 1877; the original dock was extended by the addition of the new Royal Edward Dock in the early 20th century and it is this latter facility that is illustrated here looking to the east.

The Royal Edward was the third dock to be built at the river's estuary, following on from the original 1877 dock, and opened in 1879 at Portishead. It was designed by Sir Benjamin Baker (1840–1907) and by Sir John Wolfe Barry (1836–1918), the latter being the youngest son of the noted architect Sir Charles Barry (1795–1860). Work began on the dock's construction in 1902 when the then Prince of Wales, the future King George V, cut the first sod. The new dock was opened in 1908; the work included the construction of a 267m-long graving dock (seen parallel to the lock between dock and river). The dock was provided with 27 oil storage tanks by 1911 on the north-west quay.

One of the key commodities imported through Avonmouth was grain and, to handle the trade, a number of granaries and flour mills were established on the eastern side of the dock; the scale of the trade can be gauged by the buildings visible in the background of this 1946 view. The first facility, constructed for the Co-operative Wholesale Society, was the Royal Edward Granary; this eight-storey structure was built in ferroconcrete and opened originally on 27 April 1910. During the interwar years, the facilities continued to develop and the site's importance grew during World War II. Recognising the threat posed by the German U-boats to Britain's food supplies during the Battle of the Atlantic, the government established a policy of designating 'Buffer Depots' to ensure adequate stocks of food were held; one of these was the Avonmouth complex and so a further silo and mill were added towards the end of the war. Flour production continued at Avonmouth until the mid-1980s and most of the buildings visible in the 1946 view were subsequently demolished. One of the few structures that still remain is the original 1910-built structure, although proposals for its listing were rejected on the grounds that its context had been compromised by the demolition of most of the surrounding infrastructure.

The importance of the dock grew during World War II with additional oil storage facilities added and, in 1941, the dock itself was enlarged to the north-east. Given its strategic importance, it was inevitable that Avonmouth would suffer aerial attack by the Luftwaffe during the war and, in order to make the fuel supply more secure, a pipeline was laid from the dock to London and elsewhere.

By the 1960s history was starting to repeat itself; the larger container ships then entering service were not capable of navigating the river to Avonmouth and a further new facility, the Royal Portbury Dock, was constructed in the 1970s. Once completed, traffic to Avonmouth declined but, now operated under lease from Bristol City Council by the Bristol Port Co, the Royal Edward Dock is still operational with a variety of cargoes being handled and with container services to Europe and Ireland.

EAW002060

Portishead
15 April 1972

Situated on the north Somerset coast at the estuary of the River Pill, there is evidence that Portishead had maritime connections in the 14th century but the development of the harbour illustrated here did not take place until the mid-19th century. Increasingly, by this date, larger vessels were struggling to reach the traditional quays in Bristol; this was a problem that had been recognised earlier, with Isambard Kingdom Brunel proposing the development of Portishead as a deep-water harbour as early as 1839.

Although a small stone pier was constructed in 1849 that served packet steamers, there was no further development until after 29 June 1863 when the Portbury Pier & Railway Co received the royal assent for the Act permitting the construction of the railway. This was the year after the parallel plans for the development of Avonmouth received approval but both schemes were to progress. The broad-gauge railway line was opened on 18 April 1867; it was converted to standard gauge in January 1880. In 1871 the company obtained a second Act, the Portishead Dock Act, which permitted the construction of a new wet dock alongside the mouth of the River Pill. The new facility was engineered by John Robinson McClean (1813–73) and William Croughton Stileman (1827–1915), who had also been the engineers for the construction of the original railway, with the contractors being Messrs Barnett and Gale. Work on the dock commenced in October 1873; however, construction problems resulted in work being delayed and the new dock was not opened until 28 June 1879. The first vessel to enter was the dock company's own pleasure steamer, the *Lyn*. The first commercial traffic docked on 6 July 1879, when the SS *Magdeburg* arrived with 1,000 tons of barley.

In this 1972 view, the south quay is dominated by the Albright & Wilson phosphorus factory; this plant was first announced in January 1953 and cost an estimated £4 million to construct. The location was selected due to its proximity to the two Portishead power stations, situated (but not visible in this view) on the north side of the harbour, and the deep-water harbour through which the large bulk carriers could deliver the phosphate ore required. The company continued to manufacture phosphorous here until December 1968 and so the plant was redundant when recorded here; the building was subsequently demolished and the site redeveloped.

There were two power stations at Portishead: A, which opened originally in 1929 and closed in 1976, and B, which first generated power in 1955 and survived until 1982. Although much of the coal for the two power stations was delivered by rail, as shown by the number of wagons visible, significant quantities were also shipped across the Bristol Channel from South Wales and evidence of this traffic can be seen on the north quay.

At the centre of the photograph is the new passenger station opened to serve Portishead on 4 January 1954. Originally the line extended beyond this point to serve the earlier passenger station and the pier. Although a relatively new station, passenger services to Portishead ceased on 7 September 1964 and work can be seen in the photograph of the demolition of the platform.

The closure of Portishead B power station was to see the bulk of Portishead's traffic disappear and, in 1992, the Port of Bristol Authority closed the dock as a commercial facility. Subsequently, the harbour has been transformed, as with so many others, into a marina, with some 250 pontoon berths. The area occupied by the two power stations has, like that of the phosphorous factory, been redeveloped.

EAW225597

Hartlepool
26 June 1947

At the start of the 20th century, Hartlepool was the fourth busiest port in Britain; during the course of the 19th century there had been considerable investment in the expansion of the dock's facilities on the low-lying land to the north-west of Hartlepool Bay.

Although Hartlepool had had a harbour from the Middle Ages, by the early 19th century the original dock was largely moribund; all this, however, was to change with the opening of the Hartlepool Dock & Railway through to the town on 23 November 1835. The new railway was designed to permit the shipment of Durham coal through Hartlepool. The first new dock to be completed was the Victoria Dock, visible on the right of this image, which opened in December 1840. However, there were disagreements between the owners of the railway and the docks with the result that the former, led by Ralph Ward Jackson (1806–80), promoted the development of West Hartlepool with its docks and accommodation.

The West Harbour & Dock Co received the Royal Assent for its Act on 23 September 1844. Work started on the new docks in 1845 and the first of the new docks to open was the Coal Dock, visible on the extreme left of the image adjacent to the entry locks. This opened on 1 June 1847. It soon proved inadequate and was followed by the Jackson Dock, immediately to the west of the Coal Dock, which opened on 1 June 1852 and by the Swainson Dock (not shown and to the south-west of the Jackson Dock), which opened on 3 June 1856.

The next major development came between 1875 and 1880 when the North Eastern Railway – which had acquired the original Hartlepool docks when the enlarged railway company was formed in 1854 and took over the docks at West Hartlepool on 1 July 1875 – undertook the construction of the North Basin, to the south-west of the Victoria Dock. This was linked to the original docks at West Hartlepool by the Central Dock and by the Union Dock to its south. To the west of the Central Dock can be seen a number of timber ponds; these were used for the importation of timber pit props needed by the local mining industry. While the vast amount of coal shipped out from ports such as Hartlepool is recognised, the equally vast amount of timber that the mines required to function is often overlooked.

The importance of Hartlepool as a harbour in the early 20th century was reflected by the fact that it became the first target for a German attack on British soil during World War I when, on 16 December 1914, the German navy attacked the town, killing 119. It was also to be attacked by the Luftwaffe during World War II. By this time, the docks were owned by the LNER as successor to the North Eastern Railway and the facility was to pass to BTC on nationalisation in 1948.

Today, the docks at Hartlepool are much reduced, with the timber ponds, Central and Swainson docks now infilled and the Coal, Jackson and Union docks converted for leisure activities (*see* p 263). The commercial docks, now owned by PD Ports following privatisation, are centred on the modified Victoria Dock and the surviving North Basin. The port offers five general cargo berths capable of handling products such as steel and other bulk dry cargo as well as a roll-on/roll-off facility.

EAW007972

Albert Dock, Hull
16 April 1947

With the King George Dock in the background, this view records Hull's Alexandra Dock from the west. The origins of the dock were based upon the desire of the coal mine owners of Yorkshire to break the monopoly that the North Eastern Railway had in the movement of coal to the port of Hull.

The Hull, Barnsley & West Riding Junction Railway & Dock Co – better known as the Hull & Barnsley Railway (its official name from 30 June 1905) – was incorporated on 26 August 1880 and was empowered to construct a main line from Hull towards Barnsley as well as a new dock on reclaimed land in Hull. The latter was designed by James Abernethy (1823–96) with work being carried out by James Oldham (1801–90) and George Bohn with Arthur Cameron Hurtzig (1853–1915) as resident engineer. The contactors were Lucas & Aird with the hydraulic dock machinery, including lock gates, being supplied by Armstrong, Mitchell & Co.

The completed dock, named in honour of Princess Alexandra, the Princess of Wales, was opened on 16 July 1885. The Hull & Barnsley Railway opened to freight traffic four days later. Inevitably, the dock's primary traffic was the export of coal but it was also used for the importation of timber pit props from Scandinavia. Alexandra Dock was extended at its eastern end by a further seven acres (three hectares) during 1899 and 1900 and, in 1911, a pier – West Wharf – was added. At the eastern end of the dock are two graving docks; these were occupied by Brigham & Cowan (Hull) Ltd, a business owned by Brigham & Cowan Ltd, a South Shields-based shipbuilder established in 1876 by Thomas Brigham and Malcolm Cowan.

The Hull & Barnsley Railway was taken over by the North Eastern in 1922 and both became part of the LNER in 1923; the railway-owned docks at Hull passed to the BTC at nationalisation in 1948 and thus to Associated British Ports as successor to the BTDB. In 1982, prior to ABP's privatisation the following year, Alexandra Dock closed; it was, however, to reopen nine years later although no longer rail served. The dock handles a range of products, including aggregates and chemicals.

In 2011 the dock's owners signed an agreement with the German company Siemens for the construction of a major plant for the manufacture of offshore wind turbines at Alexandra Dock. The project was given planning permission by Hull City Council in September 2014 with the proposal forming the centrepiece of the Green Port Hull development. The plans will result in the western half of the dock being infilled alongside the construction of new berths and a roll-on/roll-off ramp. Alexandra Dock was selected as a result of its proximity to a number of major offshore wind farms under development in the North Sea.

EAW004505

King George Dock, Hull
16 April 1947

One of the major exports from the port of Hull was coal from the coalfields of Yorkshire, Derbyshire and Nottinghamshire and, towards the end of the 19th century, additional capacity was required. Although the Hull & Barnsley Railway had been promoted as a competitor to the much larger North Eastern Railway, the two railway companies co-operated in the development of this new dock.

Although initially opposed by the Humber Conservancy Board, the Hull Joint Dock Act was passed in 1899. Work commenced on the dock following the plans produced by Sir Benjamin Baker (1840–1907) and Sir John Wolfe Barry (1836–1918). They were assisted by Arthur Cameron Hurtzig (1853–1915) and Cuthbert Arthur Brereton (1850–1910). Originally known as the Joint Dock, the new facility was renamed the King George Dock in honour of King George V, who, along with Queen Mary, officially opened it on 26 June 1914. Facilities at the new dock included a lock 750ft (229m) in length and 85ft (26m) in width and two graving docks.

In 1919 the reinforced concrete grain silo visible in the 1947 photograph was completed. The gradual decline in the coal traffic had resulted in new traffic passing through the dock; grain imports, partly as a result of the growth in the popularity of breakfast cereals, had risen and so dedicated facilities were required. The silos survived until demolition in 2010.

In 1922 the Hull & Barnsley and North Eastern railways merged; this was a precursor to the creation of the LNER in 1923 and to nationalisation in 1948; as with other nationalised ports, King George V Dock was privatised as part of Associated British Ports.

Since the date of the photograph, there has been much development at the dock; the story of the development of the ferry terminal is narrated on p 213. Apart from the ferry services, the dock continues to handle a considerable amount of freight. This includes paper, metals, general cargo and bulk grain. Ironically, considering its origins, the dock also handles the importation of coal and biomass for power generation.

EAW004509

Prince's Dock, Hull
6 May 1925

This view, taken looking towards the north, shows three of Hull's wet docks – Humber, Prince's to the north and Railway to the west. The latter is partially obscured by the warehouses (built by 1925) behind the large Kingston Street (Central) goods depot of the LNER (originally North Eastern Railway). Linking Prince's Dock with the Old Harbour to the east is Queen's Dock, although this is obscured by buildings.

The first phase of the development of the docks illustrated here was Humber Dock. In 1773 the Hull Dock Co – the first statutory dock company in Britain – was established by the corporation, Hull Trinity House and local merchants, and land within the town walls was passed by the crown to the company for the construction of new docks. In 1774 powers to raise £100,000 were authorised by an Act of Parliament and the development of the first wet docks commenced. Of the docks, the Queen's Dock was completed in 1778; this was known as the Old Dock once the Humber Dock was completed and the Queen's Dock from 1855. In 1802 an Act was passed to construct a new dock to relieve the pressure on the 1778 dock; John Rennie (1761–1821) and William Chapman (1749–1832) were the engineers. Work started in 1807 and Humber Dock was completed two years later. The 1802 Act included a provision requiring the construction of a third dock linking the Humber and Old docks once the annual tonnage landed reached a certain level and this was triggered in the early 1820s, with an Act covering construction passed in 1824. Work commenced on the Junction Dock in 1826 to the designs of James Walker (1781–1862) with the resident engineer being John Timperley (1796–1856). The work was completed in 1829; the dock was renamed Prince's Dock in 1854 in honour of Prince Albert. The final development was the construction of the branch Railway Dock; this was authorised under the Kingston-upon-Hull Dock Act

of 1844 and amended by a second Act the following year. The engineer was John Bernard Hartley (1814–69) and it opened on 3 December 1846.

The entrance to Humber Dock was protected by two L-shaped piers that were realigned in c 1840; on the west, the pier was further modified in the mid-1870s when Island Wharf was constructed to provide additional space for the Manchester, Sheffield & Lincolnshire Railway by partially infilling the basin that served Albert Dock. The wharf was separated from the mainland by the Albert Channel. This feature, visible in the photograph, was infilled during the 1960s and the land redeveloped in the early 21st century. At the time of the photograph the eastern pier, known as Minerva Pier from the 1920s, was constructed in wood; it was replaced by a stone walled pier in the late 20th century. On shore, to the north-east of the Minerva Pier is the Minerva Inn; this was first established in 1829.

Kingston Street depot was the original terminus of the Hull & Selby Railway; this opened as Market House Street station on 2 July 1840 and survived as a passenger station until 8 May 1848 and the opening of Paragon station. The original station was demolished in 1858 and replaced by a goods station designed by Thomas Prosser (c 1817–88), the North Eastern Railway's architect. The goods station was subsequently extended to provide additional capacity. The building shown here was demolished in 1961 as part of the development for Hull Central goods depot although there were still sidings at Kingston Street until 1984. The station site has been redeveloped for housing and is known as Freedom Quays.

The first casualty was Queen's Dock; this closed in 1930 and it was subsequently filled in to create the Queen's Gardens. Prince's Dock closed to shipping in 1968 and much of the site was used for the construction

of the Prince's Quay Shopping Centre, which opened in 1991. The modern building is unusual in that it is constructed upon piles sunk into the original dock. Although the dock still retains water, it is no longer possible to access it, with the A63 now forming a physical barrier between it and Humber Dock. Humber Dock closed to shipping in August 1967 before closing permanently in 1969 while Railway Dock also closed in 1968; Railway and Humber docks now form the Hull Marina, which opened in 1983.

EPW012696

Albert Dock and Pier Head, Liverpool
7 August 1997

This is a view of the Liverpool classic river frontage prior to redevelopment over the past 20 years. In the centre are the three famous buildings that dominate Liverpool from the River Mersey. The northernmost is the Royal Liver Building, designed by Walter Aubrey Thomas (1864–1934) and built between 1908 and 1911. The Grade I listed building was built for the Royal Liver Insurance and was one of the first multistorey, steel-framed and reinforced concrete buildings in the world. The actual ferroconcrete frame of the building was designed by the engineers L G Mouchel & Partners with the exterior clad in granite.

To the south of the Royal Liver Building is the Cunard Building, designed by William Edward Willink (1856–1920) and Philip Coldwell Thicknesse (1860–1924) and constructed between 1914 and 1917 in reinforced concrete with Portland stone cladding by Holland, Hannen & Cubbitts. The building was designed as the headquarters of the Cunard Steamship Co, who owned it until 1969, although shipping operations and the company's head office were transferred to Southampton and New York respectively earlier in the decade. The building was listed as Grade II* in 1965.

The southernmost of the three structures is the Port of Liverpool Building, constructed between 1904 and 1907 in reinforced concrete clad in Portland stone. Designed as the headquarters of the Mersey Docks & Harbour Board (MDHB) by Sir Arnold Thornely (1870–1953) and Frederick Brice Hobbs (1862–1944) in association with Frank Gatley Briggs (1862–1921) and Henry Vernon Wolstenholme (1863–1936) – following a competition in 1900 – the MDHB occupied the Grade II*-listed building until 1994.

The location of the three buildings – the Pier Head – was created following the closure of George's Basin and George's Dock in 1899 and their infilling. George's Dock dated back to 1771 and had been subsequently expanded. In 2009 a £22 million project to extend the Leeds & Liverpool Canal to the site of the former George's Basin was completed.

To the south of the three buildings are Canning Dock, with its two graving docks, Canning Half-Tide Dock, with its access to the River Mersey, Albert Dock, with its 19th-century warehouses, and Sandon Dock. The oldest of these docks is Canning, originally opened in 1737 as a tidal basin protecting the entrance to Old Dock, the world's first commercial wet dock, completed in 1815 and filled in after closure in 1826. Canning became a wet dock in 1829, being renamed after George Canning, the local MP, three years later. Canning Dock, with its two graving docks (built originally in 1765 and extended in 1813 and 1842), closed as a commercial port in 1972, and now forms part of the Liverpool Maritime Museum.

The Canning Half-Tide Dock was designed by Jesse Hartley (1780–1860); when completed in 1844 it had two lock entrances to the Mersey, but the northernmost one was sealed by a concrete dam in 1937. The southern gates remain operational. Adjacent to the site of the north locks is the Pilotage Office, completed in 1883.

Salthouse Dock was designed by Thomas Steers (c 1672–1750) and completed after his death by Henry Berry (1719–1812). The dock opened in 1753 and was used to tranship salt from Cheshire. The dock was altered in both 1842 and 1853. By 1969 virtually all the original structures had been replaced; the more modern structures in this view have subsequently been demolished.

Albert Dock was designed by Jesse Hartley and Philip Hardwick (1792–1870) and officially opened in 1846 by Prince Albert. The design was revolutionary as, for the first time, cargo was shipped directly to and from warehouses. Integral to the design of the warehouses are the massive cast-iron columns – 15ft (4.5m) in height and 13ft (4m) in circumference. In 1846 the warehouses were modified to accommodate the world's first hydraulic cranes. Although damaged during World War II, the warehouses that surrounded the dock survived until commercial trade ceased in 1971. Following a decade of dereliction, when their future was under threat, the redevelopment of the Albert Dock complex began in 1983 following the creation of the Merseyside Development Corporation two years earlier. The site was officially opened in 1988. Also to survive, at the extreme north-east of Albert Dock, are the Dock Traffic Office and the pump house, both also designed by Hartley and Hardwick.

To the north can be seen Prince's Dock, built by John Foster (1759–1827) with preliminary design work undertaken by John Rennie. Construction started in 1810 and the dock – named in honour of the Prince Regent – opened on 19 July 1821 (the date of the Regent's coronation as George IV). The dock was accessed via the Prince's Half-Tide Dock, opened in 1810, to the north or, until 1899, via George's Dock and George's Basin. The dock is now closed and has been partially filled in, making it suitable solely for canal boats accessing the extension to the canal southwards.

The classic Liverpool skyline, a UNESCO World Heritage Site, has changed considerably since 1969, most notably through the construction of new buildings to the south of the Port of Liverpool Building. These include the Museum of Liverpool, which opened in 2011. The Albert Docks complex, which represents the largest concentration of Grade I-listed buildings in the UK, is another component of Liverpool's UNESCO-listed Maritime Mercantile City. The five warehouses house museums – including the Tate Liverpool and Liverpool Maritime Museum – as well as hotels, shops and restaurants.

EAW670571

Alexandra Dock, Liverpool
3 July 1964

This view, taken looking westwards across the River Mersey with New Brighton in the distance, shows, in the foreground, two of the three branches of Alexandra Dock with Langton Dock to its south.

By the second half of the 19th century, the growth in trade and in the size of ships meant that further development was required. From the north, Hornby, Alexandra and Langton docks were designed by George Fosbery Lyster (1821–99) to be accessible at all stages of the tide by the largest liners and freighters. The trio of docks cost £4 million and were built with concrete-cement walls, hydraulic cranes, modern warehouses, transit sheds and electric lighting for night work. Langton, named after William Langton (a member of the dock committee), with the associated Langton Locks, opened in 1879; Alexandra followed in 1881 and the last, Hornby (named after Thomas Dyson Hornby [1823–89], chairman of the MDHB), came in 1884. The completion of Hornby effectively completed the expansion of the northern section of the docks in Liverpool during the late 19th century.

Visible on the extreme left of the photograph, at the western extremity of one of the graving docks serving Langton Dock, can be seen the pump house; this was also designed by Lyster in the neo-Gothic style that he adopted for the work in these three docks. The remains of the structure, which were still standing at the time of writing, were cited by the Victorian Society in 2012 as one of the year's 10 most vulnerable surviving Victorian structures.

Across the estuary of the River Mersey can be seen New Brighton and the northern extremity of the Wirral peninsula. Visible are New Brighton lighthouse and Fort Perch Rock. The lighthouse was constructed between 1827 and 1830 by Tomkinson & Co to replace an earlier structure. In use when pictured here, the lighthouse was decommissioned in October 1973 but is still extant (in private ownership) and there are plans for its light to be restored. Immediately to the south of the lighthouse is Fort Perch Rock; this coastal battery was constructed between 1825 and 1829 to provide defence for the port of Liverpool. Constructed in red sandstone, the structure, which is now listed at Grade II*, is currently in use as a museum. Also visible, to the south, is New Brighton pier; the structure in the photograph was opened in 1867 and substantially rebuilt after its acquisition by Wallasey Corporation in 1928. By the date of the photograph the future of the pier was uncertain; closed in 1965, it was reopened in 1968, only to close again in 1972. With its condition deteriorating, permission was granted in 1977 for its demolition, with work being completed later that year.

The photograph was taken shortly after the reconstruction, long delayed, of the river entrance into Langton Dock; this was completed in 1962 and at the time of writing remained one of the two surviving river entrances into the northern dock complex.

To the north, Hornby Dock was primarily employed in the importation of timber; its facilities were reduced in the 1920s with the construction of the graving dock that served Gladstone Dock. The timber trade remained significant until the 1960s but apart from the access channel along the river wall, the dock is now infilled and the reclaimed land used in connection with the coal terminal in Gladstone Dock.

Today, Alexandra Dock is largely extant and forms part of the Liverpool Freeport owned by Peel Holdings. Of the three branches, the northern (No 3) and central (No 2) are both still operational while the southern (No 1) has been infilled. There are controversial plans for the construction of a biomass power station alongside the dock. To the south, the Langton Branch Dock and the two graving docks that served Langton Dock have been partially infilled, although the gates still exist, and the site provides parking for vehicles on the Seatruck Ferries service to and from Dublin. There are proposals for the construction of a roll-on/roll-off terminal on the site. Of the transit sheds and grain warehouses visible, virtually all have been demolished, although some remain (visible on the extreme right) between Alexandra Branch Nos 2 and 3 docks.

EAW133870

Brunswick Dock, Liverpool
2 November 1980

This view taken from the south-west shows the traditional docks of Liverpool in decline. In the centre of the photograph can be seen the location of the original two locks that served Brunswick Dock – that to the north 24m in width and that to the south 30m – with the dock itself silting up. To the south was the Toxteth Dock; this closed in 1972 as had all the southern docks – and has been subsequently filled in. On the bank of the River Mersey, immediately to the north of the former locks, can be seen the Brunswick Half-Tide Dock; this had already been infilled by 1980. Beyond this is the South Ferry Basin. Immediately to the north of Brunswick Dock can be seen the Queens Docks with, from south to north, the Queens Branch Dock No 1, the Queens Graving Dock and Queens Branch Dock No 2. To the north of Queens Dock were Kings and Wapping docks.

The oldest of the docks shown is Queens Dock. This was designed by Henry Berry (1719–1815), who was Liverpool's second dock engineer, and completed by his successor Thomas Morris (c 1754–1832) and opened in 1796, primarily to serve the whaling trade. The dock as seen here had, however, been extended several times, initially between 1810 and 1816 by John Foster (Senior; 1758–1827), who was Engineer to the Mersey Docks & Harbour Board from 1799 until 1824, when he was succeeded by Jesse Hartley (1780–1860). It was further extended in 1858 and again between 1898 and 1906. The design of Brunswick Dock was undertaken by Jesse Hartley, under whose control some 160 acres (65ha) of dock were added to Liverpool's harbour facilities; the first to be completed was Clarence Dock in 1830 and the last, Canada Dock, was opened in 1859. Brunswick Dock, opened in 1832, was originally conceived as a dock for handling timber primarily; it was also enlarged in the early 20th century.

Coburg Dock, named after the ruling Saxe-Coburg family, was created in 1840 by adding gates to the small Union Basin that served the existing Union Dock; Coburg and Union docks were merged in 1858. In the early 20th century, the lock gates that served Coburg Dock were permanently closed with access being achieved via the gates that served Brunswick Dock. Among ships that used Coburg Dock were the new Cunard liners from the early 20th century. The South Ferry Basin dated to the mid-19th century; from April 1865 a ferry linked it with New Ferry on the Wirral. This was, however, short-lived and ceased to operate by 1876. Thereafter the basin was used by oystercatchers and cocklefishers, being known locally as the 'Cocklehole'. The Brunswick Half-Tide Dock was constructed shortly before the main Brunswick Dock. Toxteth Dock was built to a design of George Fosbery Lyster (1821–99), who succeeded Hartley as Engineer to the MDHB. Constructed from an earlier tidal basin, Toxteth Dock opened in 1888.

Today, there is new activity in the Brunswick and Coburg docks as the home of the Liverpool Marina. The area surrounding the docks in this view has been redeveloped with residential properties and the site of the former Half-Tide Dock is now occupied by a company selling boats and yachts. The South Ferry Basin still exists although now heavily silted up. Queens Dock and Queens Branch Dock No 1 are also still extant but Queens Graving Dock is partially covered over by an office complex and Queens Branch Dock No 2 has been infilled. The southern lock into Brunswick Dock has also been infilled although the northern lock has been re-established to provide access to the marina.

The massive grain silo, seen at the entrance from Brunswick to Coburg Dock, which was the largest grain silo in Europe when completed for the Liverpool Grain Storage & Transit Co Ltd in 1936 (and nicknamed 'The Dockers' Cathedral'), was demolished in 1986.

EAW399274

Garston Dock, Liverpool
13 September 1963

Although situated on the Mersey within the City of Liverpool, the port of Garston was developed separately from those docks controlled by the MDHB. The estuary of the Garston River had historically provided a safe refuge for fishing boats and, in the late 18th century, a salt works was established. However, the origins of the dock shown here date back to the 1830s and the competition to transport the coal from the coalfield around St Helens to the River Mersey. This traffic had earlier resulted in the creation of the first docks at Widnes (see p 115), but the competition between the Sankey Canal and the St Helens & Runcorn Gap Railway had proved ruinous for both companies, with the result that, following the passing of an Act on 21 July 1845, the two merged to form the St Helens Canal & Railway Co.

The following year, on 16 July, the new company was empowered to construct a new 12km-long line from Widnes to Garston and to construct a new dock. The new line was opened on 1 July 1852. The docks themselves did not open until 21 July 1853. The first dock to be completed was the centre dock as pictured here; this is now known as the Old Dock. This was provided with modern coal drops, as shown, but the traffic through the port was such that the original dock was soon to prove inadequate and, in 1867, a second dock – the North Dock – was opened.

By this date, however, ownership of the dock had changed. The St Helens Canal & Railway was leased by the London & North Western Railway from 1 July 1860 and formally absorbed on 29 July 1864. In addition to the traffic generated by the LNWR, through the exercise of running powers, the Cheshire Line Committee railways (the Great Northern, Midland and Manchester, Sheffield & Lincolnshire) also provided traffic to the docks. The primary traffic from Garston was coal and timber to Ireland while the port was also the main port through which bananas were imported to Britain.

The final expansion of the dock came in 1909 with the opening of the southern Stalbridge Dock; this was the largest of three docks that served Garston and its construction saw the completion of the new entrance lock as shown in this 1963 view. The dock was 84m long and 20m wide and, with the completion of Stalbridge Dock, the total enclosed area was 28½ acres (11.5ha). The construction of the dock resulted in the growth of local industry, with shipbuilding, salt-making, iron and steel, chemical and copper works all being established alongside the port. By the date of this photograph, however, most of this industry had closed down. The copper works, for example had closed in 1936 when production was shifted to Swansea.

The Port of Garston, now owned by Associated British Ports (as successors to the BTC, which had assumed ownership on 1 January 1948 on the nationalisation of the railways), remains open with a total quay length, split between the three docks, of some 2,400m and currently handles some 500,000 tonnes of freight per annum. Among the facilities that the port offers is a dedicated terminal for the import of cement while other traffic includes scrap metal and various steel products. Although there remains a railway connection to the port, this is currently disused, except for a spur serving a container terminal (which opened in the 1980s), and much of the area occupied by sidings in the 1963 view is either overgrown or has been redeveloped; at its peak there were some 150km of railway siding serving the dock.

EAW120726

Huskisson Docks, Liverpool
September 1928

Designed by Jesse Hartley, Huskisson Dock initially opened in 1852 and was named after William Huskisson (1770–1830), the former MP for Liverpool who was killed by Stephenson's *Rocket* at the Ranhill Trials of 1830. Originally designed for the timber trade, the dock was later used for grain traffic and for passenger ships used on the route across the North Atlantic. The first of the three branch docks was added in 1860 with two further ones being opened in the early 20th century. Huskisson Dock was the principal dock used by Cunard in Liverpool until the shipping line moved its operations to Gladstone Dock in 1927.

This view, taken in 1928, shows the dock at its greatest extent. As might be expected, the docks of Liverpool were a major target for the German air force during World War II and, on 2 May 1941, there was a major explosion in Branch No 2 Huskisson Dock when the munitions on board the Brocklebank Line's SS *Malakand* were ignited as a result of a fire on the ship caused by a deflated barrage balloon. The explosion resulted in the destruction of most of the buildings seen in the 1928 photograph. After the blast, Branch Dock No 2 was infilled.

In the background, running north to south can be seen the Liverpool Overhead Railway; this stretched from Seaforth & Litherland in the north to Dingle in the south and, when opened, was the first electrically operated elevated railway in the world. Known affectionately as the 'Dockers' Umbrella', the elevated line was designed to provide a passenger service parallel to the docks while not interfering with the significant network of freight-only railways that served the docks at ground level. Authorised by an Act of 24 July 1888, the line was designed and engineered by Sir Douglas Fox (1840–1921) and James Henry Greathead (1844–96). The line opened on 4 February 1893 between Herculaneum in the south and Alexandra Dock in the north; it was extended northwards to Seaforth Sands on 30 September 1894 and diverted to a new terminus at Dingle to the south on 21 December 1896. The line was constructed with almost 570 iron-built spans, the majority 50ft (15m) in length, some 16ft (5m) on average above the roadway. There were four hydraulically operated lifting sections, including one at Brunswick Dock, to ensure ease of freight traffic to the docks.

The Liverpool Overhead Railway retained its independence throughout its operational life; escaping nationalisation in 1948, the line's Achilles' heel was its method of construction. Over the years, corrosion, caused by steam and soot from the locomotives that operated on the dock railways below reacted with rainwater, seriously damaging the infrastructure. Although maintenance was undertaken, the problem grew and a report commissioned in 1955 estimated that £2 million would be required to repair the line over the next five years; this was significantly beyond the means of the railway and efforts to obtain funding from the corporation and elsewhere proved fruitless. Having obtained powers to close the line through the Liverpool Overhead Railway Act of 1956, the line closed completely on 30 December 1956 despite considerable popular opposition. Demolition of the structure commenced on 23 September 1957 and little now remains. The line of the railway is now largely followed by the alignment of the A5036.

Today, Huskisson Dock, with its two surviving branch docks, is part of the estate controlled by Peel Ports Group Ltd and remains active for general trade with oil storage facilities erected adjacent to the dock on the site of the erstwhile Branch Dock No 2. There is planning consent for the redevelopment of the site for port use and the owners are actively promoting the dock for regeneration.

EPW023590

Prince's Dock, Liverpool
27 May 1937

This view, taken looking towards the south-east, shows the network of docks constructed immediately to the north of the Pier Head.

The southernmost of the docks is Prince's; this was built by John Foster (1759–1827) and opened in 1821. A detailed history of the development of this dock can be found on p 19. To the north can be seen the Prince's Half-Tide Dock; this was also built by John Foster and originally possessed, as seen in 1937, a lock entrance to the River Mersey.

Originally a single dock designed by Jesse Hartley (1780–1860), Waterloo Dock opened in 1834 and was named after the 1815 battle. It was reconfigured between 1863 and 1868 by George Fosbery Lyster (1821–99) into East and West docks. At the time of the photograph, access to the Waterloo docks was still via the lock into Prince's Half-Tide Dock; one of the post-war improvements saw the construction of a direct river connection into Waterloo West Dock. This was opened in 1947 and survived until 1988 when all commercial traffic ceased in the Waterloo docks.

Of the buildings shown, the most prominent survival is the Waterloo Warehouse, which is situated along the eastern quay of the East Dock in this view. Designed by Lyster and completed in 1867, this brick-built structure is now listed as Grade II and has been converted into apartments. Modern construction has seen residential blocks built along the other quays of the two Waterloo docks.

Victoria Dock was one of a trio of linked docks designed by Jesse Hartley, the other two being Clarence and Trafalgar. The first of the trio to open was Clarence in 1830; this was situated slightly to the north of the scene shown here and was the first dock in Liverpool designed to handle steam ships. It was located away from the existing facilities in order to avoid any possibility of fire damaging the wooden-built vessels in other docks. Clarence was linked to Waterloo Dock by, north to south, Trafalgar and Victoria docks, both of which opened in 1836. The water level in the latter was used between 1844 and 1921 as the Ordnance Datum for the British Isles.

In 1928 Clarence Dock was closed and the site infilled. The reclaimed land, which is visible on the extreme left surrounded by the inverted L of Trafalgar Dock, was used for the construction of a new power station in the 1930s. The power station was eventually demolished in the early 1990s. Much of Victoria Dock itself was infilled in 1972 as part of the construction for the new B&I Line ferry terminal.

Of the docks shown in the photograph, none is still operational. While the four most southerly – East and West Waterloo, Prince's Half-Tide and Prince's – are still generally extant, none is in commercial use. The 1947 river connection to the river from Waterloo West Dock is still visible, albeit now heavily silted up. Trafalgar Dock to the north was largely infilled during the early 1990s; however, in 2007 work started on a £22 million extension of the Leeds & Liverpool Canal in order to extend the canal by almost 2.5km southwards to a new basin adjacent to the Pier Head. This resulted in the excavation of a new channel through the former Trafalgar Dock to connect with Salisbury and Collingwood docks to the north (the canal originally connected into the docks at Liverpool through locks leading into Stanley Dock and thus into the connected Collingwood Dock). Much of the land once occupied by dock facilities and by the power station is currently derelict although there are ambitious plans for redevelopment as part of the Liverpool Waters project.

EPW053300

Pool of London
3 May 1963

The Pool of London was the traditional core of the city's docks, with a history stretching back to the pre-Norman era; in the 7th century the Venerable Bede referred to the importance of the Pool of London. The Pool, with its wharves and warehouses, was divided into two sections: the Upper Pool, stretching from London Bridge to Bermondsey, and the Lower Pool, from Bermondsey to Limekiln Creek. This view, taken in the early 1960s, shows the section of the River Thames from Shadwell Basin in the foreground towards Tower Bridge. Closest to Tower Bridge can be seen St Katharine's Dock; this is covered in more detail on p 267.

The construction of the original London Bridge, completed in 1209, was a factor in the development of the Pool; the constriction caused by the bridge's piers to the water flow resulted in the natural dredging of the riverbed downstream of the bridge. Quays were constructed on the north bank of the river, between the Tower of London and Baynard's Castle (situated upstream on the site of the present day Blackfriars station), and the growth of London and the expansion of trade saw further development.

In 1558 an Act of Parliament established the 'Legal Quays'; this was a stretch of 446m of quays east of London Bridge through which trade had to pass for duties to be imposed in order to avoid smuggling, which had been rife up until that point. The length of the 'Legal Quays' was extended and by the end of the 18th century stretched as far as Sugar Quay. By this period, trade – both domestic (such as coal from Newcastle) and international – had grown rapidly; between 1751 and 1794, the number of vessels that docked in the Pool of London dealing with overseas trade increased from 1,682 to 3,663 and the weight of traffic carried more than doubled.

There were attempts in the late 17th century to construct the first wet docks at Blackwell and Rotherhithe, although they seem to have been used for ship repair work rather than commercial traffic. This changed in 1799 with the authorisation for the construction of the West India Docks (see p 47). In competition with the West India Docks, the London Dock Act of May 1800 authorised the construction of wet docks at Wapping. These are the two central docks seen in the 1963 photograph. The new docks were designed by John Rennie (1761–1821) and Daniel Asher Alexander (1768–1846) and the foundation stone was laid by the then Prime Minister, Henry Addington, on 25 June 1802, with the new dock complex opening on 31 January 1805.

The London Dock Co had a 21-year monopoly for a range of high-value goods, including tobacco, wine and brandy for all vessels except those from the East and West Indies. The new docks comprised the large Western Dock which was linked to the smaller Eastern Dock by the small Tobacco Dock. Access to the river was via the Hermitage Basin, on the south-west, and Wapping Basin, on the south, which both connected into the Western Dock and the later Shadwell Basin to the east that linked into the Eastern Dock. Warehouses were constructed along the quays, those alongside the Tobacco Dock and Eastern Dock handling primarily tobacco and sugar respectively. The central jetty visible in the Western Dock was added in 1831 (and subsequently enlarged). Shadwell Basin was constructed in two phases: the first, smaller, basin on the south between 1828 and 1832 and the larger, north basin, between 1854 and 1858. The new basin saw the construction of two larger locks.

The London Dock Co became part of the Port of London Authority in 1909 and the whole area of the Port of London was to suffer severe damage during World War II. Many of the early 19th-century warehouses that had once surrounded the wet docks were casualties, although some, as shown in the 1963 photograph, did survive. That the PLA believed that the traditional docks had a future was demonstrated in 1959 by the construction of installations for the handling of bulk wine. The optimism, however, was ill-founded as containerisation and the growth in the size of ships rendered the wet docks at Wapping redundant. By the late 1960s most of the warehouses had closed and the London Docks ceased to function in May 1969, although some limited commercial activity continued thereafter.

In the half-century since the London Docks closed, all, with the exception of Shadwell Basin, have been infilled and the area subject to massive regeneration with both commercial and residential development. Around three sides of Shadwell Basin, for example, there are four- and five-storey residential blocks while the basin itself is used for recreational purposes, such as canoeing. Among the handful of surviving historic structures is the Grade I listed structure at the Tobacco Dock; built between 1811 and 1813 to a design by Alexander, this single-storey building is one of the earliest in the south of England to be constructed from cast iron.

EAW110579

Canada Dock, London
30 June 1966

Following the merger that formed the Surrey Commercial Dock Co in 1865 the next phase in the development of the docks in Rotherhithe was the construction of Canada Dock, with work starting in 1875. Designed by James Adair McConnochie (1835–95), appointed engineer of the new company in 1865, Canada Dock was intended to handle the larger iron vessels then entering service. One of the challenges that McConnochie faced was the proximity of the new dock to the East London Railway (which had opened from Wapping, north of the river, via the reused Brunel Thames Tunnel to New Cross Gate on 7 December 1869). The railway, being at a lower level, was threatened by water ingress from any new dock and by possible subsidence. As a result, Canada Dock was built by its contractors, Thomas Docwra & Son of Islington, with a slight curve on its western side – visible in the photograph – and with the use of concrete walls. The new facility opened in 1876 and was primarily employed in the importation of timber from Canada.

Also visible in the view are the connections on the north side to Albion Dock, on the east to the curtailed Quebec Pond (which was reduced in size with the enlargement of Greenland Dock, a project that was completed in 1904) and on the south to Greenland Dock. The Surrey Commercial Docks were subsumed, as were the other enclosed London docks (with the exception of the Regent's Canal Dock), into the Port of London Authority following the passing of the Port of London Act in 1908. One of the functions of the PLA was the administration of the myriad lighters that were used to tranship goods from the docks to smaller wharves and upstream. Even as late as 1966, countless lighters can be seen in this view, and note the freighter in the centre; this is in the process of being unloaded. Its cargo, which seems to be rolls of paper, can be seen in lighters on both sides; the great advantage of unloading in such a fashion was that the cargo could be unloaded using the ship's own cranes in less time than being moored at a quay.

The dock, along with the rest of the Surrey Commercial Docks in Rotherhithe, was to close completely in 1970. Although ministerial approval for closure was obtained in April that year by the PLA, it was not officially implemented until the enactment of the Port of London Act in December 1970. After the closure of the dock complex, some 171ha of the 186ha of the Surrey Commercial Docks were infllled by the PLA and by the Borough of Southwark with the Greater London Development Plan of 1976 envisaging the residential redevelopment of the site. Little, however, had been achieved by 1981 when the London Docklands Development Corporation was established. Since then the area has undergone a considerable redevelopment with residential and commercial properties replacing the docks, among them the Surrey Quays Shopping Centre. Part of the old dock survives as a freshwater lake – Canada Water – which is now linked to Surrey Water via an ornamental canal constructed through the site of the former Albion Dock. The East London line remains operational; part of the London Underground network at the time that the photograph was taken, it now forms part of the London Overground, providing a connection between Clapham Junction and Highbury & Islington.

EPW164220

East India Docks, London
1 May 1962

With the opening of the West India Docks in 1802, an Act was obtained in 1803 by the East India Company for the construction of the future East India Docks. Historically, the East Indiamen, among the largest vessels to sail along the Thames, had lightened their load near Gravesend before proceeding to deep berths at Blackwall where the freight was transhipped to smaller lighters for carriage to legal quays and sufferance wharves. From these locations, the goods were then moved to the company's warehouses on Billiter Street and Cutler Street. However, this method of working resulted in the considerable loss of valuable freight by river pirates.

This problem was exacerbated by the development of London and West India docks and so the new docks were proposed. The site selected was based around the existing Brunswick Dock constructed by John Perry (1743–1810) during 1789 and 1790 with additional land purchased. To design the docks, John Rennie (1761–1821) and Ralph Walker (c 1750–1824) were employed; initially, when work started, the plans consisted of two docks – Import and Export – but during construction the plans were amended to include an entrance basin. Work started on the construction of the Import Dock in September 1803 with Hugh McIntosh (1768–1840) as the contractor. The new East India Docks opened on 4 August 1806.

In 1838 the West India Dock Co acquired the East India Dock Co and the resulting company became the East & West India Dock Co. The changed ownership saw a subtle change in traffic through the East India Docks; better able to accommodate larger ships than the West India Docks, the East India Docks increasingly came to be used for export, rather than import trade. Along with the rest of the London docks, the East India Docks passed to the Port of London Authority in 1909 and,

between 1912 and 1916, the new owners undertook improvement work at the dock. This included the deepening of the channel between the Import Dock and the dock basin, the improvement of the north quay in the Import Dock and the construction of three transit sheds on the quay to replace sheds built by the East India Company.

As the size of cargo-carrying ships increased during the 20th century, so the usefulness of the East India Docks diminished. During World War II, the Import Dock was drained and used for the construction of sections of the Mulberry harbour for use in the D-Day landings of 6 June 1944. After World War II, the Import Dock was used by ships employed on short-sea and coastal traffic, but the latter was in decline as road and rail transport came to dominate.

The Export Dock suffered severe damage during World War II and was not restored to use. Drained, the site was sold in 1946 and became the location of the new Brunswick Wharf Power Station, which can be seen on the extreme right-hand side of this view. The power station was built in stages between 1947 and 1956, although it first generated power in 1952. Coal fired initially (it was converted to oil fired during 1970 and 1971), the power station was largely constructed by Peter Lind & Co with the concrete chimneys being built by Tileman & Co. In order to receive coal, a new 261m-long wharf was constructed on the river. With the massive increase in the price of oil during the 1970s, the Central Electricity Generating Board took advantage of surplus generating capacity to close the station in 1984. It was mostly demolished during 1988 and 1989 and the site has been subsequently redeveloped.

With the shift to containerisation and the gradual loss of its coastal traffic, East India Docks became the first of the London docks to close, ceasing operation in late

1967. Since closure the Import Dock has been largely infilled and the site used for residential development. The entrance basin, however, survives and is a wildlife refuge.

EAW099748

Millwall Docks, London
2 June 1963

When photographed in 1963, Millwall Docks was approaching its centenary. The original proposals for the construction of the dock on the Isle of Dogs were made in 1863 and work on excavating the site began two years later following the passage of Millwall Canal, Wharfs & Graving Docks Act in 1864 to permit construction. Designed by John Fowler (1817–98) and William Wilson (1822–98), the original plan was for an inverted T-shaped dock but, in the event, a truncated version – a reversed L shape – was completed.

Constructed by John Kelk (1816–86) and the contractors John Aird & Son, the new dock was opened on 14 March 1868. The completed dock comprised an east–west Outer Dock linked to the River Thames by a lock and a north-south Inner Dock with a single dry dock to the south (further graving docks were planned but never constructed). With the eastern extension of the Outer Dock deferred, the eastern bank's wharf was constructed from timber during 1870 and 1871 by John Langham Reed.

Not a great success, financially, at the start, the company's name was changed to the Millwall Dock Co in 1870, but the dock's fortunes picked up with the completion of the Millwall Extension Railway in 1870. Warehouses for handling wool and other commodities were completed and, in 1876, a new method of handling grain was developed. The trade in grain was to revolutionise the dock's finances and further facilities were constructed to handle it. To the east, while the extension of the Outer Dock was again contemplated in the early 1880s, it was again deferred; in any case, the land was proving useful for depositing dredged mud – the Mudchute.

The Millwall Dock Co remained independent until control passed to the Port of London Authority in 1909. Although the plans for the eastern extension were again revived early in the next decade, the only significant change prior to the 1920s was the extension of the graving dock between 1911 and 1913. From 1909 until 1960, the PLA administered the Millwall Docks with the East and West India Docks as the India and Millwall Docks and, between 1926 and 1928, constructed the Millwall Passage that linked the north of the Inner Dock with the West India Docks. This allowed ships to enter Millwall Docks from the north, thus avoiding ships having to sail round the Isle of Dogs, and, after further work had been completed, larger ships to berth. The original entrance lock remained operational, however, until it was severely damaged on 7 September 1940 during the Blitz in World War II and not repaired.

The view recorded by the Aerofilms team in 1963 shows the dock following work undertaken in 1943 to repair wartime damage as well as modifications to the quays made both before the war and during the 1950s. The original lock was dammed in 1956 at the western end of the Outer Dock. Wholesale redevelopment of the docks was undertaken from 1957 with new warehouses being constructed on the west side of the dock. During 1962 and 1963 a new false quay was constructed on the west side of the Outer Dock.

However, the late 1960s were to witness the gradual decline of the Millwall Docks. In 1966 the graving dock was closed, despite opposition, and final closure of the Millwall Docks came in 1980. The area surrounding the graving dock was redeveloped as the Clippers Quay housing estate between 1984 and 1988. The Millwall Docks survive but the entire surrounding area has now been redeveloped. The old entrance to the Outer Dock has completely disappeared, replaced by the carriageway of the A1206 Westferry Road, although the site of the lock itself has been converted into a slipway. The Outer Dock provides a home for the Docklands Sailing & Watersports Club, while on the north side of the Outer Dock is the Telegraph & Express Print Works, one of the largest printers of newsprint in the UK.

EAW112904

Royal Docks, London
6 May 1968

Viewed looking towards the east, this complex of docks comprised, on the western side, the Royal Victoria Dock, with a small Pontoon Dock to its south, with the Royal Albert and shorter King George V docks to the east. Beyond the Royal Albert Dock was the smaller Albert Basin.

The first of the three docks to be constructed was the Royal Victoria, which was promoted originally by the London & St Katharine Docks Co. Powers for its construction were obtained in 1850 and building commenced three years later. It was opened by Prince Albert in 1855. This was the first of London's docks to be designed specifically to accommodate steamships. The dock's original traffic included tobacco, oranges and bananas. The view seen here shows the dock as modified before and after World War II. New warehousing was constructed on the south side of the docks in 1935, while in January 1937 the new 366m-long North Quay replaced the original jetties. In 1946 construction of the five warehouses visible on the North Quay started. Partially closed in 1978, the Royal Victoria finally ceased to operate as a commercial dock in 1981.

The second of the trio to be completed was the Royal Albert; this was again promoted by the London & St Katharine Docks Co with construction starting in 1874. The engineer for the project was Sir Alexander Rendel (1828–1918) with work being undertaken by Lucas & Aird. Opened by the Duke of Connaught in June 1880, the dock was designed to cater for the burgeoning trade in meat and tobacco. The Royal Albert Dock closed for commercial traffic in 1980.

In 1909, both of the existing docks passed to the Port of London Authority and it was the PLA that promoted the development of a third dock – the King George V.

Designed by Frederick Palmer (1860–1934), the dock was put out to contract in 1912 and, although construction started, this was delayed by the war and it was not until 8 July 1921 that the dock was officially opened by, appropriately, the king himself. The new facility was designed to cater for the most modern steam passenger and freight ships of the period. The Gallions Reach lock gates, at the east, were capable of accommodating liners such as the RMS *Mauretania*, which was docked in the King George V Dock in 1939. This view was taken shortly after work was completed on the reconstruction of the Gallions Reach entrance lock. Commercial traffic through the King George V Dock ceased in 1981.

Although today all three docks remain extant, virtually all of the buildings that are visible in the 1968 view have disappeared. The area once occupied by quays on the south side of the Albert Dock and the north side of the King George V now accommodates London City Airport; planning permission for the initial development of this was granted in 1982, with the first section of the runway being completed five years later. On the north side of the Royal Victoria Dock, where once stood the warehouses, is now the ExCeL exhibition centre. The redevelopment of the Royal Docks has taken longer than that of the area around the India Docks, largely as a result of the lack of public transport provision. This has, however, been rectified by the extension of the Docklands Light Railway and, from 2018, by the Crossrail link. There is a marina housed in the Albert Basin and further redevelopment is planned. A new township – Royal Wharf – is planned to provide almost 4,000 new homes around the Royal Docks with additional commercial developments.

EAW182493

Surrey Commercial Docks, London
29 July 1963

The Surrey Commercial Docks were both, in origin, the oldest of London's wet docks and also the only commercial docks established on the south side of the river. Located at Rotherhithe, development of the site started in the late 17th century. This view records, from the east, the southern element of the docks – Greenland (in the centre), South (to the south), Norway, Russia, Quebec and Canada (all to the north) – with the Surrey Canal running north to south through Greenland Dock and linking it with Russia Dock.

The first dock was initially laid out between 1695 and 1699 after its construction was sanctioned by parliament in 1695; it was named the Howland Great Wet Dock after John Howland, who had passed the land originally to the Russell family as part of his daughter's dowry. The dock was designed by John Wells (1662–1702) to handle ships belonging to the East India Co. In 1725 the dock was leased to the ill-fated South Sea Co but, more importantly, from that decade the dock was widely used to handle whale blubber, with large blubber boiling houses erected on the dock side. The importance of this trade was reflected in the fact that the dock was renamed Greenland Dock following its sale by the 4th Duke of Bedford in 1763. By the start of the 19th century, Greenland Dock had been supplemented by a small Mail Pond to the south; this became known as the East Country Dock.

However, the major stimulus to the development of the docks in Rotherhithe came with the opening of the Grand Surrey Canal from Old Kent Road in 1807 (subsequently extended to Camberwell in 1810 and Peckham in 1826). This was one of a number of schemes designed to link Surrey with the River Thames.

Authorised in 1801, the canal's plans were modified the following year to permit the construction of a small dock with a lock into the River Thames at its northern terminus. The new dock opened on 13 March 1807.

The same year saw the formation of the Commercial Dock Co by William Richie (a Greenwich timber merchant) and the East Country Dock Co and, in 1808, the Greenland Dock was purchased, refurbished and renamed the Commercial Dock. Four years later the Norway Dock was added (as was the Baltic Dock further to the north) immediately to the north of Greenland Dock. In 1850 the old East Country Dock was enlarged and renamed South Dock. In 1864, the various companies that owned the south London docks were amalgamated into a single company – the Surrey Commercial Dock Co; this company would retain ownership until 1909 and the creation of the PLA. Between 1895 and 1904 the Greenland Dock was extended to the west, straddling the Grand Surrey Canal (which ran south to north, and incorporating the older Commercial Basin). From the north-west corner of the enlarged Greenland Dock a connection through to Canada Dock was opened. The work in expanding the Greenland Dock cost some £940,000 and was engineered by Sir John Wolfe Barry (1836–1918), who had completed his work on Tower Bridge in 1894. The dock, with its newly enlarged lock (170m long by 24m wide and 11m deep), was suitable not only for the largest cargo vessels of the period but contemporary passenger liners as well.

During World War II, Greenland Dock suffered significant damage, with its locks being hit and most of the quayside warehousing being destroyed. Following post-war restoration the dock had a final decade of prosperity before changing working practices saw the timber trade, by then its principal business, start to decline.

After more than a decade of decline, commercial traffic into the Surrey Commercial Docks ceased in December 1970 and the following year the bulk of the timber docks were filled in prior to redevelopment. The site was sold to Southwark Borough Council in 1977 and two years later construction began on new housing over much of the site.

At the time of writing, the enlarged Greenland (Commercial) Dock remained largely intact, although all of its quayside warehouses have been demolished. It remains connected to the South Dock. The latter and the eastern section of Greenland Dock now act as a marina with access to the river via the lock into South Dock. The Surrey Docks, following closure, remained largely derelict for a decade but in 1981 were transferred to the London Docklands Development Corporation. This resulted in massive redevelopment with the Surrey Quays complex replacing the wet docks to the west and north of Greenland Dock and significant residential development replacing the quayside warehouses.

With the demise of the docks, the Grand Surrey Canal also fell into decline. The southernmost section into Camberwell was abandoned in the 1940s, with the remainder closing with the Surrey Docks. The bulk of the canal has been reclaimed although traces, such as in Camberwell, still survive.

EAW118732

Thameshaven
24 February 1967

Along the River Thames, in addition to the various wet docks that were constructed, there were also numerous private wharves that catered for individual types of traffic. One of these facilities was the quay that served the Shell oil refinery at Shell Haven on the north bank of the river in Essex. From the late 19th century onwards, the handling of volatile products, such as petroleum, was shifted downstream for safety reasons. Shell Haven was the name of the locality; the name Thameshaven (or Thames Haven) came in the 1850s with the construction of a branch by the London, Tilbury & Southend Railway in the 1850s and the establishment of a small port.

In 1912 a licence was obtained by Royal Dutch Shell – through its subsidiary the Asiatic Petroleum Co Ltd – to establish a facility to store petroleum at Shell Haven and four years later a refinery was established to provide fuel for the Admiralty during World War I. This plant was converted to produce bitumen in 1919 and during the interwar period the range of products manufactured at Shell Haven increased. After World War II, when Thameshaven and the other oil refineries were inevitably enemy targets, the site was considerably expanded and in 1948 approval was given for the construction of a new refinery with much of this facility being commissioned two years later. Further investment continued during the 1950s and 1960s. In 1967, shortly after the date of this photograph, a second catalytic reformer was installed and investment continued thereafter. For example, in 1981 a new bitumen plant was completed. By the 1990s, the facility was served by five jetties and covered some 2,000 acres (809ha).

The oil tanker shown is the *ESSO Portsmouth*, which was one of 12 'City'-class tankers constructed between 1957 and 1960. Built by Vickers-Armstrong (Shipbuilders) Ltd at High Walker on the River Tyne, the *Portsmouth* was launched on 6 January 1959 and completed in July the same year. Just one year later, on 9 July 1960, the tanker was severely damaged in an explosion and fire at Milford Haven. Deemed repairable, the *Portsmouth* returned to the Tyne where the tanker was dry-docked. A new 200ft (61m) section was constructed by Vickers-Armstrong and fitted by Swan Hunter in the dry dock at Hebburn. The rebuilt tanker entered service in December 1961 and, as seen here in 1967, was in its rebuilt form with modified stern structure and increased grt (25,715). The *Portsmouth* was to remain in service with ESSO until 1972 when it was sold to Winson Tankers and re-registered in Panama as the *Winson*. Its new career was, however, not to last long; on 12 January 1975 the ship, now used for transporting wheat, grounded in the South China Sea heading for India. Refloated on 6 August 1975, the ship sank the following day while under tow.

The Shell refinery closed in 1999 and was progressively decommissioned thereafter; the bitumen plant remained operational, however, until 2010. The site of the refinery was acquired by DP World in 2006; in May the following year, planning permission was granted for the redevelopment of the site as a new deep-water port – London Gateway. The intention is that, once completed, the new facility will provide 2,700m of quays, six deep-water quays and 24 giant cranes.

The Shell facility was not the only oil terminal on the Thames at this point; slightly to the east was the Coryton oil refinery. This dated to 1953; sold by BP to Petroplus in 2007, the refinery closed in 2013 after its new owner filed for bankruptcy the previous year. This facility is still extant and there are plans to convert it into a diesel import terminal.

EAW168667

Tilbury Docks, London
26 March 1981

Prior to 1909, when the Port of London Authority was established, there was intense competition between the existing dock companies, most notably between the London & St Katharine Dock Co and the East & West India Docks Co. When the former opened its new Royal Albert Dock downstream of its existing facilities in 1880, it gained a competitive edge in providing a deep-water quay. The development of Tilbury was the East & West India Docks Co's response.

Powers to construct the new dock were obtained by an Act of 3 July 1882 and construction commenced on 17 July 1882 under the engineer Augustus George Sackville Manning (1837–1910) with Kirk & Randall succeeded by Lucas & Aird as the contractors. Costing some £2.8 million, the new facility was officially opened on 17 April 1886 when the *Glenfruin* entered carrying invited guests. The original dock is to the south of this view, although the three branch docks – East, Centre and West – can be seen on the extreme right. When opened, the dock had a tidal basin with a lock, some 214m by 24m (the largest on the Thames), from the basin into the main dock.

The view recorded here, looking towards the north-east, shows some of the extensive work undertaken by the PLA during the 1920s and the 1960s. During 1929 and 1930 a new Western lock (300m in length and 34m in width) was completed. In addition, but again out of view, a third dry dock was added at the same time. The dock's major expansion occurred between 1963 and 1966 when a fourth dock branch – which dominates this view – was completed. During the 1960s the original lock was closed along with the tidal basin and both were eventually filled in; the latter is now used as the site of a terminal for the import and export of cars.

The importance of Tilbury grew as ships grew larger and less able to access the traditional docks upstream and as containerisation developed. In 1967 the PLA funded a new £30 million container terminal at Tilbury, although opposition from the unions meant that full operation did not commence until April 1970. A limited operation by United States Line had, with agreement, started two years earlier. In 1978, a deep-water riverside berth was completed on reclaimed land at Northfleet Hope; this is seen clearly in the view when only three years old.

In the view a container ship, the *Tricolor* of Scanmel, can be seen being guided into the entrance lock laden with containers. More evidence of the growing container traffic through the dock can be seen between the new branch built in the 1960s and the 1978 deep-water terminal. It was the massive shift from conventional cargo handling to containerisation that resulted in the demise of the traditional London docks upstream of Tilbury.

Today, Tilbury, now a subsidiary of Forth Ports (having originally been privatised in 1992), is one of the UK's main container ports, competing with Felixstowe and Southampton for trade. It also handles a considerable amount of non-container traffic, such as cars and newsprint.

EAW404063

Viewed looking towards the east, the West India Docks complex straddles the northern part of the Isle of Dogs. To the south, but out of view, are the Millwall Docks (*see* p 37).

The development of the West India Docks, the first commercial wet docks to serve London, was the result of concern among traders with the British colonies in the West Indies over the level of pilferage that ships docked at the riverside wharves suffered. In 1780 the London Society of West India Planters and Merchants was established to promote the interests of those trading with Jamaica primarily and it was two of the main proponents of the society – Robert Milligan (c 1746–1809) and George Hibbert (1757–1837) – that were at the forefront of the campaign to construct a wet dock surrounded by a high wall for security.

Construction of the new docks was authorised by the West India Docks Act of 1799 and construction of the complex commenced following the laying of a foundation stone by the then Prime Minister, William Pitt the younger (1759–1806), and Lord Chancellor, Lord Loughborough (1733–1805). The dock was designed by William Jessop (1745–1814) and Thomas Morris (c 1745–1832) with John Rennie (1761–1821) acting as a consultant. The new docks, which then consisted of the two northerly docks, formally opened on 27 August 1802.

As a result of a clause in the Act permitting the construction of the docks, the West India Docks had a monopoly of the West India trade for 21 years. When originally completed, the northern dock (later North Dock) dealt with imported goods, while the southern (later Middle Dock) was employed with the export trade; the total area of wet dock was some 54 acres (22ha). There were locks and basins at both the east (Blackwall Basin) and west (Limehouse Basin). The Import Dock was surrounded by five-storey warehouses designed by George Gwilt (1746–1807) assisted by his son, also George (1775–1856). As goods were generally loaded on receipt in the Export Dock, there was less need for warehousing. The whole site was surrounded by a 6m-high wall for security.

Also authorised by the Act of 1799 was the construction of the City of London Canal across the Isle of Dogs, immediately to the south of the West India Docks. This was intended to improve access to the upper reaches of the river and was formally opened on 9 December 1805. It was, however, not a financial success and was sold in 1829 to the West India Dock Co. The City of London Canal was to form the basis of the third of the West India Docks, the South Dock, which was built to a design of John Hackshaw (1811–91) and completed in 1869. Initially the South Dock was not connected to the other two docks; this was changed following the creation of the Port of London Authority in 1909. Cuts were made that linked the South Dock to the Middle and North Docks to the north and to the Millwall Docks to the south; the main entrance to the West India and Millwall docks complex was through the lock at the eastern end of the South Dock thereafter.

The 1964 view sees the three West India Docks hard at work; the western – Limehouse – basins and locks have, by this date, disappeared, with access primarily through the enlarged lock at the eastern end of the South Dock. By this date, however, trade was gradually in decline as a result of containerisation and the disappearance of the local industries. There was some investment in the West India/Millwall complex in the late 1960s and 1970s – including the installation of a container-handling crane in 1979 (which was never used due to industrial problems and later relocated to Tilbury) – but final closure for the West India Docks came in 1980.

Much of the original fabric of the docks was lost during World War II; however, a block of the Gwilt-designed warehouses can be seen standing at the north-west end of the North Dock. Today, now listed at Grade II, this is still present and part accommodates the Museum of London Docklands. Other listed buildings include the Grade II two-storey Excise House; this was built in a neo-Classical style in brick and stone to a design by Thomas Morris (c 1754–1832) and completed in 1808. In 1810, two circular guard houses were built; one of these, visible immediately to the west of the surviving warehouses, survives and is now listed at Grade II. Following closure, the land was transferred to the London Docklands Development Corporation and today accommodates Canary Wharf and other developments. The South Dock, however, remains functional and often plays host to visiting ships, including warships on courtesy visits to London, as it is possible for these vessels to be turned in the dock.

EAW130034

London Docklands and Greenwich
10 November 2000 and 25 July 1996

As the traditional docks in London declined, so the issue of how the increasingly deprived areas could be regenerated arose. A vast number of jobs had disappeared and the population was moving away. Without action, a vast swathe of land, both north and south of the river, would be wasted. The issues, apart from the disappearing jobs and the poor quality of much of the existing housing stock, included lack of much of the social infrastructure, such as banks and decent public transport links, that could aid the development of the area.

In 1981 the government decided to create the London Docklands Development Corporation to promote the regeneration of this area. Between then and 1998, when the corporation was wound up, it oversaw the transformation of much of the traditional dockland areas. The first of these views (facing page), looking towards the west, shows redevelopment taking place on the Isle of Dogs. Running from east to west are the three docks that comprised the West India Docks – South Dock, Export Dock and Import Dock – with the Blackwall Basin at the east end. To the south can be seen the Inner Dock of the Millwall Docks. Already operational is the Docklands Light Railway, which opened its first lines in 1987, while construction work was taking place on the Canary Wharf development; work on this had started in 1988 and marked the beginning of the process by which financial and other companies expanded their operations to the docklands area. Alongside the new jobs, vast numbers of residential blocks were either built new or converted from existing warehouses and other buildings.

The second image shows the Greenwich peninsula with the Royal Docks stretching into the distance on the north bank. The LDDC created a new airport – London City – where once freighters had docked in the Royal Albert. Initially proposed by the LDDC in 1981, the first aircraft landed on the new runway on 31 May 1987 with commercial traffic commencing in October the same year. Today, with expansion, the airport is the 15th busiest in the United Kingdom.

In the foreground, is the peninsula itself. This was originally drained in the 16th century by Dutch engineers to create pastureland. During the 19th century, the peninsula became increasingly industrialised with shipbuilding, cement manufacturing and linoleum production. Much of the site, however, was dominated by the town gasworks of the South Metropolitan Gas Co. The largest town gasworks in Europe, the East Greenwich factory possessed two massive gas holders. Originally the gas was manufactured by coal, requiring vast quantities of coal to be shipped in, but in the 1960s manufacture of gas from oil began. However, the development of the North Sea and the arrival of natural gas resulted in the site becoming redundant. With the demise of the gasworks and the closure of much of the other industry during the 1970s and 1980s, the peninsula became virtually a barren wasteland as evinced in this 1986 view. However, the site was chosen to house the Millennium Dome project; despite controversy and less than favourable press, the dome opened on 31 December 1999. Today, as the O2 Arena, it continues to host sporting and artistic events and was one of the venues used in the hugely successful London Olympics of 2012. Much of the surrounding land has also now been redeveloped following the acquisition of land by English Partnerships in 1997.

EAW687121/EAW659284

Dunston Staithes
10 September 1947

In the history of England's maritime trade no single traffic was perhaps more significant than the movement of vast quantities of coal from the north-east of England to London; indeed, it is one of the few trades that has resulted in idiomatic use – the phrase 'carrying coals to Newcastle' being regarded as epitomising a pointless action. Such is the history of the trade in coal from the Newcastle area that the phrase was first recorded in 1538 when some 15,000 tonnes of coal was being shipped annually from the Tyne.

The massive growth in London resulted in the demand for coal from the Durham and Northumberland coalfields increasing exponentially during the 18th and 19th centuries. As a result, dock and port facilities to handle the trade increased in size and complexity; this was not only to affect the River Tyne but places like Hartlepool also developed to cater for the booming coal traffic. One of the ways in which coal was transhipped from wagon to coaster was via staithes and one of the most significant of those to be constructed in the late 19th century is shown here.

The staithes at Dunston were constructed by the North Eastern Railway, with work starting on the first piles on 26 August 1890. The staithes and the associated 4km-long railway branch that served them opened on 16 October 1893, having cost some £230,000 to build. The staithes themselves were originally 521m long and had three shipping berths and two sets of side-tipping spouts through which the coal was dispatched to the coasters. In 1903 a second set of staithes was completed, increasing the capacity to six berths. The staithes continued in operation until 26 May 1980, although increasingly in a state of disrepair, when they and the line to Norwood Yard closed completely; by this date the decline in the coal industry and the increasing use of merry-go-round trains from the surviving collieries rendered the traditional equipment obsolete.

During the 1980s the staithes underwent restoration and were, in 1990, to form one of the centrepieces of that year's garden festival, but the structure, which is believed to be the largest wooden-built structure in Europe, was seriously damaged by fire in 2003 and was listed on the English Heritage Buildings at Risk Register. Now owned by the Tyne & Wear Building Preservation Trust, the Grade II listed structure, which is also a scheduled Ancient Monument, is now the subject of a major restoration project, part funded by the Heritage Lottery Fund, that will open the staithes to the public.

Across the River Tyne can be see the Elswick Works of Vickers-Armstrong Ltd. The factory was first established by William George Armstrong (1810–1900) in 1847. Initially the business of W G Armstrong & Co was the manufacture of cranes but, in 1854, the business started to manufacture armaments and it was this trade that came to dominate production at Elswick. Vickers-Armstrong Ltd was formed in 1927 and the factory eventually passed to BAE Systems. The factory was finally to close in 1982, the victim of the reduction in Britain's defence procurement. The site has been subsequently cleared and has been redeveloped for residential purposes.

EAW010681

Newcastle
August 1935

The use of the River Tyne for the shipment of goods can be dated back to the Roman era, when it was used to supply materials and provisions to the legions stationed along Hadrian's Wall. By the start of the 13th century there is the first evidence of the construction of jetties and by the final quarter of that century, Newcastle was the sixth largest exporting port in England; while coal was significant – with a royal licence being obtained in 1350 – other goods, such as wool, were equally important. From the 17th century onwards, as demand for coal grew, so did the port of Newcastle with some 400,000 tonnes per annum being exported by the middle of that century. However, increasing problems with navigation caused by the silting of the Tyne led, following Royal Assent to its Act on 15 July 1850, to the creation of the Tyne Improvement Commission. The new commission took over the responsibility for the river and its docks from the City of Newcastle and, under its aegis, the river was improved and significant investment undertaken. This resulted in the construction of new docks downstream, although the quays in Newcastle remained active. The commission was to survive until 31 July 1968 when it was replaced by the Port of Tyne Authority.

The quay on the north was, as shown in the 1935 photograph, served by a branch railway line. This had been agreed in 1845 but the short – 1.2km – and steeply graded line was not opened until 1 June 1870 by the North Eastern Railway. Originally steam operated, the gradient and the presence of the Trafalgar Street tunnel made operation difficult and resulted in the line's electrification. Two electric locomotives were built in 1904; these were to survive until the branch was dieselised on 29 February 1964 and one was subsequently preserved. Declining traffic to the quays resulted in the closure of the branch and the associated railways goods station on 16 June 1969.

In the foreground on the south bank of the river can be seen the British Ropes Ltd factory; this was originally the Tyne Wire Drawing Co's plant. This company was a subsidiary of Haggie Bros Ltd of Gateshead, which was one of the eight companies that combined on 6 June 1924 to form British Ropes Ltd (known as Bridon Ltd since 1974 and now owned by the Ontario Teachers' Pension Fund). Part of the site was originally occupied by the Park Iron Works of John Abbot & Co and the rope works was developed after 1909 following the closure of the ironworks.

Rope works were a common feature of many ports and harbours, particularly in the age of sail, but Gateshead has a special place in the history of wire ropes (albeit not at the site illustrated here). The Dundee-born Robert Stirling Newall (1812–89) took out a patent on 17 August 1840 for the manufacture of wire rope. In partnership with Lewis Dunbar Brodie Gordon (1815–76), a one-time assistant of Isambard Kingdom Brunel, and Charles Liddell (1813–94), he set up a business – R S Newall & Co – for the manufacture of wire rope. A decade later the company got involved in the production of coated cables for use in the developing network of undersea telegraph cables.

Today this view is radically different. The decline in commercial shipping using the upstream quays resulted in increasing dereliction by the end of the 1980s and, during the following decade, work started on the wholesale redevelopment of the riverside area on both the Gateshead and Newcastle sides, resulting in an area now branded as the 'Quayside'. On the Newcastle side, virtually all the surviving industrial and quayside structures were swept away, to be replaced by a mixed development of residential and commercial properties. On the Durham side of the river, two major art complexes were built: the Baltic Centre for Contemporary Art, housed in a converted flour mill, and the Norman Foster-designed Sage, which was opened in 2004. The Baltic Flour Mill, which houses the former, was completed in 1950 and thus post-dates the photograph. It was designed by Sir Alfred Gelder (1855–1941) and Llewellyn Kitchen (c 1870–1948) on behalf of Rank Hovis. Linking the redeveloped quays across the river is the Millennium Bridge, which was designed by Wilkinson Eyre, the London-based architectural practice, and opened in 2001.

EPW048818

Salford Docks and Manchester Ship Canal, Salford
25 May 1947

The impetus for much investment in transport in Britain has often been the desire on the part of business to escape from what were perceived as exorbitant charges imposed by contractors. One of the most notable examples of this was the Manchester Ship Canal and the dock complex built to serve Salford and Manchester.

Frustrated by the charges imposed by the docks at Liverpool and by the railways, the businessmen of Manchester proposed the construction of a 58km-long ship canal from Eastham Locks on the River Mersey to central Manchester. Powers were obtained, despite considerable opposition, following an Act of Parliament in August 1885 and work commenced in 1887. Opened in January 1894, the canal terminated in two dock areas – Salford, as shown here, and, further to the east, the Pomona Docks. The complex at Salford comprised four large docks – numbered six to nine – of which No 9 was the largest and the last to be completed (in the early 20th century); the remaining five were situated at Pomona. During the first decade of the 20th century the Ship Canal was deepened by two feet to permit larger vessels. The importance of the docks in Manchester can be gauged by the fact that, in the immediate post-war years, they were the third busiest in Britain; traffic through the docks peaked in 1958 and, despite the creation of a dedicated container facility in No 9 dock on behalf of Manchester Liners in 1968, tonnage declined inexorably thereafter.

The Ship Canal, with its restricted size, was only capable of accommodating vessels of up to 183m in length and 20m in beam; the growth in the size of vessels and the development of containerisation resulted in the gradual decline of traffic along the ship canal and the demise of the docks at Manchester and Salford, with the last closing in 1982. Commercial traffic, however, continues to a container port at Irlam where current owners of the Manchester Ship Canal, Peel Holdings, have plans for a significant expansion. Much of the original dock area in Salford has now been redeveloped, with the BBC and ITV both occupying space at Salford as part of the Salford Quays development.

EAW006236

Southampton Floating Dock
June 1930

The concept of a floating dry dock dated back to the late 18th century but it reached its pre-World War II apogee with the construction of the floating dock at Southampton with its lifting capacity of 60,000 tonnes. The principle was that the dock was sunk to allow the ship access and the hollow base and sides of the dock was then pumped dry to raise the enclosed ship out of the water.

Ordered on 13 October 1922 by the London & South Western Railway (but delivered to its successor, the Southern Railway) and designed by Clark & Standfield, the dock was built by Armstrong Whitworth on the River Tyne and completed on 14 April 1924. Following its tow from the Tyne, the new dock arrived at Southampton on 21 April 1924 where it was berthed to four reinforced concrete piles via 341m-long steel lattices. Officially opened by the Prince of Wales on 27 June 1924, the dock was used until the completion of the new King George V Dry Dock in January 1934. The floating dock remained at Southampton until 27 February 1940 when it was towed to Portsmouth for use as an Admiralty Floating Dock (AFD 11). Declared surplus to Admiralty requirements and offered for sale, the floating dock was sold to the Rotterdam Drydock Co in 1959 and was based in the Netherlands until 1983 when it was sold to a Brazilian business; however, it was wrecked the following year while being shipped to South America. The four concrete piles, which were used as part of BOAC's Maritime Air Terminal between 1948 and 1950, remain extant.

Apart from the floating dock, this view also records the Town Quay and the Trafalgar Dry Dock. The former was begun in 1803 when the Harbour Commissioners, then newly established, demolished the old Watergate quay, which dated originally to 1411. A customs house was constructed in 1847 and six years later the pier was extended. As can be seen in this 1930 view, the Town Quay was served by the railway and handled a variety of cargo. The Town Quay still exists today, although the southern end of the jetty has been converted into a car park and the centre section modified to provide a ferry terminal for services to Cowes and Hythe. Redevelopment has resulted in new shops, restaurants and offices on the northern section, and a marina now operates to the east of the structure.

The Trafalgar Dry Dock – Dry Dock No 6 – was constructed in 1905 and officially opened by the Marquis of Winchester on 21 October 1905, the date being the centenary of Nelson's famous victory. When built, the dock was the largest dry dock in the world, but as the size of ships continued to grow, it was extended in 1913 (to accommodate the RMS *Olympic*) and again in 1922 (for the SS *Berengaria*). When originally constructed, it was fitted with steel gates but these were replaced by a sliding steel caisson in 1913. The dock remained in use until 1989; the bulk of the dock, except for the extreme southern portion, has been infilled to provide parking and all the structures shown in the 1930 photograph have been demolished.

EPW032342

Eastern Docks, Southampton
10 October 1950

Viewed from the south, this complex of docks comprised Southampton's Eastern Docks. The Southampton Dock Co was established by Act of Parliament which received the Royal Assent on 19 May 1836 and, following a meeting on 16 August of that year, it was decided to construct the new docks on mud-land to the east of the existing town quay. On 12 October 1838 the foundation stone of the new dock was laid by Sir Lucius Curtis (1786–1869).

The tidal Outer Dock saw its first occupants in late 1842, when two P&O ships (the *Liverpool* and the *Tagus*) arrived; the formal opening, however, was not until 1 July 1843. Three dry docks – built between 1846 and 1854 on the south side of the dock – were provided. As trade increased, encouraged by the development of the railway network (the line to Southampton Terminus station had opened on 11 May 1840), the Inner Dock was added; this was opened in 1851.

The next phase of the Eastern Docks' development occurred after 1873. The construction of the Itchen Quays, running down the west side of the River Itchen to the south of the Outer Dock, was spurred on by the growing inadequacy of the existing facilities. The shortage of accommodation led Cunard to abandon Southampton in 1875, although the problem was to be relieved the following year when the first of the Itchen Quays opened. It was not until 1895 that the last of these quays was completed; by then, the docks had changed hands and construction started on a third dock.

By the late 1880s, the finances of the original Southampton Dock Co had deteriorated and the only means by which the new dock could be funded was by entering into an arrangement with the London & South Western Railway, which led to the railway assuming ownership on 1 November 1892. The new dock was named the Empress Dock after Queen Victoria, who formally opened the facility on 26 July 1890. At the southern end of the new dock a graving dock, named after the Prince of Wales who opened it in 1895, was provided.

Under the LSWR's ownership, development of the Eastern Docks continued; quays were constructed down the east side of the River Test and at the south end of the promontory. The Test and South quays were completed in 1902. To the west of Empress Dock and to the north of the Test Quays, the White Star (later Ocean) Dock was completed in 1911, following the transfer of White Star Line's transatlantic services to Southampton in 1907. It was from this dock that the ill-fated RMS *Titanic* set sail on its maiden voyage in April 1912.

Berthed at the north quay of the Empress Dock is the troopship *Empire Ken*. This had originally been built by the Hamburg-based shipbuilder Blohm & Voss in 1928 for the Deutsche-Ost-Afrika Line and requisitioned by the Kriegsmarine in 1939. The liner had been captured by the British at Travemünde in May 1945 and transferred to the Ministry of War Transport. Fitted out as a troopship and renamed the *Empire Ken*, the ship was to see service through the 1950s, including the Suez invasion of 1956, before being scrapped finally at Troon, where the hulk arrived on 16 December 1957.

In the 67 years since the photograph was taken, there has been a dramatic change. Virtually every structure illustrated along the various quays has been demolished, to be replaced by a network of roads and storage compounds. The Ocean Terminal, covered in more detail on p 61, has also been demolished while the southern end of the Test Quays is now dominated by the Queen Elizabeth passenger terminal; this was originally constructed in 1966 and modernised in 1988. In 1963 the entrance to the old Outer Dock was enlarged and the Inner Dock infilled. A new car ferry terminal, opened by Princess Alexandra on 3 July 1967, and named after her, was built; this, however, ceased to be operational in 1984 and the Outer Dock is now used as a marina. The dry docks in both the Outer and Empress docks have disappeared. Empress Dock is still extant; the north quay, with berths Nos 26 and 27, is now occupied by the National Oceanography Centre.

EAW033408

Ocean Terminal, Southampton
21 April 1964

One of the most spectacular buildings constructed to serve the great liners that served Southampton was the Ocean Terminal, which is seen here in a photograph taken in 1964. It was in 1907 that White Star Line transferred its operations from Liverpool to Southampton, ultimately occupying a new facility then called the White Star Dock, which was built by the dock's owner, the LSWR, between 1908 and 1911. When, after World War I, Canadian Pacific and Cunard also based their operations in Southampton, the facility was renamed Ocean Dock.

Although there had been moves to construct a new prestigious facility to serve the ocean-going liners that used the dock for some time, it was not until 1950, under the auspices of the British Transport Commission, that the new Art Deco Ocean Terminal was formally opened by the then Prime Minister, Clement Atlee. The new structure was built in concrete; initially this was white, but over time, it became discoloured. The building was provided with two platforms for trains: one was located within the building while the other was alongside the building on the far side. The upper floors provided various waiting halls and other facilities, including bars, buffets and shops.

However, while long in planning, by the time that the terminal was finished, the traffic for which it was designed was under threat. The rise in air travel, particularly with the development of jet aircraft, meant that traffic declined from the 1960s. The Ocean Terminal closed in 1980 and, despite opposition, was demolished three years later.

To the east of the Ocean Terminal is the Empress Dock; this was opened in 1890 by Queen Victoria (*see* p 59). The modern Ocean Cruise terminal occupies the berths on the west side of Ocean Dock.

EAW086604

Southampton Royal Pier
21 August 1957

With the works of Harland & Wolff (which closed in the 1960s) in the background at the northern end of the Trafalgar dry dock, this view shows the Royal Pier.

In 1803 an Act established Southampton's Harbour Commission; this body was tasked with the management of the town's existing harbour situated in front of the Water Gate. The first development was the Town Quay; this was to be used by sailing ships on cross-channel services and, from 24 June 1820, paddle steamers on services across the Solent to the Isle of Wight. However, the new quay could only be used at high tide and, following pressure, in 1829 the Commissioners approved the construction of a pier. The Royal Victoria Pier – later simply the Royal Pier – was designed by Edward L Stephens, a naval officer, and officially opened by the Duchess of Kent and her daughter Princess Victoria on 8 July 1833.

The original pier, however, was constructed using wooden piles; this proved unsuitable and had to be replaced five years later. The wooden piles had to be replaced again in 1864 and 1871 and, in 1892, the structure was again rebuilt, this time using cast iron. On 26 September 1871 an extension from Southampton Terminus station saw horse-drawn passenger trains serve the pier with a passenger station established on the eastern side of the structure; from 21 September 1876 these were steam hauled. The station and line were rebuilt and reopened on 2 June 1892 following the reconstruction of the pier. The line closed on 1 October 1914 and there is no evidence of the line along the pier in this 1957 view. Evidence of the extensive railway network that once served the docks can, however, be seen on Town Quay as steam-hauled freight heads eastwards.

The structure seen here had been modified in 1950 with the addition of a vehicle bridge to provide access to the ferries that were still using the pier. The pavilion, which dated to 1894 on an extension to the original, was extended in 1947. The two-storey entrance building (which is now listed Grade II) was completed in 1937; of all the buildings on the pier seen in this view, it is the only one that still stands. At the time of writing it was occupied by a Thai restaurant. The pier was to be closed on 2 January 1980 when its then owners, the British Transport Docks Board, deemed it no longer economically viable. Four years later, the land at the Town Quay end was acquired by Red Funnel ferries for use as car parking for the vehicle terminal quay established to the east of the Royal Pier and from where ferries to East Cowes now depart. The pavilion was severely damaged by fire on 4 June 1987 and further fires have followed and, although the basic structure remains, it is now derelict. There are plans for the wholesale redevelopment of this area of Southampton docks but any redevelopment would see the removal of the remains of the Victorian pier.

To the north and east of the pier are two significant structures that still exist. The six-storey Geddes Warehouse, which is now listed as Grade II, was designed by and for Donald Geddes, surveyor to the Harbour Board, and built by H W Bull, being completed in 1866. Constructed primarily in red brick, the structure is one of the few old warehouses to survive in Southampton. To the east can be seen the Edwardian baroque building that once formed the Harbour Board offices. This was completed in c 1910 and was constructed in stone on the ground floor and brick on the first, with stone cupola and central pediment. Now listed as Grade II, this structure, at the time of writing, was a club. Between the buildings, on the corner of the road junction, can just be seen the Water Gate Tower, one of the surviving elements of Southampton's medieval town walls. The gate, which was the southern entrance to the town, dates to the 14th and 15th centuries and is now listed at Grade II.

EAR030076

Container Terminal, Southampton
30 April 1972 and 8 July 1987

These two photographs, taken 15 years apart, show the dramatic expansion of the container terminal at Southampton from the period when the facility was nearly new. The process of development has continued since the 1987 view, with the eastern bank of the River Test now developed and with long-terms plans for the development of the western bank of Southampton Water. Most recently, in March 2014, a new deep-water container terminal was formally opened; this represented a £150 million investment and gives Southampton the second largest container quay – after Felixstowe – in Britain. The new facility is capable of accommodating the largest container ships currently in service.

The foreground of the earlier view (facing page) sees the King George V dry dock, which was built at the western extremity of the original Western Docks. The dry dock, also known as No 7, was designed by Sir Francis Wentworth-Shields (1869–1959) and built by John Mowlem & Co and Edward Nuttall & Co. Construction of the facility, which required the removal of two million tonnes of earth with the dock being constructed of concrete with granite dressings, took some two years, with the facility being officially opened by King George V and Queen Mary on 26 July 1933 (although work was not finished until 1934 when the White Star Line's *Majestic* was the first use it). When completed, it was the largest graving dock in the world; it was to retain this distinction until the 1960s. The King George V dry dock closed in 2005 and its lock gates were removed. The following year, the dry dock and associated pump house, also designed by Wentworth-Shields were both listed as

Grade II; the dock, now open to Southampton Water, is still used to accommodate ships.

Across Southampton Water can be seen the original Marchwood Power Station; construction of this began in 1952 and although the first power was generated in 1955, it was not until 1959 that the power station was completed. Originally planned to be coal-fired, the decision was made to make it oil-fired, with the fuel being piped in from the oil refinery at Fawley to the south. The power station closed down in 1983 and was subsequently demolished; the adjacent research laboratories operated by the CEGB closed six years later.

The development of the container terminal at Southampton was the product of the decline in the traditional port traffic. Following a government inquiry, the Rochdale Committee of 1965, Southampton was selected as the site of a container port and work started in February 1967 on the construction of the first quay. The first phase, berth No 201, was opened in October 1968 and a second berth, No 202, followed soon afterwards. The 1972 view records these first two berths in operation; as container traffic continued to expand, the 1970s saw further development, resulting in the opening of new berths – Nos 203–205 during 1972 and 1973 and No 206 in 1976 – with the entire complex being named the Prince Charles Container Port in April 1979. This is the condition of the terminal as illustrated in 1987; the next new berth, No 207, was opened during the 1990s. The container terminal is currently operated by DP World Southampton.

EAW229813/EAW516637

Bideford
August 1932

Located some four miles upstream of the estuary of the River Torridge, Bideford was, in the 16th century, the third busiest port in England and remains one of the few ports in the country to retain a traditional town centre quay.

It was in the 16th century that the harbour's importance developed. The first mention of a quay is in 1619; prior to that date vessels were beached on the foreshore. Controlled by the Grenville family from the middle of the 16th century, it is believed that Sir Walter Raleigh, a cousin of Sir Richard Grenville, landed his first – but not the first to reach Britain – cargo of tobacco at Bideford. The port prospered as a result of the trade with the New World and was also prominent in the exploitation of the cod found off the coast of Newfoundland. On four occasions between 1706 and 1758 the fishermen of Bideford were among those petitioning the government for improved defences on Newfoundland to protect the island against the French and the native tribes. Another source of trade was the importation of wool from Ireland. Bideford was also a centre for shipbuilding, with a significant number of wooden-hulled vessels being constructed. Among vessels constructed during the 19th century were a number of warships for the navy, but the importance of Bideford as a shipbuilding centre declined when iron and steel came to dominate. The last wooden ship was launched into the Torridge in 1912 from a yard at Hubbastone.

Crossing the river upstream from the quay is the Long Bridge. This was originally constructed in timber in the late 13th century; requiring regular reconstruction, it was replaced gradually by a stone bridge between 1460 and 1500 with the stone encasing the original wooden structure. The bridge was widened between 1792 and 1810 by James Green (1781–1849) and again, by Thomas

Page of London (1803–77), between 1864 and 1866. A further widening occurred in 1925. In 1949 the bridge was listed Grade I. Following the collapse in 1968 of the westernmost arch as a result of flooding, the Department of Transport took on ownership from the Bideford Bridge Trust and commissioned Freeman Fox & Partners to replace the missing arch and undertake further repairs and strengthening. Further work, following the introduction of a weight limit and the construction of a new bridge to the north, was begun in 2008.

This view in 1932 was taken looking towards the north-west with the quay on the west of the river with wharves and warehousing on the east side. Adjacent to the eastern end of the Long Bridge is Bideford railway station; this was opened on this site on 10 June 1872, the railway having originally reached the town on 2 November 1855. The station closed on 4 October 1965, although the line through the town remained open for freight until March 1983. The disused railway now forms the route of the South West Coastal Path, although track has been reinstated at Bideford station as part of a preservation scheme.

Today the port at Bideford is controlled by the Bideford Harbour Board, on behalf of Torridge District Council, and it is still regularly used for the shipment of aggregates, raw materials and clay extracts, with fertiliser being brought in. All freight for shipment out of the port is brought to the quay, which is about 1.5km long, by road for loading. In addition, the harbour is also one of the two departure points – the other being Ilfracombe – for the ferry service across to the island of Lundy. Access to the quay, which was refurbished in 2006 to give improved flood protection, is dependent upon the tide and the maximum vessels handled are about 1,500 grt. It has, however, been known for ships to get stuck. The warehousing on the eastern side of the river has been

largely demolished and in late 2014 planning permission was given for the redevelopment of the Brunswick Wharf site, immediately adjacent to the Long Bridge.

EPW039893

Blyth Harbour
15 April 1948

For several centuries one of the major commodities shipped from the ports of north-east England was coal, with London a major market. The most important port handling this traffic for much of the past 200 years was not Newcastle but Blyth in Northumberland and evidence of the facilities required for shipping coal can be seen in this view looking towards the south-west.

The first historic record for a port at Blyth dates to 1138 when salt from pans constructed on the north bank was shipped out by the monks of Newminster Abbey. The coal used in making salt was itself first shipped out during the 14th century; this trade grew significantly over the next 300 years and in 1682 the first purpose-built quay – Bishop's (or Blyth) Quay – was constructed on the north bank. This still survives and is located under the Cowpen Coal Co's coal staithes at the bottom of the photograph. By 1730 coaling and ballast quays had been constructed along with a lighthouse; these were followed in 1765 by the construction of the first breakwater – the North Dyke – and, in 1788, by the first elevated coal staithe. Shipbuilding first appeared by 1813 and in 1822 the original breakwater was rebuilt.

In 1854 the Blyth Harbour & Dock Co was established; this survived until, by Act of Parliament dated 19 June 1882, the Blyth Harbour Commission was created; this body still manages the modern port. The Act also permitted funds to be raised to construct a new South Dock, which is situated downstream of the scene shown here. Upstream, other facilities, not shown in this view, include the Battleship Quay, so named as it was the location of a ship dismantling yard that scrapped Royal Navy warships among other vessels.

Visible in this picture are, on the east bank of the river, the Cowpen Coal Co's staithes; these were completed in 1868. Further upstream on the east bank are the North Staithes; these were officially opened on 13 July 1896. On the opposite bank, part of the South Staithes is shown; these were first completed in 1884 and extended four years later. In the period leading up to World War II, Blyth became Europe's largest port for the handling of coal. The coal traffic peaked in the early 1960s but there was an inexorable and rapid decline thereafter, with the consequent closure and demolition of the coal staithes; all except the West Staithes were closed during 1964. The North Staithes were demolished in 1972 following the construction of a new terminal, first used in June 1971, on the site for the import of material for the Alcan aluminium works.

Blyth also possessed a significant shipbuilding industry and evidence of this is clearly shown in the view on the south bank of the river. The first ships were constructed in 1811; in 1880 the first iron ships were built and on 2 March 1883 the Blyth Shipbuilding & Dry Docks Co Ltd was registered. This company survived until the post-World War I decline led to its closure in 1925. Under new ownership the yard reopened but again failed in 1930; it was again revived in 1937 and constructed a number of frigates and corvettes for the Royal Navy during World War II.

After the war, the yard, which had by this date four berths and five dry docks, manufactured tankers and bulk carriers with one of the dry docks being extended in 1954 to accommodate the construction of larger vessels. The yard closed in 1967; much of the site was cleared to provide a storage area for the paper and timber that represented much of the inward traffic through the port.

Although coal traffic disappeared from the 1960s onwards with the closure of the local mines, the port at Blyth remains busy. Apart from its shipping facilities, the port now includes a significant coastal wind farm located along the harbour's east pier.

EAW014447

Boston
May 1930

If any single port demonstrates how commercial fortunes can change, it is the port of Boston in Lincolnshire. At the end of the 13th century, it could claim to be the chief port in England but by the early 16th century, its importance had declined and by the time the town got its charter from King Henry VIII in 1545, the harbour was virtually silted up.

It was after the Norman conquest that Boston started to develop as a port, with wool, lead and salt being the principal exports and luxury goods being imported from Europe. In the middle of the 13th century the Hanseatic League, the commercial confederation of merchant guilds that dominated trade in northern Europe, established a warehouse in Boston and by the end of the century more than one-third of England's wool exports – the country's principal export of the period – was being shipped through Boston. However, the Hundred Years War was to lead to a dramatic decline in trade, with wine imports largely ceasing and, by the mid-15th century, the loss of much of the wool trade. The importance of Boston to the Hanseatic League declined with the result that the last merchant visited during the second decade of the 16th century.

By the middle of the 16th century, Boston's port served merely local trade; its international importance had ceased and this was to persist for some 200 years. By the middle of the 18th century the River Witham had become largely silted up, with the result that only vessels with a shallow draught could reach the town. However, spurred on by the draining of the vast Holland Fen, in 1762 powers were obtained by Act of Parliament to embank and straighten the fenland stretch of the River Witham; this, combined with revived dredging of the Haven – the stretch of the Witham through Boston – resulted in the revival of the port's fortunes as agricultural products were shipped out.

The early 19th century witnessed a revival of trade, but this renewed prosperity was undermined by the opening in 1848 of the Great Northern Railway's first line to the town as the railway offered a quicker route to market than the existing coastal ships. The survival of Boston as a port was largely the result of investment undertaken by the corporation in the second half of the 19th century that resulted in improvements to the Haven and the construction of a new enclosed harbour; the latter, measuring 82ft (25m) long and 560ft (171m) wide, was opened in 1884 and is the central feature of this view, taken looking towards the west, in 1930. Now owned by the Victoria Group Ltd, the port at Boston remains active, providing – in a re-creation of its Hanseatic past – a connection between England, Scandinavia and the near continent.

EPW031904

Exeter
September 1928

When recorded by the Aerofilms photographer in 1928, the harbour at Exeter was still in commercial use, linked to the estuary of the River Exe by the Exeter Ship Canal. Surrounding the canal basin was light industry, and the branch railway line, opened by the South Devon Railway on 17 July 1867 (initially as a broad-gauge route), provided a link to the main line from Exeter to Plymouth.

With the River Exe originally navigable and tidal, a harbour at Exeter existed in Roman times and by the 13th century it had become a significant regional port. However, during the last quarter of that century, Isabella de Fortibus (1237–93), Countess of Devon, installed a weir in order to improve the water flow to power her mills; although the navigation through to Exeter was restored in 1290, a second weir, built for Hugh de Courtenay (1276–1340), 9th Earl of Devon, in 1317, along with his promotion of Topsham as an alternative harbour, resulted in Exeter's decline as a port due to tolls that de Courtenay was able to exact for shipping on the river.

Although the merchants of Exeter petitioned to have the river passage restored, it was not until 1550 that this was acceded to; unfortunately, by this date, the river had silted up and was no longer navigable by large ships. As a result, in 1563 a canal was promoted to provide an alternative route bypassing the silted-up river. Sanctioned by an Act of Parliament in 1564, the canal was constructed by John Trew of Glamorgan and completed by the spring of 1568. The canal – which saw the first use of pound locks in Britain – was, however, only 5m wide and 1m deep, so was not adequate for larger vessels. The canal was improved in 1677 when it was extended and the entrance moved downstream. It was not, however, until 1701 that the canal was deepened and widened, with the number of locks reduced from three to one; the 18th century saw the

port at its most prosperous as the wool trade provided a staple export with wine and tobacco among the imported goods. It was not until the 1820s that the canal as it exists today was completed; again widened and lengthened, this time under the supervision of James Green (1781–1849), the County Surveyor, the improved canal was formally opened by Humphrey Pinhey, Lord Mayor of Exeter, on 19 April 1825. The final improvement came with the completion of the canal basin itself, following a second Act of Parliament in 1829; the new basin was opened on 29 September 1830.

By this date, however, there was a new threat to the prosperity of the port – the arrival of the railway age. On 1 May 1844 the Bristol & Exeter line to the city was opened, to be followed on 30 May 1846 by the opening of the first section of the South Devon Railway. The decline of the port was such that by the 1920s and the era of the photograph, only three vessels regularly traversed the canal to the port. Trade continued until December 1973 when a cargo of timber represented the last commercial traffic into the port.

Of the site shown in the 1928 image much still remains, although the railway branch is closed and there has been considerable provision of new residential accommodation in and around the harbour area. Maclaine's Warehouse, located between the River Exe and the canal basin, still stands; between 1969 and 1997 this building was occupied by the Exeter Maritime Museum, as was 60 Haven Road, the twin-gabled structure across the basin. The latter, which is also still extant, dates to c 1830. Behind this building, is the Haven Road generating station of the City of Exeter Electric Co, which was owned by the corporation and constructed under powers obtained in 1903. The power station was opened in 1905 and remained operational until 1955. The chimney was removed in March 1960

and the turbines the following year. The building still survives, although having had a somewhat chequered career in recent years, and at the time of writing housed apartments and an indoor climbing area.

Since 1981 much of the work to ensure the survival of the canal and the remaining historic structures that surround the basin has been promoted by the Exeter Canal & Quay Trust Ltd working in co-operation with Exeter City Council.

EPW024101

Falmouth
24 June 1928

Until the mid-16th century, Truro, 16km upstream from Falmouth, was the primary harbour serving this part of Cornwall. However, the growing size of ships meant that Falmouth, which claims to have the third deepest natural harbour in the world, grew in importance. It was, however, only in the mid-19th century that the development of the port became significant.

In 1858 James Abernethy (1814–96) was appointed engineer for the port and he produced a scheme for five graving docks. The following year, following approval of its Act of Parliament, the Falmouth Docks & Engineeering Co was established and on 28 February 1860 the foundation stone of the new dock was laid by Viscount Falmouth.

The work included the construction of a short Western Wharf, which was completed in 1861, along with the associated Northern Arm and a longer Eastern Breakwater that was finished six years later. Two graving docks – Nos 1 and 2 – were completed west of the East Breakwater in 1861 and 1863, respectively. In 1870, again following an Act of Parliament, the Falmouth Harbour Commissioners were established as a statutory body to control the harbour.

The scene as illustrated here had undergone significant change over the previous decade. During World War I the Admiralty started to construct a third graving dock – No 3; this was completed in 1921. Two years later the Western Wharf was lengthened and repaired and the Eastern Breakwater repaired and strengthened. During the 1920s, No 2 graving dock was slightly enlarged and a new graving dock, No 4, was completed in 1926, shortly before the date of the photograph; work was undertaken between 1926 and 1928 on the Northern Arm.

In the decade after the photograph, two new wharves were added to the west of the Western Wharf; these were the Empire Wharf, built between 1931 and 1933, and the King's Wharf, completed between 1935 and 1937. Although shipbuilding at Falmouth ceased in 1930, No 1 graving dock was extended to allow for ship repair work. In 1938 work started on the Queen's Wharf, at the extreme western end of the Western Wharf; this was completed in 1942 at the same time as the Northern Arm was restored. During World War II the docks played a significant role in the D-Day landings of 6 June 1944, with US forces embarking en route to Omaha Beach.

The final phase in the major development of Falmouth harbour occurred in the 1950s. As a result of the growing size of ships requiring repair, No 2 graving dock was enlarged between 1955 and 1958. It was formally opened by the Duke of Edinburgh on 16 May 1958 when it became known as the Queen Elizabeth Dock. Two new wharves, again to the west of the Western Wharf, were constructed the same year; County and Duchy wharves form an inverted V.

The headland above the port is the location of Pendennis Castle; this was one of a number of coastal fortifications built between 1540 and 1542 to protect England from possible French invasion during the reign of Henry VIII. The estuary of the river was protected on this shore by Pendennis Castle and on the eastern side by a second castle at St Mawes; both are now managed by English Heritage.

The port, which was owned by British Shipbuilders at the time (the Falmouth Dock Co having been nationalised in 1977), was privatised in 1985; it is now owned by A&P Group Ltd – one of only two significant ship repair companies remaining in the UK – and three of the graving docks – Nos 2 to 4 – remain operational while there are about 700m of operational wharves for commercial traffic. The port is also used by cruise ships, with about 40,000 passengers per annum passing through.

EPW021716

Glasson

1 May 1972

Problems with ensuring the navigability of the River Lune to Lancaster in the late 18th century resulted in the Lancaster Port Commission deciding to build a replacement facility at Glasson in 1779. Land was purchased the following year and by 1782 a pier had been constructed, but this proved unstable and led to a dispute between the Commissioners and the contractor who had built it. Thomas Morris (c 1754–1832) was brought in to assist and he produced plans in November 1783 to replace the existing quay and add a second pier and gates so that a new wet dock could be completed. With Morris acting as engineer, work was completed by March 1787.

Shortly after the completion of the dock, earlier plans for the construction of the Lancaster Canal were revised with a final survey being carried out by John Rennie (1761–1821) at the end of 1791. On 11 June 1792 the Royal Assent was granted to an Act for the construction of a canal running south from Kendal via Lancaster to Preston on the one hand, along with a second – detached – section south from Preston. There were plans in Rennie's original scheme for a connection to Glasson Dock but no work took place until after the Napoleonic Wars; a further Act was passed in 1819 that allowed funds to be raised for the 4km-long branch, with work commencing in 1823. The canal was completed in December 1825 but the additional wharves were not completed immediately. Other buildings, such as the Custom House (1834) and the Watch House (1836), were added later.

By the date of the photograph, many of the facilities that had once served Glasson Dock had disappeared. The railway line, opened originally in 1883, had lost its passenger services on 5 July 1930 and closed completely on 7 September 1964. The dry dock, which had been completed in December 1840 and which had been used by the shipbuilders Nicholson & Sons until 1907 and then for ship repair work, was closed in 1968 and filled in the following year. Although much of the harbour is now devoted to a marina, a limited amount of commercial traffic, such as coal to the Isle of Man, is still handled. The entrance to the dock is protected on the east side by a late 18th-century lighthouse, which is now listed as Grade II.

EAW228113

Gloucester
May 1932

Looking south-westwards along the Gloucester & Sharpness Canal, this view shows to good effect the docks that served Gloucester. At the bottom right of the image is the Main Basin; this has a connection, via a lock, with the River Severn. To the east of the Main Basin is the Victoria Dock and in the middle distance, on the west side of the canal, can be seen Monk Meadow Dock. On both sides of the canal from the Main Basin to Monk Meadow Dock are quays: that on the west side is Llanthony and on the east Bakers.

Although the earliest records of a harbour at Gloucester date to the Roman era, Gloucester's importance grew from the late 18th century with the construction of the canal. Promoted by the architect and civil engineer Robert Mylne (1733–1811), construction of the canal commenced in 1793, but problems with finance resulted in delays. Mylne was sacked in 1798, to be replaced by James Dadford (c 1768–1804), who had been employed since 1795 and who was also to be dismissed in November 1800 when the funds dried up. By 1799 only 8.5km of the projected 26.5km canal had been completed, along with the actual canal basin in Gloucester itself. Additional funds raised allowed for improvement works on the basin at Gloucester in 1813 but it was not until after 1817, and the terms of the Poor Employment Act, that work on the completion of the canal commenced with the route opening throughout in April 1827.

The success of the docks meant that expansion proved necessary. In 1824 a small addition to the basin – the Barge Arm – was added on the east side of the basin (slightly to the south of the site of the future Victoria Dock). Bakers Quay – privately funded by Samuel Baker – was added in the 1830s, while the continuing growth in traffic required the opening of the new Victoria Dock in 1849. The small dry dock at the western end of the basin

was supplemented by a second – larger – dry dock in 1853. Llanthony Quay was also added in the early 1850s by the Gloucester & Dean Forest Railway Co, with the broad-gauge railway connection opening on 20 March 1854. This railway became a subsidiary of the GWR following an Act of 30 June 1874. Further south Monk Meadow Dock was added in 1892; this was constructed to handle the booming timber trade that had seen a number of timber yards established on the canal-side quays. The final development of the dock – Monk Meadow Quay to the south of Monk Meadow Dock – was completed in 1965, long after this photograph was taken.

The 1932 view records the massive brick-built warehouses that were constructed around the basin and Victoria Dock. The earliest of these dated from 1827 and internally were constructed with wooden floors carried on cast-iron tubular columns. Although the traditional use for these warehouses has now ceased, a significant number of them have been listed and have found alternative uses.

The triple block adjacent to the barges at the north-east corner of the Main Basin – Herbert, Kimberley and Philpotts warehouses – were all designed, it is believed, by the local architect John Jacques (1800–68) and completed in 1846. Listed Grade II, this trio of warehouses were restored and converted for the local authority in 1985.

On the east side of the canal, adjacent to the Llanthony Road bridge across the canal just south of the Main Basin, is the Llanthony Warehouse; this Grade II listed building, built in 1873 to the design of another local architect, Capel Nankivell Tripp (c 1844–83), was converted into a museum – originally the National Waterways Museum and subsequently the Gloucester Waterways Museum – in the late 1980s. Many of the warehouses alongside the Victoria Dock and Bakers

Quay have more recently been converted into residential blocks. These include Albert Warehouse (again probably designed by Jacques and completed in 1851), Philpotts Warehouse (designed by Jacques and completed in 1846) and Biddles Warehouse (designed by William Franklin and completed in 1830).

The canal was nationalised in 1948 and control passed to the British Waterways Board, which was established in 1962, and then to the Canal & River Trust when this charity was established in 2012 to take over British Waterways' responsibilities. Commercial traffic along the canal largely ceased in the 1980s and the canal is now largely used for leisure purposes with a marina, for example, established in Victoria Dock.

EPW037834

Goole
20 April 1949

Situated some 72km inland, Goole is now England's furthest port from the sea and, handling some 2 million tonnes of cargo per annum, is one of the most important on the East Coast.

The origins of the port stretch back some 300 years to the draining of Hatfield Chase by the Dutch engineer Cornelius Vermuyden (1595–1677). In order to drain the marshland, he diverted the River Don northwards between 1626 and 1629 and created a new navigable channel – known as the Dutch River – that enabled coal to be shipped from the Yorkshire coalfield to ports on the Humber. The Dutch River is the southernmost of the waterways in this 1949 view of the port of Goole looking towards the west.

During the late 17th and 18th centuries, there were proposals, some of which were completed, for work to make the rivers Aire and Calder navigable to serve the growing industrial centres around Leeds, Bradford and Wakefield. One of these schemes was the Aire & Calder Navigation. In 1820 the company obtained an Act for the construction of a canal from Knottingley to Goole with the survey work being undertaken by John Rennie (1761–1821), who advocated shortly before his death the construction of a port at Goole rather than a simple lock into the River Ouse.

Work started on the construction of the port and canal at Goole on 28 September 1822 under Rennie's successor, George Leather (1786–1870), and the dock opened on 20 July 1826, the first vessel having passed along the canal on 25 July 1825. The port was provided with locks at both entrances; that into the river was 120ft (36.6m) in length and just under 34ft (10.4m) in width. The canal was not to have a monopoly of traffic for long; the first railway reached the town in 1840 and competition for the all-important coal traffic became intense, particularly after 1846 when the railway, which

became the Lancashire & Yorkshire the following year, gained powers to construct coal staithes. The canal responded to the competition by increasing, between 1860 and 1867, the length of the canal locks by 22ft (6.7m) to permit the use of longer barges. More significant was the development of sectional boats, proposed by the canal's chief engineer William Hammond Bartholomew (1831–1919), that could be lifted via hydraulic hoists to unload into ships. Evidence of the sections, nicknamed 'Tom Puddings', and hoists can be clearly seen in the 1949 view; this type of traffic was to survive until 1986 and one hoist remains extant on the south side.

During the late 19th century the port expanded, with steamer services operating to the Low Countries and Scandinavia (these were taken over by the L&YR once the railway obtained powers to run shipping services following the Royal Assent to its Steam Vessels Act on 15 August 1904). A second entrance lock to the River Ouse – the Victoria Lock – was completed in 1888; this was followed by a third lock – Ocean Lock – completed in 1938. This new lock, 37ft (11.3m) by 80ft (24.4m), permitted the use of the port by much larger vessels.

Across the Dutch River from the port is the shipyard, which dated to 1917, of the Goole Shipbuilding & Repairing Co Ltd. This business had originally been established in 1901 by the Craggs family when the Victoria Yard on South Street, previously owned by Thomas Scott, was acquired. Scott himself had previously acquired the site from the Goole Shipbuilding & Engineering Co in 1876 and the origins of the shipbuilding and repairing industry in the port can be traced back to the opening of the facility. The yard primarily constructed trawlers and small merchant vessels, three of which can be seen on the slipways. The company retained its independence until 1967

when it was sold to Swan Hunter, becoming part of the latter's Small Ships Division. As such it was nationalised in 1977, forming part of British Shipbuilders. Renamed Goole Shipbuilders in 1982, the yard closed on 27 April 1984. Briefly resurrected by Cochrane & Co later that year, a further four vessels were completed before construction work ceased. Thereafter the yard was used for shipbreaking and the site has subsequently been redeveloped.

Nationalised in 1948, the port at Goole remains one of the subsidiaries of the now-privatised Associated British Ports. With the loss of its coal and much of its timber traffic – the timber ponds at the western extremity of the port have been converted into a marina – Goole now handles a variety of bulk products such as cement, agricultural products and scrap metal.

EAW022510

Immingham
13 June 1950

At the start of the 20th century there were few railway companies more ambitious than the Great Central Railway. Its London Extension, to Marylebone, had just been completed and it was about to embark on a further major project – the construction of its docks at Immingham.

Proposals for the development of a port at Immingham first emerged in 1874 when the engineer Charles Liddell (1813–94) undertook some test borings for the Manchester, Sheffield & Lincolnshire Railway, one of the GCR's predecessors. Work did not commence, however, but in 1900 Sir John Wolfe Barry (1836–1918) confirmed Liddell's findings and, despite considerable opposition, the Humber Commercial Railway & Dock Act received the Royal Assent on 22 July 1904.

Work commenced officially on 12 July 1906 with the facility being designed by Sir John Wolfe Barry & Partners and actual construction being undertaken by Price, Wills & Reeve of Edinburgh. The wet dock was officially opened by King George V on 22 July 1912 although the western jetty had been in use from 1910 for the shipment of coal. As completed, the docks comprised a lock with three sets of lock gates (with a maximum length of 840ft [256m] and width of 90ft [287.4m]) along with a wet dock with a water area of 45 acres (18ha) and just over 9,000ft (2,743.2m) of quay space. The two jetties were both originally rail connected; the western jetty handled coal while the eastern served a passenger terminal with a station – Immingham Eastern Jetty – opening on 17 November 1913 to serve the GCR's steamer services. By the date of the 1950 photograph the link to Eastern Jetty had closed; services ceased during 1939. In addition to the wet dock, the facility also included a graving dock (parallel to the entrance lock and, at the time of writing, still extant but largely silted up at its northern extremity with a further quay cut to its immediate west).

During World War I, Immingham was used as a submarine base by the Royal Navy. In 1923, the harbour (along with the GCR) passed to the LNER at the grouping and in 1948 was nationalised, passing to the BTC. While Immingham was a relatively minor port when recorded in 1950, over the succeeding years its importance has grown with the result that, at the time of writing, it was the UK's largest in terms of tonnage handled. Although the original wet dock is still very active, much more significant are the deep water jetties that have been constructed both north and south of the entrance lock seen in the 1950 view.

Owned by Associated British Ports, the docks at Immingham are still rail served, with some 300 train movements per week, with coal and other bulk goods, container traffic, oil, steel and timber being among the traffic handled. There is also a significant roll-on/roll-off facility with services linking the port with Scandinavia and the Low Countries. Among the few buildings to survive from the GCR period is the Immingham Dock Office; this is the three-storey brick-built building visible on the east side of the entrance lock in the 1950 view.

EAW030245

Ipswich
5 October 1950

Located on the River Orwell, Ipswich has been a port since the 7th or 8th centuries and was one of the principal harbours of the Anglo-Saxon period. Until the early 19th century the quays were along the banks of the original alignment of the river through the town – effectively the north-eastern side of the wet dock – but towards the end of the period, these quays suffered from silting and from the unwillingness of larger ships to navigate the twisting river through the town.

It was in the late 18th century that William Chapman initially proposed investment in improving the facilities, but it was not until the early years of the 19th that practical efforts were made to upgrade the facilities, following the passage of an Act of Parliament in 1805 that established the River Commissioners. Initially this involved dredging the existing river channel but, in 1837, a further Act empowering the Commissioners to divert the river (the New Cut) and construct a new wet dock was passed. The construction of the new facility was overseen by David Thornbory of King's Lynn (although not without dispute between him and the Commissioners). When completed in 1842, the new wet dock was the largest in Britain. However, the continuing growth in the size of vessels using the port required a further Act of 1877 to permit the construction of a new lock downstream of the original lock; this facility was opened in 1881 and was to suffice until the early years of the 20th century.

In 1913 a further Act, the Ipswich Docks Act, was passed to permit the construction of a new dock entrance as well as quays both within the wet dock and downstream of the facility. Theoretically, work had to be completed within 10 years but, as a result of World War I, a further Act was passed in 1918 allowing for an extension. In the post-war environment, it was decided that the expense of enlarging the lock could not be justified and so the 1881 structure was retained while other work, including the construction of new quays, was completed in the mid-1920s. The view taken in 1950 illustrates the wet dock very much as it had been upgraded after World War I. Since then, there has been considerable investment in the port of Ipswich although the bulk of this has gone into facilities downstream of the wet dock.

Today, the wet dock is used largely as a marina, although there is still limited commercial traffic to the quays on the west side. The main commercial activity of the port, owned by Associated British Ports since 1997, is now concentrated on quays located on the Orwell downstream of the scene recorded in 1950. Of the area surrounding the wet dock there has been considerable modern work undertaken on the northern and eastern quays, although the old Custom House, designed by local architect John Medland Clark (1813–49) and completed in a neo-Classical style in 1844, remains and is listed as Grade II*. This building is visible in the 1950 view on the north-east quay of the wet dock.

EAW033332

King's Lynn
June 1928

As with Boston (*see* p 21), the importance of King's Lynn – known as Bishop's Lynn prior to 1537 – as a port dates back to the Middle Ages and the Hanseatic League. The first settlement occurred towards the end of the 11th century and the town's first charter was granted in 1204. In 1271 the Hanseatic traders received their first trading privileges in the town although these were subject to dispute until confirmed in 1310. The export trade was dominated by salt (produced locally in copper pans), wool and grain, while timber, fish and iron were imported. Through the Hanseatic League, connections were established with a number of northern ports, most notably Danzig, Bergen and Lübeck and merchants from Lynn were based in a number of ports, just as foreign merchants had their own properties in Lynn, and there was also a considerable interchange of artisans. In 1474, following the Treaty of Utrecht (which settled a dispute between England and the League), King Edward IV conveyed a quay and tenements in the town to the League; the following year, Hanse House was completed. This, now listed as Grade I, and the Grade II* listed Marriott's Warehouse are the only two substantial remains of the Hanseatic League in existence in England.

From the 16th century, the importance of the Hanseatic League declined, although Lynn retained trading links with the Baltic, as the East Coast trade of coal from Newcastle to London and corn came to dominate. The trade in wool, however, largely disappeared. Lynn's position was ideal, particularly for the export of corn from the agricultural area that surrounded it. Lynn, like a number of other East Coast ports, suffered from the growth of London in the 17th and 18th centuries as well as from the increasing importance of trade to ports such as Bristol and

Liverpool that were better placed to serve the burgeoning commerce with the Americas and Africa.

The original port area was located to the south of the view recorded here by the Aerofilms photographer. It was in the mid-19th century that the impetus came for the construction of a modern dock. The King's Lynn Docks & Railway Co was incorporated under an Act of Parliament dated 19 June 1865 to construct a new wet dock with linking railway. The new dock – named after Princess Alexandra who formally opened it in 1869 – was accessed off the Great Ouse by a lock capable of taking vessels of up to 46ft (14m) in beam. A second wet dock – Bentinck Dock – was added in 1883, taking the total water area to 17 acres (7ha) with more than 5,000ft (1,524m) of quay berths.

As with other railway-owned ports, King's Lynn was nationalised in 1948. Privatised when Associated British Ports was sold, the port remains one of those controlled by the business. The two wet docks and the 720m-long Riverside Quay remain operational, with traffic comprising agricultural and forest products as well as steel and other metals. Of the quayside buildings seen in the 1928 view, all have disappeared – although most were still standing in the early 1960s – with the exception of the two single-storey blocks with curved roofs to be seen on the south side of Central Road (to the south of Alexandra Dock). When recorded in 1928 the docks were still served by rail; all freight to and from the port now uses road transport exclusively with the rail connection having fallen into disuse in the early 1990s. The local council has undertaken a consultation process with a view to safeguarding the route – and others within its area – for either recreational or transport use in the future.

EPW021482

Maryport
August 1930

Situated at the mouth of the River Ellen and known until 1756 as Ellenfoot, Maryport's importance as a port grew from the decision of local landowner Humphrey Senhouse (1705–70) to create a new port to rival that established at neighbouring Whitehaven.

In 1749 an Act of Parliament was obtained 'for repairing, enclosing and preserving the harbour at Ellenfoot in the County of Cumberland' along with the creation of a new town. The town was renamed Maryport in honour of Senhouse's wife, Mary. The work included the widening of the river channel and the construction of a new pier; this stands and is now known as the North Pier. In 1765 the first shipyard was opened – ship construction survived until 1914 – and trade continued to grow during the second half of the 18th century as a result of the expansion of the iron and coal industries. In 1833 a second Act was obtained in order to expand the harbour and to see its management under a Board of Trustees; this resulted in the construction of South Quay. In 1838 a Custom House was established in the town; this was replaced by a new structure in 1898 and the town retained a Custom House until closure in 1960.

The next phase in the port's development came with the construction of the Elizabeth Dock; this was formally opened on 20 October 1857. It is this dock, 180m long and 73m wide, that forms the foreground of this view taken in 1930. At the time, Maryport was suffering a significant loss of trade; a new deep-water dock had been opened at Workington in 1927, with the consequent transfer of raw materials for the Workington Iron & Steel Co away from Maryport, which compounded the decline in the local coal and iron industries. Such was the parlous state of the local economy that 20 men from Maryport joined the Jarrow March of 1936.

The Elizabeth Dock was not the final development of the facilities in the town; the dock was not capable of handling the increasing trade and the larger ships of the late 19th century, with the result that the Senhouse Dock – visible in part at the bottom left of the photograph – was constructed between 1880 and 1884. The engineers for the project were Sir John Hackshaw (1811–91) and his partner Harrison Haytor (1825–98).

The docks at Maryport enjoyed a brief revival during World War II, when coal from north-east England was routed via the port rather than via the more vulnerable East Coast ports, but traffic declined in the 1950s and the port ceased to deal with cargo vessels during the 1960s. The port had always had a fishing fleet, primarily for herring, and this trade continues to operate from the Elizabeth Dock, while Senhouse Dock has been converted to act as a marina.

EPW034441

Middlesbrough
11 April 1981

Until the mid-19th century Middlesbrough was no more than a small village, but with the coming of the coal and iron industries, it was to experience significant growth.

In the late 1830s it was becoming clear that the existing dock facilities upstream from Middlesbrough were proving inadequate and Thomas Cubitt (1788–1855) was approached to survey a new dock. He undertook the work, consulting George Leather (1786–1870) who had undertaken work previously on harbour facilities on the River Tees, and work commenced on construction in early 1840. The builder was George Turnbull (1809–89), who had worked closely with Thomas Telford (1757–1834) earlier in his career. The new dock was officially opened on 12 May 1842 and proved to be an immediate success, although not without problems as the lock proved too small for some of the vessels that desired to dock in Middlesbrough. The success of the dock meant that it was enlarged in size on three occasions – between 1869 and 1873, between 1878 and 1889, and between 1898 and 1904. The final work, which was undertaken on behalf of the North Eastern Railway – the dock had been railway-owned since the 1840s – resulted in an improved entrance lock and the enclosed dock extending over 25½ acres (10ha). As with other railway-owned docks, Middlesbrough passed to the ownership of the BTC in 1948 on nationalisation.

Visible straddling the river is the transporter bridge; this is one of only three such structures that remain extant in Britain and is now listed Grade II. In 1907 an Act was secured to permit the construction of the bridge to the design of the Frenchman, Georges Camille Imbault (1877–1951), the chief engineer of the Darlington-based Cleveland Bridge & Engineering Co Ltd. Work commenced on the bridge's construction in 1907 with the contract placed with the Glasgow-based Sir William Arrol & Co. The completed bridge was officially opened on 17 October 1911 by Prince Arthur of Connaught (1883–1938). It was designed to replace the existing ferry service across the river while not impeding shipping heading upstream to the port of Stockton. The bridge underwent a major refurbishment between 2013 and 2015 with the work being undertaken by Balfour Beatty.

The date in the photograph is significant. In the mid-1960s, a new facility – now known as Teesport – was established downstream of the existing dock at Middlesbrough. Much of the traffic that had made use of Middlesbrough now used the new harbour and, by the late 1970s, the dock at Middlesbrough was losing money. As a result the owners – the Tees & Hartlepool Port Authority (established by Act of Parliament in 1966) – decided to close the dock at Middlesbrough. The last ship to use it was the *Evpo Wave* on 24 July 1980 and the dock was officially closed seven days later. Demolition of the cranes commenced in September of the same year and so, by April 1981, the dock was effectively derelict. Since then, there has been some regeneration; most notably, the construction of Middlesbrough's new football ground – the Riverside Stadium – was completed on the south side in 1995. At the western end of the dock, Middlesbrough College has been built over part of the infilled dock. The docks themselves remain largely extant but unused.

EAW405234

Northfleet
April 1927

Alongside small ports and harbours, the coast and river estuaries often played host to wharves designed to deal with specialist traffic, where the bulk of raw materials travelling inwards, usually coal or iron ore, or finished goods out – cement, for example, as seen in this 1927 view of Bevan's cement works at Northfleet – justified the investment.

With its ready supply of chalk and water, north Kent was the centre of the UK cement industry from the early 19th century. In 1824 Joseph Aspdin (1778–1855) was granted a patent for a new type of cement – Portland cement (so-named as its manufacturers wished to suggest it was similar to Portland stone) – and his son, William (1815–64), moved from Yorkshire to north Kent to establish a cement works at Rotherhithe. William Aspdin then established a partnership with Messrs Robins and Maude to build a cement works at Northfleet in the 1840s. In 1852 Aspdin sold his share of the partnerships and seems to have invested in a rival concern that constructed a second cement factory immediately to the east of the original site. This was the origin of the plant seen in this 1927 view; owned by Knight, Bevan & Sturge, production started in 1853. In 1900 ownership passed to Associated Portland Cement Manufacturers Ltd, a combine established that year to take over the interests of some 24 separate businesses, with its Blue Circle trademark.

In the early 1920s APCM decided to upgrade the facility at the Bevan's works; the redevelopment started in 1922 and, as a result of the restricted site, could only be completed by the demolition and replacement of the existing kilns. The work was completed in 1927 and so this view records the plant at the point at which this major investment was being completed. Also, between 1925 and 1928, a new deep-water wharf was built at the plant to service the increased capacity; the engineer in charge was Oscar Faber (1886–1956), who was a pioneer in the use of reinforced concrete. His other work included Rhodes House and South Africa House, both in London, and the Queen's Hotel in Leeds. The photograph shows the new facility in use. The Bevan's cement factory was never rail-connected and so the wharf was essential in the exporting of the finished product from what was, when the rebuild of the 1920s was completed, one of the largest cement works in Europe, capable of producing up to half a million tonnes of cement per annum.

In 1970 the old Bevan's site and a number of other cement works in the area owned by APCM were closed, to be replaced by the new Northfleet works, although the existing cement handling and wharves at the site remained operational. In 1978 APCM became Blue Circle Industries and in 2001 Blue Circle was acquired by the French company Lafarge. The Northfleet cement works closed in 2008 and the site was cleared. Today, the wharf as seen in the 1927 view is still extant although disused and the site of the Bevan's cement works has been cleared, as has the more recent Northfleet works; much of the land released is still to be redeveloped although some of the neighbouring chalk pits have been incorporated into the massive Bluewater shopping centre.

EPW017640

Plymouth Millbay Docks
11 August 1953

As well as the naval dockyard at Devonport, Plymouth possesses a number of non-military facilities; these include Millbay Docks, Cattewater Harbour and Sutton Harbour. This view shows Millbay Harbour in the early 1950s when it was owned by the successor to the GWR, the BTC.

Situated to the west of Plymouth Hoe, Mill Bay, a natural tidal inlet, derived its name from the grain mills that existed in the vicinity from the 12th to the late 16th centuries. In the mid-18th century John Smeaton (1724–92) used the harbour as the base from which to construct the Eddystone Lighthouse. By the 1830s there was a small dock, Union Dock, located to the north of the bay; this had been the work of Plymouth engineer James Meadows Rendel (1799–1856), who was also involved in the first plan to create a non-tidal dock in Mill Bay itself. Following plans drawn up by Rendel in the late 1830s, Thomas Gill (1788–1861) obtained an Act of Parliament in 1840 to permit construction. Work commenced on the pier, now known as Millbay Pier, which was completed in 1844.

Two years later a further Act saw the Great Western Dock Co established and Gill sold his interest to the new company, becoming a director of it. He and Isambard Kingdom Brunel (1806–59) were also both involved with the South Devon Railway and it was the latter that came to design the new Millbay Docks. The first addition was a floating pontoon pier, which was completed in the early 1850s for the Irish Steamship Co's services. The Inner Basin, with its entrance lock and dry dock, was opened in February 1857. Between Millbay Pier and the Inner Basin a further pier, Trinity Pier, was also completed.

In 1874, the Great Western Dock Co was taken over by the South Devon, Bristol & Exeter and Great Western railways and, over the next few years, further investment was undertaken, including the construction of the West Wharf, to the south of the Inner Basin, and the East Wharf. The GWR took over operation of the other two railways in 1876.

From 2 April 1849, trains ran between Plymouth Millbay station (adjacent to the freight yard to the east of the Inner Basin in this view) and the non-timetabled platform, Plymouth Millbay Docks adjacent to Millbay Pier, carrying passengers who used lighters to connect with the transatlantic liners that docked in Plymouth Sound. Millbay station closed on 23 April 1941 as a result of wartime damage. Plymouth Millbay Docks, visible in the scene with coaching stock, opened in 1882 and was to survive until closure overnight on 18/19 October 1963 when mail and passenger traffic was last handled via this facility.

The 1953 image records the harbour following considerable change during the first half of the 20th century. In November 1902 a new central entrance lock was opened slightly to the west of the original facility. At the same time Trinity Pier was widened and lengthened. In 1903 Millbay Pier was also lengthened. A decade later the West Wharf was rebuilt, this time in concrete, and during the 1920s the dry dock and North Quay were improved, with the latter being fitted with electric cranes and better facilities for handling mail.

Today the harbour remains active as a subsidiary of Associated British Ports; ferry services operate from the harbour to Roscoff and St Malo in France and to Santander in Spain. The western half of the now Grade II listed Inner Basin and the dry dock have been reclaimed, the latter filled in during 1972 and 1973, and the land used to provide additional parking and facilities for the ferry terminal; the first roll-on/roll-off ferry terminal opened in the early 1970s and a second facility followed in 1986. The gates to the Inner Basin have disappeared and the western part of the surviving section of the wet dock has silted up. The new King Point Marina opened in the inner dock in 2013 and the dockside area is subject to a regeneration scheme. On the eastern side of the outer docks, the middle pontoon pier has disappeared and a marina now occupies the site between Millbay Pier and the new jetty. The impressive grain silo, which had been built for grain imports during World War II and which was long a familiar indication of the harbour's entrance, was demolished in 2008.

EAW051361

Preston Docks
July 1932

This 1932 photograph shows the Albert Edward Dock at Preston viewed from the west, with the River Ribble heading towards the town. The development of a port serving Preston commenced in the early 19th century when the first of three navigation companies started the process of creating quays alongside the river within the town and by 1880 some 1,100 acres (445ha) of land had been reclaimed and quays established. However, the increasing size of ships led to the realisation that major investment would be required to ensure that the port remained viable.

In 1883 the Ribble Navigation & Preston Dock Act passed control of the port to the corporation and permitted the construction of a new dock. Work commenced in 1884 with the foundation stone of the new basin being laid in July 1885. The work, designed by the engineer Edward Garlick (1822–1900), was achieved by the diversion of the river to a new channel and the construction of the basin on the original alignment of the river. When completed, the new dock had a water area of some 40 acres (16ha), one of the largest basins in the world, with the lock entrance being 550ft (167.6m) long. Not all were impressed with the scheme, however; an editorial in *The Engineer* on 23 March 1888 described it as 'rash and ill-considered', citing the distance from the sea and the quantity of dredging required as being factors that would cost the operators a considerable amount. Despite these concerns and the additional sums required to fund the work, the docks were completed and the dock was officially opened on 25 June 1892 by Prince Albert Edward, later King Edward VII.

The completed basin is that seen in this view; the oil storage tanks were initially erected in 1914. The port's facilities enabled it to handle a wide range of goods – cotton, timber, china clay and agricultural products being regular traffic – but the finances of the port declined during the interwar years – evinced, perhaps, in this view by the lack of ships at the quays – before trade improved after World War II with the port pioneering the development of roll-on/roll-off ferries. Such was the success of this traffic that the port was at its busiest during the period from 1960 to 1972. But the good times were not to last.

Following strikes by the dock workers in 1969 and 1970 and as vessels grew in size, so the viability of the docks at Preston diminished, particularly given the high cost of dredging the Ribble to maintain access, and the port was formally closed following the Preston Dock Closure Act of 31 October 1981. This opened up the site for regeneration and, over the past 30 years, with the disappearance of the oil terminal, closed by Petrofina in 1992, the site has been converted into the Riversway development, with a marina occupying the western half of the old basin and housing, office and retail redevelopment occurring on the quays. The railway line to the dock is now preserved, following the loss of the final traffic (to Lancashire Tar Distillers) in 1999, as the Ribble Steam Railway.

EPW038882

Sharpness Harbour
September 1929

Viewed looking towards the north, this scene records the harbour at Sharpness, in Gloucestershire, in the late 1920s. The rise of Sharpness as a harbour began in the late 18th century with plans for the construction of a canal from the River Severn to Gloucester; the construction of the Gloucester & Berkeley Canal was authorised by an Act of 1793. Although work on the canal started quickly, financial problems meant that only one-third of the 26.5km route had been completed by 1799 when work effectively ceased. Work recommenced in 1817 and the entire route was opened in April 1827. Initially, there were limited cargo handling facilities at Sharpness in the first – later known as the Old – dock. The original entrance lock and Old Dock are not visible in this 1929 view, which features the new basin and harbour opened in 1874.

By the middle of the 19th century it was evident that the existing lock was inadequate to handle the larger ships then appearing. The new work included breakwaters, a tidal basin with lock gates, entrance lock, dry dock, harbour and quays as shown in the view; the work was undertaken by the engineer John Baldwin and his son Arthur Ernest (1854–1902). The lock was 320ft (97.5m) long but larger vessels could be accommodated through the use of the locks on the tidal basin. Unusually, the port at Sharpness was served by two railways: the Midland Railway from the south opened on 2 August 1875, while the Severn & Wye Railway came over the Severn Bridge from the Forest of Dean and opened on 17 October 1879. The latter railway was primarily involved in the transport of coal and the view shows well the coal tip and viaduct that the Severn & Wye Railway, which had become a joint railway controlled by the Great Western and Midland railways in 1893, constructed in ferroconcrete in 1909 to supplement the original wooden structure.

In 1905 the Old Dock ceased to be used and four years later the original lock gates were sealed permanently; they were, however, to be replaced by new gates supplied by Vickers-Armstrong Ltd in 1940 in case the new entrance was damaged by enemy attack. The replacement gates were operational in 1942. Today, although the Old Dock still survives and is in use as a marina, the original entrance lock was sealed permanently in the 1990s.

In 1948 the canal and railways were nationalised and the port was subsequently privatised. The port at Sharpness, now owned by the Victoria Group, continues to handle commercial traffic. Of the structures visible in the 1929 photograph, virtually all have disappeared. The only 19th-century warehouse to survive is that visible between the concrete coal viaduct and Sharpness station and even this is now under threat as it no longer meets modern standards. Some of the buildings to the south of this warehouse were destroyed by fire shortly after the photograph was taken and a grain silo, which still stands, was constructed on the site in 1934.

The railway connection across the River Severn disappeared following a collision on 25 October 1960 when two barges, which had missed the entrance to Sharpness Docks, collided with the Severn Bridge, resulting in the partial collapse of the structure. The coal viaduct and tip were subsequently demolished. Theoretically, there is still a railway connection via the erstwhile Midland Railway but this has not been used regularly for some years. Another survivor, but not visible in the view, is the Old Dock House, situated adjacent to the 1827 entrance lock, which was at the time of writing occupied by the Severn Area Rescue Association.

EPW029346

Shoreham Harbour
23 March 1948

Located at the mouth of the River Adur in Sussex, Shoreham has been the site of a port since Roman times. Its importance grew following the Norman conquest of 1066 when its proximity to France made it both a useful route linking England with Normandy but also a potential channel for invasion – a channel exploited by King John in 1199 who landed his army there when securing the English throne. During the early 13th-century a royal prison and an arsenal were established in the town and shipbuilding commenced; in 1346, for example, no fewer than 26 ships were supplied to King Edward III to move his army to France during the Hundred Years War. Another royal encounter occurred in 1651 when Prince Charles fled through Shoreham to Fecamp, thus evading his parliamentarian pursuers.

One of the problems with the harbour was that the estuary kept shifting as a result of the build-up of shingle and, following an Act of 1760, the first Commissioners of Shoreham Harbour were appointed and a new entrance, protected by piers, created. This was not successful, however, as a storm of 1763 destroyed the piers; as a result, the harbour entrance continued to shift eastwards so that by 1815 it had migrated 2.5km to the east. A second Act of 1816 resulted in a new entrance being completed in 1821 slightly to the west of that built in 1760. It is this entrance, modified over time, that remains the entrance to the harbour.

In 1840 the railway first came to the town with the opening of the LB&SCR branch from Brighton; this was subsequently extended westwards to Chichester. Initially, Shoreham, which had had a weekly packet service to Dieppe since the 1790s and a steam packet service since 1826, was considered by the LB&SCR for development as a railway port; agreement between the railway and commissioners, however, proved impossible and led to the railway's development of Newhaven (*see* p 219).

In 1826 the first Middle Pier was constructed on the north bank and was followed between 1850 and 1855 by the construction of the first lock, thus allowing the water level in the harbour to be regulated for the first time. This lock was to survive until replacement by the Prince George Lock, opened in 1933, and was converted into a dry dock with access from the enclosed harbour. It is this stage of the harbour's development that is shown in this view taken in 1948. In 1958 a new lock – the Prince Philip Lock – was opened to the south of the existing lock; both this and the Prince George Lock are still in use. At the same time as the new lock was under construction, new East and West breakwaters were also constructed.

In the photograph, work can be seen on the construction of Brighton B coal-fired power station; this was the second power station to be built at Southwick and followed on from Brighton A, which was opened originally in June 1906. The location was ideal for both stations as the harbour allowed coal to be shipped in as well as providing a plentiful source of water for cooling. The two power stations were to survive until 1976 (A) and 1987 (B); it was the closure of the two power stations with the consequent loss of coal traffic that led to a decline in the port's fortunes.

EAW014021

South Shields
16 December 1927

This view, taken from the south-west, shows Tyne Dock at South Shields. This was once described as 'the greatest coal shipping dock in the world' (William Weaver Tomlinson [1858–1916] in his book *The North Eastern Railway: its rise and development* first published in 1915), exporting no less than seven million tonnes of coal per annum at its peak, but its history reflects the changing fortune of the staple industries of north-east England.

The development of Tyne Dock had its origins in the growing trade in the shipping of coal from the north-east. Backed by the Stanhope & Tyne Railway Co, the Tyne Dock Co was authorised to construct a dock by an Act of 1 July 1839 with capital of £150,000. However, despite issuing tender notices later that year, the financial problems of the Stanhope & Tyne precluded the start of construction. In 1847, George Hudson (1800–77), the 'Railway King', obtained a new Act for the construction of a dock and work commenced on 24 February 1849; however, Hudson's fall from favour later that year resulted in work being suspended. Five years later, the North Eastern Railway-backed Jarrow Dock & Railway Co was authorised to build the dock, designed by John Plews (1795–1861), and in July 1855 the contractors Jackson, Bean & Gow began construction work. In January 1859 the first vessel entered the new wet dock and on 3 March 1859 the facility was formally opened.

As completed, the dock was 50 acres (20ha) in extent with a 9½-acre (4ha) entrance basin. There were originally two entrances: an 80ft (24.8m) tidal entrance and a 60ft (18.3m) lock. Both had gates supplied by Robert Stephenson & Co. By the date of the photograph, the entrance arrangements had been altered. In November 1894 a new 70ft (21.3m)-deep water entrance was added and, in 1923, new gates were installed on the 60ft (18.3m) lock, while the tidal entrance was permanently closed and sealed. The dock was served by four coal staithes, visible on the right, the last of which was added in 1872. Unlike earlier staithes, which had required the use of either horse or steam power to move the wagons, the staithes at Tyne Dock operated via self-acting inclines. Apart from the transfer of coal, Tyne Dock was also used for the importation of timber, and by the date of this photograph a 5-acre timber pond had been established.

In 1923, the North Eastern Railway, along with Tyne Dock, passed to the LNER. In 1936, however, an Act was passed for the purchase of the dock by the Tyne Improvement Commissioners (replaced by the Port of Tyne Authority on 31 July 1968); this was effected in April 1937. By this date, however, coal traffic was in decline and by 1948 only two of the staithes remained open. New traffic, however, was to come through the importation of iron ore for the steelworks at Consett and a new quay became operational in 1954 for this traffic. For a number of years, until the demise of steam operation in north-east England, the Tyne Dock to Consett iron ore trains were in the hands of British Railways Class 9F 2-10-0 locomotives.

Today there is very little to remind people that Tyne Dock once existed. The final coal staithe closed in 1967 and in 1974 the importation of iron ore was transferred to the Tees. By that year the staithes had been demolished and the dock was in terminal decline. The dock and timber pond have both now been fully infilled, using material from the construction of the second Tyne river tunnel (which was officially opened on 18 July 2012), although there remains evidence of the entrance locks.

EPW020191

Stanlow Oil Refinery
12 July 1946

Alongside cement (*see* Northfleet on p 93), another commodity that resulted in the construction of a number of dedicated dock facilities around the coast of the British Isles was oil. One of the major sites developed was that at Stanlow, on the Manchester Ship Canal. The oil industry was very much a product of the late 19th century; production of crude oil in the USA, for example, increased from 2,000 barrels in 1859 to 126.5 million barrels between 1859 and 1906, and the development of the internal combustion engine pushed up demand. Britain, until the development of the North Sea, had effectively to import all its oil and, as a result, from the early 20th century a number of coastal facilities such as Stanlow were built; other notable examples in England were the refineries at Fawley in Hampshire, the largest in the country, and Shellhaven and Coryton, both of which were in Essex (*see* p 43).

This view records the facility in 1946, just after the cessation of hostilities, and shows the structure still with evidence on the roofs of a number of buildings of the wartime camouflage scheme designed to protect it from aerial attack.

The refinery at Stanlow was opened by Shell in 1924, initially as a small plant for the production of bitumen. Among the facilities provided was a new dock for handling ships delivering the crude oil to the terminal. The dock, constructed in concrete, had a length of 600ft (182.9m), a width of 100ft (30.5m) and a depth of 30ft (9.14m); it also possessed a caisson to prevent burning oil floating from the dock into the Manchester Ship Canal in the event of a fuel leak and fire. This is the dock visible across the canal from the refinery shown in the 1946 view.

One of the major stimuli for the development of the refinery came with World War II, with Stanlow being one of the major reception points for oil imports to support the war effort. Such was the increase in the workforce that a new railway station, Stanlow & Thornton, was opened for the staff on 23 December 1940; initially for use by the workers only, it became an advertised station available to all on 24 February 1941. Among the products developed at Stanlow during the war was 'Teepol', a liquid-based detergent that represented the first manufacture of a petroleum-based organic chemical in Europe.

After the war, the increasing size of oil tankers made the wharf at Stanlow a problem for Shell and, in March 1974, a pipeline was opened from the Anglesey Marine Terminal at Amlwch. This was a floating platform that could handle the then largest oil tankers afloat; this was to survive until the late 1980s. Today Stanlow receives all its crude via a 24km pipeline from the Tranmere Oil Terminal, a facility that opened originally on 8 June 1960.

Shell continued to own the Stanlow refinery until 2011 when it was sold to Essar; the facility remains operational and is the second largest in capacity terms in the United Kingdom after that at Fawley. Although the site was rail-connected in 1946 when the photograph was taken, today the rails have largely disappeared and the site's products are shipped out either by road, by ships on the Manchester Ship Canal or by pipeline.

EAW001909

Sunderland South Dock
2 October 1985

In the 19th century the competition among ports in the north-east for the lucrative coal traffic from the Durham and Northumberland coalfields was intense, with both Newcastle and Hartlepool expanding during the period. Unless there was investment in the facilities at Sunderland, it was possible that Wearside might have lost its share of the trade as the existing quays – such as those serving the North Dock – were increasingly inadequate.

Central to the development of the South Dock was the town's MP, the controversial 'Railway King' George Hudson (1800–71), who promoted the Sunderland Dock Co to develop a series of docks on the south side of the river with backing from the railways, primarily the York, Newcastle & Berwick, of which he was also chairman. The construction of the docks required considerable land reclamation on the eastern side in order to accommodate the wet docks.

The initial design work for the new docks was undertaken by the engineer to the River Wear Commissioners, John Murray (1804–82), with Robert Stephenson (1803–59) acting as an early consultant. The original scheme envisaged a tidal harbour inlet from the river leading through two gated entrances to a half-tide dock and then a single wet dock. The latter was planned to have a second – southern – exit, but this was not constructed until later.

Appropriately, Hudson laid the foundation stone of the half-tide basin on 4 February 1848 and on 20 June 1850 the new wet dock was formally opened; this was named Hudson Dock after its promoter. Work started in late 1850 on the construction of the southern entrance; this was to open in 1856. Concurrent with this project, work on the extension of Hudson Dock southwards was underway. This commenced in August 1853 and the enlarged dock was opened on 24 November 1855. The investment was worthwhile as coal traffic increased by more than 50 per cent during the first half of the 1850s and there were eventually 13 coal staithes on the western side of the harbour exporting the coal from some 20 collieries.

In 1859 the docks were acquired by the River Wear Commissioners and the final phase of their development took place under the aegis of the Commissioners' engineer Thomas Meik (1812–96). Between 1864 and 1867 a small enclosed dock – Hendon Dock – was constructed to the south of Hudson Dock. Meik was succeeded by his pupil Henry Hay Wake (1844–1911), who undertook the final enlargement of Hudson Dock following his appointment in 1868. During Wake's tenure, Sir John Coode (1816–92) produced plans for the conversion of the half-tide basin into a sea lock. Designed by Wake, construction of the new facility commenced in 1877 and was opened on 21 October 1880; this is the sea lock visible in the 1985 photograph.

Immediately to the north of the sea lock, but infilled by the date of the photograph, was a graving dock; this was occupied from 1871 by the shipbuilding company Bartram, Haswell & Co (and then by its successors) and claimed to be the only shipyard to launch ships directly into the North Sea. The shipyard closed in March 1978 and the site was reclaimed.

Today the port of Sunderland remains active although the vast majority of the dockside buildings seen in the 1985 view – in particular the two grain warehouses dating from 1856 and 1863 and designed by John Dobson (1787–1865) which succumbed in 1992 – have been demolished, as has the final remaining coal staithe. Among the few that survive are those located around the graving dock, which remains active as a ship repairing facility. The last coal to be handled by the port was in 1986. The railway lines, which latterly served a Petrofina oil terminal at the docks (itself now closed), ceased to be used commercially in the late 1990s but are still intact and in 2014 it was announced that they were to be restored to use. The lock between the tidal basin and the southern end of Hudson Dock has been filled in and all access to the dock is now via the river entrance, although the tidal basin itself with its piers remains, albeit silted up on the landward side.

There are two listed structures extant as portrayed in the photograph. The older of the two is the dock office constructed by John Murray for the Sunderland Dock Co and completed in 1850; this was modified in the mid-1870s when a hydraulic accumulator for the bridge at the north end of Hudson Docks was installed by Sir W Armstrong & Co. The building is listed at Grade II. Also listed at Grade II is the associated swing bridge – known as Gladstone Bridge – along with its associated walls, abutments and locks. The hydraulic equipment to operate the bridge was also supplied by Sir W Armstrong & Co, although the steel lock gate is a replacement dating to 1955.

EAW493267

Teignmouth

23 July 1990

Situated at the mouth of the River Teign in Devon, Teignmouth has possessed a small harbour since the end of the 13th century at least, and by the early 14th century was second only to Dartmouth in the county. In 1340 the port was attacked by the French during the Hundred Years' War, and seven years later seven ships sailed from Teignmouth as part of the English assault on Calais.

During the 16th and 17th centuries, the importance of the harbour at Teignmouth declined, partly as the result of silt, although the Newfoundland cod trade remained important. On 26 July 1690 Teignmouth was to suffer the last invasion of the English mainland when French troops, under the command of Admiral Anne Hilarion de Tourville, landed briefly and destroyed much of West Teignmouth. Some of the buildings destroyed at the time still survive in rebuilt form, as does the Jolly Sailor Inn (listed Grade II), the only building from pre-1690 still standing in the immediate area of the harbour.

The development of the modern harbour started in the 18th century. The major impetus to the port's development was the export of clay; this had begun at the start of the century and had reached almost 10,000 tonnes per annum by the mid-1780s. The Old Quay in the town was constructed in the mid-18th century and a further boost to the harbour came with the completion of the Stover Canal in 1792; the canal eased the movement of ball clay from the mines to the harbour. By 1820 additional traffic through the harbour came in the shape of granite from the Haytor quarries on Dartmoor. This was routed to the Stover Canal from the Haytor Granite Tramway.

The growth in trade required the construction of a second quay – the New Quay – which was built between 1821 and 1825 under the auspices of George Templer (1781–1843) the son of James Templer (1748–1813) (who had promoted the Stover Canal). This structure is still extant to the south of the modern port. At this date, the harbour at Teignmouth was still under the control of the Port of Exeter; it was not until 1852 that the Lords Commissioners of the Treasury agreed to the creation of independent Harbour Commissioners to control the harbour at Teignmouth. In 1886, management of the harbour passed to the Teignmouth Quay Co. The years after World War I proved difficult and the port declined; a further change of management in 1932 resulted in considerable investment going into the redevelopment of the Old Quay and the expansion of the dock's facilities. The creation of the modern port took place between then and the mid-1960s.

The harbour at Teignmouth continues to be active and remains under the control of the Teignmouth Harbour Commission, a statutory body created primarily by the Teignmouth Harbour Order of 1924 but amended by the Teignmouth Harbour Revision Order of 2003. Traffic through the port benefited from the end of commercial traffic through the dock at Exmouth in 1989. There are two quays (Eastern and Western – of 119m and 300m respectively – that straddle the site of the Old Quay) – that are capable of accommodating up to four vessels of a suitable size. Locally mined ball clay remains the principal export, with inward traffic including timber, animal feed and other bulk items. The port itself is owned by Associated British Ports and currently handles about 400,000 tonnes per annum.

EAW583221

Whitehaven Harbour
June 1933

This view, taken looking towards the east, shows the harbour at Whitehaven in Cumbria. Although the origins of the harbour stretch back to Roman times, the physical development of the port started in 1634 with the completion of the Old Quay by Robert Storey; this structure still survives and the quay stretches towards the north-east from West Strand to create the South Harbour. This was extended after the Restoration of 1660 by Richard Caton. The original quay was designed to facilitate the export of coal and salt for Sir Christopher Lowther (1611–44) who owned the harbour.

The early 18th century witnessed further development of the harbour. A second quay – Bulwark – was constructed as a breakwater; this was relocated in 1711 to the north-east of the harbour. A lighthouse – now disused – was erected at the end of the Old Quay by 1721 and two new quays – the Sugar Tongue and Lime Tongue – were constructed in 1733 to 1735 and 1754 respectively. This work created Custom House Dock. An L-shaped quay – Old New Quay – was constructed to the west of the Old Quay between 1739 and 1742 to provide a breakwater; between the Old and Old New quays is the Old Fort. This was constructed in 1639 and its remains are now listed Grade II. It was this structure that was attacked by the American revolutionary John Paul Jones during his celebrated raid on Whitehaven in April 1778. Whitehaven was a logical target for Jones as it was one of the main ports dealing with trade between Britain and New England; it was the loss of this trade that undermined the finances of the port in the late 18th century until it was replaced by the booming coal trade. The Old New Quay was also provided with a lighthouse, also now no longer in use.

In 1768 John Smeaton (1724–92) recommended the construction of the Old North Wall Pier; this was completed in 1785 and extended in 1804, at which time the Bulwark Quay was also extended. This work created a North Harbour. Further proposals resulted in the construction of the West Pier between 1824 and 1830 and the North Pier between 1833 and 1841. The West Quay, after considerable pressure, was provided with a lighthouse as was the North Quay; these are both still in use (although the latter is not visible in this view). The scale of operation in the mid-19th century can be gauged by the fact that 400 wagons per day were being handled on the Sugar Tongue. The next development occurred in 1876 by the creation of the Queen's Dock; this was designed by Sir James Brunlees (1816–92) and resulted in the creation of a wet dock with a single set of wooden dock gates as shown in this view in the north-east corner of the harbour.

The photograph shows some of the network of railway lines serving the harbour. Two things are noteworthy about the harbour's railways. First is the course of the early wagonway zig-zagging down to the staithes on the south side of the harbour. An early painting of it includes the first known representation of a moveable point blade, so it represented an important part of the history of the very earliest stages of railway development. Second, on the east side there is a swing bridge to carry railway traffic over a launching slip from a shipbuilding yard. It is still there and is believed to be a unique device.

Since this view was taken, the original wooden lock gates to the Queen's Dock were replaced with steel (in 1938) and have subsequently been removed entirely. In 1998 work was completed on the construction of a new £8.5 million sea lock linked to the extension to the Old Quay; this has effectively created a much larger wet dock with the advantage of providing better protection to the town from tidal flooding. Regular commercial traffic through the port ceased in 1992 but much work and investment has gone into the rejuvenation of the harbour as a marina and for other leisure activities.

EPW042101

Whitstable
June 1937

Whitstable, on the north Kent coast, had been famous for oysters and other seafood since Roman times, but it was not until the opening of one of the country's pioneering railways lines – the Canterbury & Whitstable Railway – that a dock was actually constructed to serve the town. In the mid-18th century, transport links with London, via ship, and with Canterbury, via a new turnpike road, saw the town develop as a seaside resort, while the oyster and seafood business continued to prosper.

On 2 November 1824, a committee, chaired by John Brent, proposed the construction of a railway between Canterbury and Whitstable and a bill to permit construction was introduced on 17 February 1825 following plans produced by William James (1771–1837). Receiving Royal Assent later the same year, construction started with George Stephenson (1781–1848) as engineer, assisted by Joseph Locke (1805–60) and John Dixon (c 1795–1865). The line opened throughout on 3 May 1830 but it was to be a further two years before the dock, engineered by Thomas Telford (1757–1834), was officially opened on 19 March 1832.

The scene here shows the harbour with the railway, nicknamed the Crab & Winkle, stretching towards the south. Financially never successful, operation of the line was taken over by the South Eastern Railway in 1844 and the SER took ownership nine years later. The town was also served by the SER main line, which opened to a temporary station in 1860, and it was the arrival of this railway that further undermined the finances of the C&WR as it meant that freight could be shipped less expensively by rail than by ship and passengers could reach London more speedily. Passenger services over the line were withdrawn on 1 January 1931 but the port remained open to cater for coal, grain and timber. In 1936 a plant to manufacture tarmacadam was established on the east side of the harbour and this is visible in the photograph.

During World War II the harbour was busy, with munitions being shipped through it, but traffic was to decline significantly after the war and closure of the C&WR – by now nationalised – occurred on 1 December 1952, with a brief reprieve following the floods of 1953. In 1958 Whitstable UDC purchased the port from the British Transport Commission. Following the sale, the UDC invested in improving the dock's facilities with a new East Quay being opened on 22 July 1963 (and upgraded in 2006) and the West Quay being expanded. The tarmacadam works of 1936 have expanded on the East Quay and the harbour is home to fishing vessels that continue to exploit the rich oyster beds. The harbour is run by a Harbour Board appointed by Canterbury City Council.

EPW054080

Widnes
July 1952

Viewed from across the Mersey with the Manchester Ship Canal in the foreground, the town of Widnes can be seen on the north bank of the river.

The photograph shows two distinct installations; one in use and one already disused. Immediately to the west of the railway bridge on the north bank is West Bank Dock. This was opened in 1864 largely to cater for traffic from the chemical industry; it and docks at Garston were major factors in the demise of the first wet dock at Widnes, which was established to the east of the bridges at the point where the Sankey Canal connected into the River Mersey. The dock, which was the first in the country to provide a rail-to-ship facility, was promoted by the St Helens & Runcorn Gap Railway, which was authorised on 29 May 1830. The railway line to the dock opened officially on 21 February 1833 but the dock itself was not to open until August the same year. When the Sankey Canal realised that the railway offered significant competition, its owners obtained parliamentary approval to extend the canal to the Runcorn Gap at Widnes; the extension from Fiddlers Ferry opened on 24 July 1833. The St Helens & Runcorn Gap Railway was taken over by the London & North Western Railway on 31 July 1864. The original dock at Widnes lost traffic to the West Bank and to the new dock as Garston (see p 25), and was to close commercially in 1931. By the date of the 1952 photograph, the dock and entrance lock had already been infilled. The sidings, however, were still very much in use at this stage.

The transporter bridge seen in the centre of the photograph was both the first of these structures to be constructed in Britain and was also the largest to be built in the world, stretching for some 300m across the river and canal. In 1900 an Act of Parliament was obtained by the Widnes & Runcorn Bridge Co for the construction of the bridge. Designed by John Webster (1845–1914) and John Wood (1849–1932), construction of the bridge commenced in December 1901 and the structure was formally opened by Sir John Brunner (1842–1919), standing in for the indisposed Edward VII, on 29 May 1905. The bridge became increasingly inadequate and, following the opening of a new fixed link, the transporter bridge was closed and demolished in 1961. There are, however, still traces of the structure, most notably the power house that was located on the north bank; this is now listed as Grade II*.

The railway bridge across the Mersey was originally authorised in 1846 but was not progressed. In 1861 the LNWR obtained parliamentary approval for the bridge and work started on its construction in 1863. Designed by William Baker (1817–78), the railway's Engineer in Chief, the viaduct was formally opened on 10 October 1868, although the first freight train did not cross until 1 February 1869 and the first passenger train exactly two months later. Also known as the Ethelfleda or Britannia Bridge, the viaduct is still extant and now carries the electrified West Coast main line services from Crewe to Liverpool. The viaduct is also listed as Grade II*.

West Bank Dock finally closed in the 1970s and the land has been subsequently reclaimed; today there is very little evidence that a dock ever existed there. The sidings adjacent to the end of the Sankey Canal – Marsh Sidings – remained operational until 4 November 1968, ceasing operation with the closure of the line from Widnes Dock to Widnes Dock Junction. The site of the dock has been converted into an area of parkland called Spike Island, which opened in 1982. Although the wet dock had been infilled when photographed in 1952, it has been partially recreated as part of the Spike Island project and this, with traces of the entrance lock, survive.

The Sankey Canal, which closed for commercial traffic in 1959 with the cessation of sugar traffic to Earlestown, is still accessible from the Mersey and there is a marina adjacent to the parkland.

EAW044937

Prince of Wales Dock, Workington
29 June 1953

Situated on the banks of the River Derwent, Workington was one of a number of towns that provided a channel through which coal could be exported from England to Ireland. However, its importance grew in the mid-19th century following the development of the steel industry through the invention of the Bessemer Converter by Sir Henry Bessemer (1813–98). When first developed Bessemer's technique required the use of haematite iron ore, a substance found in profusion in and around Workington and this led, in 1857, to the establishment of the Workington Haematite Iron Co Ltd, the world's first commercial producer of mild steel.

The development of the steelworks led to the construction of the new Lonsdale Dock on the north side of the River Derwent to the design of Alexander Meadows Rendel (1828–1918). However, this first dock, with restricted river access, was to prove inadequate once local supply of haematite declined and the works was forced to rely on the importation of raw materials. As a result, in the early 1920s, the existing dock was enlarged by 50 per cent (to 2.5ha) and deepened. The design work was undertaken by Rendel, Palmer & Tritton and the initial contractor was Kirk & Randall. However, the contractors failed in March 1926 and the work had to be completed by Sir Henry Japp (1869–1939). On completion the enlarged dock was opened by the Prince of Wales, later Edward VIII, and renamed in his honour.

At the time of the photograph, the dock was still busy with traffic to and from the steelworks. The extensive railway sidings, with specialist steel-carrying wagons, are evident. However, the decline in the iron and steel industry resulted in the last of the Bessemer Convertors being blown out in 1974, although it was not until 2006 that work finally ceased at Workington, when the rolling of railway track from reheated steel blooms was transferred to Scunthorpe. Today, the port, now owned by Cumbria County Council, is still busy, handling some 600,000 tonnes of freight annually. The dock is still rail-served, although the sidings are now much less extensive than they were in 1953.

EAW050235

T W Ward Ltd premises on Frog Island, Rainham Marshes
7 June 1921

After the cessation of hostilities in November 1918 and the subsequent Treaty of Versailles, there was a rapid decommissioning of much military equipment. Apart from the disposal of the German fleet, which had surrendered at Scapa Flow, some 500,000 tonnes of scrap was realised through the disposal of surplus Royal Navy warships. In order to cater for this a number of new scrapyards were opened, including this facility at Rainham Marshes in the Thames estuary by Thos W Ward Ltd in 1919. In all, this company, which had first established itself in the ship scrapping business in 1894 at Barrow-in-Furness, possessed at least 13 yards by the early 1920s.

Of the vessels visible, the two most complete are both Admiralty 'M'-class destroyers. While that closest to the camera is unidentifiable, the pennant number on the easternmost of the two – D41 – identifies it as HMS *Myngs*. This was built by the Jarrow-based shipyard of Palmers Shipbuilding & Iron Co, being launched on 24 September 1914 and completed the following year. HMS *Myngs* was one of the six of the type constructed as part of the Naval Programme for 1913/4 with the bulk of the type being constructed as part of the Emergency War Construction Programme. In all, including variants, some 85 'M'-class destroyers were completed. HMS *Myngs* was one of a large number of naval vessels rendered surplus by the Armistice and was sold for scrap on 9 May 1921, less than a month prior to the date it was recorded at the scrapyard.

The massive expansion in the ship scrapping industry in the years immediately after World War I was a relatively short-lived phenomenon; by the middle of the 1920s relatively few warships were sold for scrap and it is probable that the Ward yard at Rainham Marshes closed during this period.

Also visible in the view are the remains of the cement works established at Rainham in 1881 by the Rock Cement Co. Taken over eventually by Allied Portland Cement Manufacturers in 1900, the works were to close two years later. Almost two decades later the site of the factory, located slightly to the west of the scrapyard, was largely intact. Cement works, with their heavy demand for coal, were often sited on the coast so that raw materials could be easily supplied by sea.

EPW006567

Woolston Shipbuilding & Engineering Works, Southampton
16 March 1928

One of the most important shipyards of southern England was situated at Woolston, Southampton, where, from 1904 until closure in 2003, John I Thornycroft & Co Ltd and its successors constructed some 600 ships.

John Thornycroft (1843–1928) first established a shipbuilding business at Chiswick, on the River Thames, in 1866, with the company being formally registered in 1901 in order to pay off the heirs of his late partner John Donaldson (1840–99). In 1904 the company took over the yard at Woolston, previously owned by Mordey, Carney & Co (Southampton) Ltd, in order to build larger ships. Five years later the site at Chiswick was closed and in 1929 the Day, Summers & Co Ltd yard at Northam, in Southampton, was acquired.

Thornycroft acquired a considerable reputation for the construction of warships both for the Royal Navy and for export and it is this latter activity that is recorded in this view of the yard taken in March 1928. The company was in the middle of constructing six 'Serrano'-class destroyers for the Chilean Navy. At the date of the photograph, two of the six had been launched – the *Serrano* on 25 January 1928 and the *Orella* on 8 March 1928 – and these are visible being fitted out. Three further destroyers are under construction – the *Riquelme*, launched 28 May 1928, the *Hyatt*, launched 21 July 1928, and the *Videla*, launched 16 October 1928. The last of the group, the *Aldea*, was only laid down in March 1928 and so probably not visible in this view. The destroyers were long-lived; the last was not decommissioned until 1967.

John I Thornycroft & Co Ltd remained independent until 1966 when it was taken over by Vosper Ltd, becoming Vosper Thornycroft Ltd. As a result of the Aircraft and Shipbuilding Industries Act of 1977, Vosper Thornycroft was nationalised and became part of British Shipbuilders. During 1982 the yard played a significant role in the creation of the task force established to retake the Falkland Islands following the Argentinian invasion, preparing both the *Canberra* and the *QE2* for their roles as troopships. In 1985 a further change of ownership came with the privatisation of the business and its sale to its management as VT Group. In 2003 ship construction at Woolston ceased with the transfer of warship work to a new facility at Portsmouth naval dockyard. With the reduced expenditure and the decision to construct the new Type 26 frigates on the Clyde, the facility at Portsmouth was itself to close in 2014.

EPW020528

Engineering and Boatbuilding Works off Thetis Road, Cowes
August 1928

Situated on the west bank of the River Medina on the Isle of Wight, the shipyard at Thetis Road was officially opened on 1 October 1815 and was one of two shipyards in Cowes controlled by Thomas White (1773–1859), who had moved to the island from Broadstairs in Kent in 1802. The White family had a long tradition of shipbuilding and Thomas White's move to Cowes coincided with the increased demand for warships that resulted from Britain's involvement in the French Revolutionary and Napoleonic wars.

By the date of this photograph the yard was owned by J Samuel White & Co Ltd, which had been incorporated in 1898 and was named after Thomas's grandson John Samuel White (1838–1915), under whose auspices the yard had expanded during the second half of the 19th century. In 1912 the yard's facilities were further enhanced by the erection of an 80-ton-capacity hammerhead crane supplied by Babcock & Wilcox of Renfrew in Scotland; although the shipyard is long closed, the hammerhead crane still remains and is now the only surviving pre-World War I hammerhead crane in England.

J Samuel White & Co Ltd specialised in the construction of smaller warships and merchant vessels, such as the warship being fitted out in this view. The ship is believed to be one of the three 'Mendoza'-class destroyers built by J Samuel White & Co Ltd for the Argentine Navy. Given the date, it is most likely to be the ARA *Mendoza*, which was launched on 18 July 1928. The other two warships were the ARA *Tucuman*, launched in October 1928, and the ARA *La Rioja*, launched in February 1929. All three remained in service until being decommissioned in April 1962.

Shipbuilding continued at the company's yards until the 1960s; the first to close, that on the east bank of the river, succumbed in 1964 and the yard illustrated here in the following year. Engineering work continued, however, with the site being sold to the US-based Elliot Corporation in 1972. The hammerhead crane was last used in 2004 and was listed as Grade II* the following year.

EPW023056

The Deptford Shipbuilding Yard, Sunderland
6 June 1946

The involvement of the Laing family, originally from Fife in Scotland, in shipbuilding on the River Wear at Sunderland started in 1793. Following the use of a number of sites, Philip Laing (1770–1854) established himself at Deptford in 1818, having moved to Sunderland from Fife in 1792; the first ship to be completed at the yard was called *Anne*. In 1843 the business passed to James (1823–1901), Philip's son, and in 1853 the yard's first iron-built ship, the *Amity*, was completed. In 1865 the Laing family became ship owners as well as shipbuilders. In 1898, following James's knighthood in 1897, the private company Sir James Laing & Sons Ltd was registered. However, following the death of Sir James in 1901 and his son Philip in 1907 the company had financial problems and had to be rescued by Sir James Marr (1854–1932) in 1909. As with other shipyards, World War I resulted in the yard being kept busy and by 1918 the facilities included the graving dock, which originally dated to the mid-19th century, and five building berths.

In 1930, following the Wall Street Crash, lack of orders resulted in the yard being closed; shipbuilding was not to resume until 1935 when the yard benefited from the government's 'scrap and build scheme'. Unlike many other yards, Deptford was employed almost exclusively in the construction of merchant vessels and it was the building of tankers and bulk carriers that kept the yard busy both during and after World War II. A total of 36 tankers, for example, were completed between 1946 and 1966. In 1954 the company formed a consortium – Sunderland Shipbuilding, Dry Docks & Engineering Co Ltd – with seven other companies controlled by the Marr family. In turn the consortium was acquired by the Doxford & Sunderland Shipbuilding & Engineering Co Ltd in 1961.

In 1966 Sir James Laing & Sons Ltd's independence ended when the Doxford & Sunderland Shipbuilding & Engineering Co Ltd bought out the subsidiary companies; in turn, following nationalisation in July 1977, this enlarged company became a subsidiary of British Shipbuilders. Work continued on a number of bulk carriers thereafter; however, on 3 May 1985, with the launch of the *Mitla*, no further ships were laid down at the Deptford yard and shipbuilding work ceased. Heavy engineering continues at Deptford, the current occupant of the site being Liebherr, which is one of the British subsidiaries of a large Swiss-owned group. All evidence of the shipyard, including the graving dock, has, however, disappeared.

EAW001030

Smith's Docks, North Shields
15 May 1947

Dominating this view of the north bank of the River Tyne at South Shields is the shipyard of the Smith's Dock Co Ltd with the Albert Edward Dock beyond.

The first graving dock to be constructed on the future Smith's Dock Co site was built in the 1750s by the landowner Edward Collingwood (1734–1806) to the south of the Bull Ring (which resulted in the yard becoming known as the Bull Ring Graving Docks). In 1883, the South Shields-based shipbuilder Harry S Edwards & Sons (originally established in 1768), acquired the site in order to expand the company's business and immediately undertook development, with the construction of a new river frontage and two new graving docks to replace that built in the 18th century. The new docks were completed in 1885 and 1889. In 1899 the company merged with two other companies with facilities in North Shields adjacent to the Bull Ring site: Edwards Brothers and T & W Smith. The new, publicly quoted, company that resulted, Smith's Dock Co Ltd, was to become one of the most important ship repairers in Britain.

In 1906 the new company bought a site on the River Tees and four graving docks were built there; as a result of this investment, shipbuilding at North Shields ended in 1910 with the construction of the 286grt *Mountcharles* in January 1910 (although one further vessel was constructed; this was the unpowered 600grt oil storage barge *Rose Shell*, which was completed in 1920 for the Anglo-Saxon Petroleum Co Ltd of London). Although new construction was transferred to the company's shipyard on the Tees, investment still went into the North Shields Yard. In 1910 a further graving dock was constructed and one of the earlier graving docks extended. By 1930 there were four graving docks in operation and two further were acquired immediately after World War II from Baird Brothers. By the early 1960s, the graving docks at North Shields ranged in size from 55m by 12m to 216m by 27.4m.

Although there had been earlier proposals, construction of the Coble Dene Dock was authorised by the Tyne Improvement (Coble Dene Railways and Docks) Act of 18 July 1872. The dock was designed by Philip John Messent (1830–97) and John Francis Ure (1820–83). Work started the following year but financial problems resulted in construction being suspended in 1876. Following a further Act in 1877, work resumed and the new dock was formally opened by the Prince and Princess of Wales in 1884. The new facility was renamed Albert Edward Dock in the Prince of Wales's honour. The dock had a water area of 22½ acres (9ha) and was used for the export of coal and the import of timber for pit props. With the decline of traditional traffic, the dock closed in the late 1980s.

From 1990 onwards the erstwhile dock has been redeveloped as a marina with shops and residential property and is now branded as the Royal Quays. The locks and lock gates are listed as Grade II while the accumulator tower, visible between the lock and the dock itself, is listed at Grade II*. The latter is the only surviving example on the River Tyne of the type of hydraulic machinery first developed in Newcastle by William Armstrong (1810–1900), the founder of Armstrong Whitworth and the owner of Cragside House (now owned by the National Trust).

The shipyard remained active for more than four decades after the 1947 photograph. In 1966 the company merged with Swan Hunter and, as part of the Swan Hunter Group, was to be nationalised as part of British Shipbuilders in 1977. After some years of troubled operation, the shipyard on the Tees was closed in February 1987, with some 900 vessels having been built there between 1910 and closure. The ship repair work at North Shields was, however, to continue until the 1990s when the site became derelict. The site has been cleared, although three of the graving docks remain. There are plans for a £140 million regeneration of the area, with up to 800 houses being constructed to link the historic Fish Quay area with the area around Royal Quays.

EAW005502

The Middle Docks & Engineering Co Ltd, South Shields
9 August 1947

This view along the River Tyne shows the south bank of the river dominated by the graving docks of the Middle Docks & Engineering Co Ltd of South Shields. This company was one of a number of companies with facilities on the Tyne at this point. The company's prime business was in ship repairing, undertaking the routine maintenance of vessels in order to keep them seaworthy.

The origins of Middle Dock, South Shields, date back to the late 18th century; the first reference comes via a sale announcement in 1772. By 1799 a second dock had been completed; ownership of the two docks was split until the 1840s when both passed to the ownership of the Middle Dock Co. The docks were used for the importation of timber and for the maintenance of wooden vessels, although at least two wooden sailing ships were also constructed in the docks. In 1899 the Middle Dock Co was sold by its owner, G E Henderson, and a new company – the Middle Docks & Engineering Co Ltd – established.

The docks as seen in this post-World War II view were largely the result of expansion during the first half of the 20th century. A third graving dock – 460ft (140m) long by 62½ft (19m) wide – was opened in 1909 with a fourth, built on the site of the yard previously owned by J T Eltringham & Co, involved the infilling of the Metcalfe's Dock. This work was completed between 1914 and 1917 and resulted in a dock 630ft (192m) in length by 80ft (24m) in width. Between the two world wars the original two docks were extended and, in 1941, the fourth dock was extended by 10ft (3m). The scale of the business was such that, in 1961, it employed some 1,100 staff.

During the 1960s the company merged with Brigham & Cowan Ltd and Mercantile Dry Dock Co Ltd to form North East Coast Ship Repairers Ltd; this company was to be taken over by Court Line to become part of Court Line Shipbuilders Ltd. The entire Court Line business failed in August 1974 and the business was formally taken over by the government on 19 September 1974. With the nationalisation of the shipbuilding industry in 1974, the Middle Dock complex passed to the ownership of British Shipbuilders; closure, however, was not long in coming and all work ceased at the docks in 1982. Today, the four graving docks still remain, although the surrounding area is largely derelict. Slightly to the north of the Middle Dock complex, the Customs House, a neo-Classical building dating to 1848 built on the historic mill dam, is now a local arts centre.

EAW008937

Swan Hunter & Wigham Richardson Ltd, Wallsend
10 September 1947

The name Swan Hunter is undoubtedly one of the greatest in the history of shipbuilding in England. Based on the River Tyne, the company was to build many of the great passenger liners – such as the *Mauretania* (*see* p 185) – and Royal Navy ships, such as the most recent ship to carry the name *Ark Royal*.

The name Swan Hunter dated back to 1879 when George Burton Hunter (1845–1937) entered into a partnership with Mary Kelly Swan (1839–unknown), the widow of Charles Sheridan Swan (1831–79), to take over the management of the yard in Wallsend run by Swan's brother-in-law Charles Mitchell (1820–95) since 1873. C S Swan & Hunter was incorporated in 1895 and in 1903 merged with the neighbouring shipbuilder – Wigham Richardson & Co – to form Swan, Hunter & Wigham Richardson Ltd in order to bid for the construction work on the *Mauretania*.

Wigham Richardson & Co had been established in 1860 by John Wigham Richardson (1837–1908) to take over the existing yards owned by the Scottish-born John Henry Sangster Coutts (1810–62), who had first built ships in 1842, and Miller & Ravenhill at Wallsend. The yard as acquired occupied some four acres (1.6ha) and had three berths. By the date of the merger, expansion between 1895 and 1901 had seen the Neptune Yard expand to 18 acres (7.3ha). The combined yard following the merger and the acquisition the same year of the Tyne Pontoons & Dry Docks Co Ltd was 80 acres (32.3ha), with a river frontage of some 4,000ft (1.2km). This is the site as recorded in this 1947 photograph.

The newly merged company continued to expand its interests, opening a new yard in Sunderland in 1912 and acquiring businesses in Scotland, Northern Ireland and England during the inter-war years. In 1966 the company merged with the Teesside-based Smith's Dock Co Ltd to form Associated Shipbuilders, which was renamed Swan Hunter Group later the same year. Further acquisitions followed and the shipbuilding interests were transferred to a new company Swan Hunter & Tyne Shipbuilders Ltd – later shortened to Swan Hunter Shipbuilders Ltd.

Following nationalisation in 1977, Swan Hunter became part of British Shipbuilders but was to be privatised through a management buy-out a decade later. In 1994, following the company's failure to win the contract for the construction of HMS *Ocean*, Swan Hunter went into receivership but the Wallsend Yard was acquired by a Dutch millionaire and work was undertaken primarily on ship repairs and conversions. In 2000 Swan Hunter was awarded the contract to build two ships – RFA *Lyme Bay* and RFA *Largs Bay* – for the Royal Fleet Auxiliary. It was problems with the construction of these two vessels that led to the decision to cease shipbuilding at the yard in November 2006 with work on the incomplete RFA *Lyme Bay* being transferred to the Clyde. With much of the yard's equipment sold to an Indian shipbuilder, work on the site's clearance took place from 2007 onwards and today the once busy yard awaits redevelopment. A minimal Swan Hunter presence remains in the erstwhile offices concentrating on ship design and management.

EAW010662

Buccleuch Dock, Barrow-in-Furness
15 October 1948

Buccleuch Dock, situated to the east of the original Devonshire Dock at Barrow-in-Furness, was the second of the enclosed docks to be completed and opened in 1872. At 152.4m in width and with a depth of 7.3m, the new dock was exactly the same size as its predecessor. The Buccleuch Dock also included a graving dock capable of accommodating ships of up to 5,500 tonnes. In charge of construction was Frank Stileman (1851–1912), who was the Resident Engineer for the Furness Railway (which owned the dock complex at Barrow). Now a subsidiary of Associated British Ports Holdings Ltd, the docks at Barrow remain active, although trade has declined as the local steel industry has diminished, with Buccleuch being one of four enclosed docks still in use.

Seen alongside the dock is SS *Himalaya*, which had only been launched from the Vickers-Armstrong yard 10 days earlier and was being fitted out. The *Himalaya* had been ordered by P&O in 1945 and had been laid down on 26 February 1946. Completed in August 1949 with a grt of 27,955, the ship undertook its maiden voyage on 6 October 1949, sailing from Tilbury to Sydney via Bombay. The ship spent its entire career operating between the UK and Australia, being taken out of service on 30 October 1974 and sold for scrap.

Shipbuilding began in Barrow in 1852 and in 1871 the Iron (later Barrow) Shipbuilding Co was incorporated; this was taken over by Vickers & Sons in 1891. Becoming Vickers Ltd in 1911 and Vickers Armstrong Ltd in 1927, following the merger with Armstrong Whitworth, the company remained independent, although undergoing further name changes, until nationalisation in 1977. Following the decision of the Conservative government under Margaret Thatcher to privatise the shipbuilding industry, the Barrow yard was the first to be sold, being acquired by its management in March 1986. Further changes of ownership have resulted in the yard now being owned by BAE Systems.

EAW019736

Cammell Laird, Birkenhead
29 June 1950

The Birkenhead shipbuilder Cammell Laird was one of the great names of English shipbuilding and, despite the vicissitudes of the past 40 years, remains in operation today, albeit at a much lower level of activity than shown in this view from 1950.

The origins of the shipyard date back to 1824 and the establishment by William Laird (1780–1841), William Hamilton (c 1839–1912) and John Forsyth of the Birkenhead Ironworks. This partnership was dissolved four years later when Laird went into business with his son John (1805–74) as William Laird & Son. In the same year the business received its initial order for an iron ship. Further work followed. In the 1850s the original yard was acquired by the Mersey Docks & Harbour Board for the expansion of Birkenhead Docks and the company moved to a new yard – the North Yard – shown in this view. In 1860 the company became John Laird, Sons & Co as John brought his sons William (1831–99) and John (1834–98) into the business prior to retiring the following year. In 1862, the business became Laird Brothers as Henry Hyndman Laird (1838–93) joined the company.

The company produced both merchant vessels and warships for both domestic and international customers. During the 1890s armour-clad warships were built for the Royal and other navies; the armour plating was manufactured by the Sheffield company Charles Cammell & Co, and this led to a closer relationship between the two businesses and, in 1903, to a merger that resulted in the name Cammell Laird & Co Ltd emerging for the first time. The business continued to manufacture both warships and civilian vessels thereafter; the first submarines were constructed during World War I and the yard was to become one of the main submarine builders in the UK alongside Vickers in Barrow.

Among the ships seen under construction in the 1950 photograph, the most prominent in the wet basin is HMS *Ark Royal*. This was one of two members of the 'Audacious' class of aircraft carriers ordered during World War II – the second being HMS *Eagle* – and was laid down on 3 May 1943; production was delayed as a result of the cessation of hostilities in 1945 and *Ark Royal* was not actually launched until 3 May 1950. She is in the wet basin being fitted out. Commissioned into the Royal Navy on 25 February 1955, *Ark Royal* was to serve until decommissioned on 14 February 1979. She was scrapped at Cairnryan in Scotland, arriving there in September 1980.

As with the bulk of the British shipbuilding industry, Cammell Laird was nationalised in 1977; privatised in 1986, the yard was sold to Vickers Shipbuilding & Engineering Ltd but, following the completion of HMS *Unicorn*, one of the 'Upholder' class of nuclear submarines in 1993, the new owners closed the yard with submarine work being concentrated at Barrow. This was not, however, the end of the story as the site was leased by Coastline Group as a ship repair facility; over the past 20 years the ownership of the yard and the operational lease have passed through a number of hands. In 2005 the lease was taken on by Northwestern Ship Repairers & Shipbuilders, in which Peel Holdings had a significant shareholding; Peel Holdings also acquired the freehold of the site two years later. On 17 November 2008, having acquired the rights to use the name, Northwestern renamed itself Cammell Laird Ship Repairers & Shipbuilders Ltd. While Peel Holdings has plans for the regeneration of much of the Birkenhead Docks, this work includes the retention of the historic Cammell Laird shipyard.

At the time of writing, the facilities at the yard comprised a large fabrication hall (built on the west side of the slipways visible on the southern half of the site in the 1950 photograph), the non-tidal wet basin and four dry docks – Nos 7 to 4 – that run south to north; No 6 dock was extended considerably in the 1960s. Since the yard's revival, the bulk of the business has involved ship repair work but, recently, shipbuilding has returned with the construction of two new ferries for a Scottish operator.

EAW030649

The Goole Shipbuilding & Repairing Co Ltd, Goole

29 June 1950

The Goole Shipbuilding & Repairing Co Ltd was established in 1902 by the Craggs family to take over production from T Scott & Co Ltd, a company that had been founded in the 19th century. Much of the company's reputation was based upon the construction of coasters, tugs and trawlers. The yard illustrated in this view dates originally to 1917 when the company relocated to the New Shipyards following a fire at its earlier premises; the new yard, which was on land leased from the Aire & Calder Navigation, also had the advantage that ships could be launched directly into the River Ouse.

The company maintained its independence until November 1967 when it was taken over by Swan Hunter; as such, following the Aircraft and Shipbuilding Industries Act of 1977, it passed into state ownership becoming known as Goole Shipbuilders in 1982. The yard closed on 27 April 1984 although was briefly to be resurrected under the ownership of Cochrane &

Co, shipbuilders of Selby, from late 1984. Under the new ownership, a number of vessels were completed, culminating with the building of the tug *Lady Sybil* that was launched on 8 October 1987 and completed the following January.

This picture taken in the summer of 1950 sees a number of vessels under construction. From the date of the photograph and from the available records of the company's production, the two larger vessels under construction would appear to be, closest to the camera, the 816grt *Christine*, which was launched two days after the date of the photograph (on 1 July 1950), and, further away, another dry cargo vessel, slightly larger at 1,142grt, the *Beeding*. These were yard numbers 474 and 475 respectively. The latter was scrapped in 1977 but the fate of the *Christine*, which was still active in 2006, is uncertain.

EAW030613

Southampton New (Western) Docks
April 1933

In 1923, at the grouping of the railways, ownership of the London & South Western Railway passed to the new Southern Railway. Among the assets the new company inherited was the LSWR's interest in Southampton Docks. This was the golden age for transatlantic passenger traffic and in 1925 P&O liners returned to Southampton. As a response to the increase in traffic, the SR gained powers in 1927 for the reclamation of the area to the west of Southampton's Royal Pier. The plans envisaged the construction of a 7,500ft (2,286m)-long quay plus a new No 7 dry dock – the King George V Dock – which was, at the time, the largest graving dock in the world and was designed to accommodate the larger liners – such as the RMS *Queen Mary* – then entering service.

On 19 October 1932 work on the construction of the new quay had progressed to the point where the first ship to use the new quay – RMS *Mauretania* – used the facility. In all, the work required the reclamation of 400 acres (162ha) and cost some £10 million by the time work was completed in 1934. Also visible at the extreme eastern end of the new docks is the small single-storey storm water pumping station; of all the buildings visible in this view, this is the only one to survive at the time of writing.

This view shows the new docks looking towards the north-west. The new graving dock is located at the extreme western extremity of the site and can be located in the distance. The graving dock was designed by Francis Wentworth-Sheilds (or Shields) (1869–1959), constructed in concrete and steel by John Mowlem & Co and Edward Nuttall Sons & Co and was formally opened by King George V and Queen Mary on 26 July 1933.

The new quay provided eight new berths – Nos 101 to 108 – which were provided initially with long single-storey transit sheds; of these, that serving Nos 101 and

102 is seen completed in the foreground of this view. Each of these transit sheds had facilities for handling passengers, and boat trains serving the new sheds commenced soon after completion, with all berths being served by the end of 1934. In 1937 Imperial Airways commenced the operation of flying boats from a pontoon served from Nos 107 and 108; these continued until just after the end of World War II when they were relocated to the Eastern Docks

Development of the facility continued after the date of the photograph; the remaining three transit sheds were completed and the land behind the dock was completely drained and redeveloped. One of the companies that took advantage of the newly released land was Rank; the company constructed the Solent Flour Mills immediately inland of the transit shed serving Nos 101 and 102, with the first phase opening in 1934 and linked to the transit shed by overhead conveyor belts. Other business to be established on the land included General Motors, Cadbury's and Heinz.

During World War II the Western Docks suffered considerable damage; in 1940, for example, the General Motors plant was hit, as was the transit shed serving Nos 101 and 102 shown in the 1933 view. The latter was rebuilt after the war, with the new facility opening in 1956; this also served as a terminal for the Union-Castle Line's passenger services. Of the factories opened, only the Solent Flour Mills remained extant at the time of writing; much of the land reclaimed for the Western Dock scheme is used for the storage of containers and for vehicles, either destined for export or import.

With the reduction in passenger traffic through Western Docks, the last boat train to serve the facility ran on 10 January 1992 but, with the Port of Southampton increasingly being used by cruise ships, boat trains resumed in 2010 to a new temporary platform. At the

western end of the quay, the graving dock ceased to be used as such in 2005 and the caisson gates and keel blocks were removed; the dock, along with its associated pump house, were both listed Grade II and are currently used as additional capacity for Nos 107 to 109. The Western Docks, owned by Associated British Ports, remain an important facility for Southampton with the City Cruise Terminal now standing on the site of the transit shed that served Nos 101 and 102, the Mayflower Cruise Terminal occupying Nos 105 and 106, and further land reclaimed to the north-west for the container port (operated by DP World).

EPW041062

Parkeston Quay West railway station under construction
August 1933

This is a view of the estuary of the River Stour looking towards the east and shows the new quay and railway station at Parkeston Quay under construction in 1933. The new station was formally opened on 1 October 1934 although it did appear in Bradshaw's timetable in September 1934. In addition to the construction of the railway station and quay, all the land between the construction site and the existing shoreline was subsequently reclaimed.

When the Great Eastern Railway initially operated steamer services to the continent, these sailed from Harwich. However, as traffic grew, a new facility was required and powers were obtained in 1872 to reclaim land at Ray Farm and construct a new quay; this was opened in 1883 when the existing passenger line to Harwich was diverted to serve the new Quay station. The name adopted was a tribute to the then chairman of the Great Eastern Railway, Charles Henry Parkes (1816–95).

Ownership of Parkeston Quay passed via the LNER to the BTC in 1948; on 1 October 1972 Parkeston Quay West station was officially closed although it had been out of use for some time prior to that date with all services concentrated on the original 1883 station. The site of the 1934 quay and station is now used for truck and container parking. Privatised in the mid-1980s, the port, now known as Harwich International, is still used for the ferry across the North Sea to Hook of Holland and the facilities have been improved to facilitate roll-on/roll-off ferry services.

Also visible at the eastern extremity of the north shore of the estuary is HMS *Ganges* at Shotley; this was a facility that existed between 1902 and closure in 1976 for the training of boys enlisted in the Royal Navy. The first buildings were erected in 1902 and the following year the training ship HMS *Ganges* was transferred from Harwich to Shotley. The shore-based facility was initially known as RNTE *Shotley*, being renamed formally HMS *Ganges* in 1927.

Moored mid-stream are a number of ships; these include at the extreme east one of the three train ferries operated between Harwich and Zeebrugge that had originally been constructed in 1917 for use on military traffic from Richborough and transferred to the Harwich-Zeebrugge service in 1924 and SS *Sheringham*. This was a cargo-only ferry built for the LNER by Earle's Ship Building & Engineering Co Ltd of Hull in 1926.

EPW042608

Felixstowe Docks
29 June 1972 and 2 July 1997

Although the port of Felixstowe has its origins in the late 19th century when the Felixstowe Dock & Railway Co, established by Act of Parliament in 1875 (under a slightly different name with the current title being adopted late in 1879), opened its dock basin in the town in 1886, its prominence owes much to the creation of a major port dealing with containers in the mid-1960s. The first roll-on/roll-off berth was completed in 1965 and the following year work commenced on the construction of the Landguard Container Terminal, which was destined to be the UK's first dedicated container terminal when the first phase opened in July 1967. When the initial work was completed, the quay stretched for 1,500ft (457m) and was equipped with two Paceco cranes; a second roll-on/roll-off berth was also added during 1968.

In 1972, when the view of the old and new ports at Felixstowe was taken (facing page), work had just commenced on a 700ft (213m) extension of the Landguard terminal. This was completed in 1973 and saw the installation of a third Paceco crane. Since this date the facilities offered by Felixstowe have continued to expand; at the time of writing, there were two main container terminals – Trinity and Landguard – and the quays stretched for almost 2.4km with 29 ship-to-shore

gantries as well as the roll-on/roll-off berths. Future development work is designed to ensure that the port can continue to handle the massive new container ships currently under construction.

Less than 50 years ago, Felixstowe was a minor port as trade was transported by traditional freighters and handled by conventional docks and ports. The container revolution has seen the decline of many of these traditional ports, with consequences both for the workers employed and for the structures used. While container ports are still dominated by cranes, the once impressive ranks of quayside warehouses, such a feature of the traditional dock landscape, have been replaced by the vast numbers of containers awaiting onward movement.

In the foreground of this photograph taken in 1997 can be seen Landguard Fort; this dated originally to 1540 when it was known as Langer Fort. Extended in the early 17th century, the building that survives today, in the care of English Heritage, is largely the result of the construction in the 18th and 19th centuries, culminating in the building of interior barracks and a new river frontage in the 1870s.

EAW235566/EAW670704

Dover Eastern Docks
10 June 1976

Following the development work of the early 20th century at Dover, with the construction of the Eastern Arm, the Southern Breakwater and the Admiralty Pier extension, a significant body of water was enclosed. Linked to the Eastern Arm was the South Jetty, which, combined with the West Jetty, formed a smaller enclosed area known as the Camber. During World War I, this was the home of the Dover submarine flotilla and its depot ship, HMS *Argonaut*, and after the war, until 1925, the Admiralty used the Camber for dismantling redundant warships. This work continued in private hands after 1925; in 1928 the first car ferry service, owned by Captain Stuart Townsend, a former artillery officer, started to operate from the Camber. During World War II, the Camber was the base for Royal Navy motor torpedo boats and, as in 1918, once peace was restored, shipbreaking resumed.

After the war, car ferry services also resumed from the Camber, using the *Forde*, an ex-Royal Navy minesweeper (HMS *Ford*) that had been acquired to launch the new service in 1928. This vessel, although fitted with stern doors for loading cars, could only be operated with vehicles being craned on and off; it was not until 1953 and the construction of the first link span at Dover that roll-on/roll-off traffic could commence (a similar facility had been built in Calais in 1951). Continued growth resulted in the original facilities becoming inadequate and a new terminal was opened in 1970 (*see* p 201). Even this, however, was soon to prove inadequate and the scene recorded here portrays the development of the Eastern Docks in the mid-1970s.

Under construction is the new link from the A2 that provided improved transport connections from the docks to the road network; when opened in 1977 the road was named Jubilee Way in honour of the queen's Silver Jubilee. During the 1960s much land had been reclaimed to the west of the West Jetty to facilitate the expansion of the ferry operations. This process of reclamation has continued unabated since the mid-1970s; while in 1976 the approach viaduct descended over the water, it is now completely landlocked, with development of the site extended through to the Eastern Arm.

Despite the opening of the Channel Tunnel, Dover remains a major ferry terminal and the Eastern Docks are now effectively operating at full capacity; as a result, in 2006, the Port of Dover Master Plan included proposals for the development of a new ferry terminal to be constructed to serve the Western Docks.

EAW317159

Submarine works under construction, Barrow-in-Furness
11 May 1985

One of the most significant recent investments undertaken in Britain's shipbuilding industry occurred in Barrow-in-Furness through the construction of the Devonshire Dock Hall. This structure was built between 1982 and 1986 by Alfred McAlpine plc for Vickers Shipbuilding & Engineering (now BAE Systems Maritime – Submarines) and was designed to permit the construction of Britain's next generation of nuclear-powered submarines, including those destined to carry the Trident nuclear deterrent, under cover and thus away from the prying eyes of spy satellites. Facilities include a 24,300-tonne-capacity ship lift that permits completed boats – the Royal Navy always refers to submarines as boats rather than ships – to be lowered and raised from the water. With a covered area of 25,000sq m, the Devonshire Dock Hall is the second largest indoor shipbuilding facility in Europe.

The new facility was built at the western end of the existing Devonshire Dock at Barrow and required the infilling of part of the dock to accommodate the new build. Devonshire Dock was the oldest of the main docks constructed at Barrow in the 19th century and was formally opened on 19 September 1867. Owned by the Furness Railway, the dock complex at Barrow – which ultimately included six enclosed docks and a total water area of 279½ acres (113ha) – passed to the LMS in 1923 and to the BTC on nationalisation in 1948. It is now one of the subsidiary ports owned by ABP following privatisation in 1983.

There has been a long tradition of naval shipbuilding at Barrow-in-Furness. The first submarine built was constructed for the Ottoman Empire in 1886. Since 1963 the yard at Barrow has constructed all but three of the Royal Navy's nuclear-powered submarines; until 2003 the yard was also capable of constructing surface warships but a reorganisation within the parent BAE Systems group resulted in this work ceasing at Barrow with the yard concentrating on the construction of submarines.

In late 2014 work commenced on a further redevelopment of the facilities at Barrow-in-Furness to permit the construction of the new generation of submarines capable of carrying Britain's nuclear deterrent to replace the existing four 'Trident'-class submarines in the next decade. Work costing some £300 million will see the construction of a new Central Yard Complex; at 15,300sq m this will be two-thirds the size of the Devonshire Dock Hall.

EAW496011

Britannia Royal Naval College, Dartmouth
September 1928

With the expansion of the Royal Navy during the 19th century, the existing training facilities, both onshore and on the training ships, were increasingly inadequate to provide the officers that the growing navy required. In 1863, the hulk of HMS *Britannia* was transferred from Portland to Dartmouth in Devon, where the ship was moored in the River Dart. A second ship, HMS *Hindustan*, arrived the following year. For the next 40 years these ships – with the original *Britannia* being replaced by HMS *Prince of Wales* (renamed *Britannia* for the purpose) in 1869 – provided the accommodation required for the training of naval officers. In March 1902, however, the foundation stone for a new purpose-built college was laid by HM King Edward VII. The new building, designed by the architect Sir Aston Webb (1849–1930) – who also designed part of the Victoria & Albert Museum in London – and built by Higgs & Hill was completed three years later, with the first cadets arriving in September 1905.

When originally completed, the college took cadets from the age of 15; this was raised to 16 in 1948 and to 17½ in 1955. Today, the college takes officer cadets from the age of 18 up to 32; while some come straight from school, the majority come after completing university education and includes recruits both for the Royal Navy and from overseas. Following closures elsewhere, Dartmouth is now the only naval college in the United Kingdom. The impressive building is seen here in a photograph taken in September 1928.

EPW024215

Royal Naval College, Greenwich
1946

Now listed Grade I and regarded by UNESCO as a World Heritage Site, the Royal Naval College at Greenwich is one of the finest architectural ensembles in the country. Its origins lay in a Tudor royal palace, the Palace of Placentia, where the future queens Mary and Elizabeth were born in 1516 and 1533 respectively, like their father, Henry VIII, in 1491. In 1613 James I passed the palace to his queen, Anne of Denmark, and in 1616 Inigo Jones (1573–1652) designed the Queen's House – set back from the river and in the centre of the photograph – as probably the first Italianate house in England. However, this building was not complete by Anne's death in 1619 and work ceased until 1629 when Charles I thought it suitable for his queen, Henrietta Maria. Work on the building was completed in 1637; the building as it exists today reflects additional work undertaken after the restoration in 1662 by John Webb (1611–72), Jones's son-in-law, to eventually provide additional accommodation for the returning Henrietta Maria.

During the Commonwealth, between 1649 and 1660, the palace suffered severely and, following the restoration, Charles II decided to rebuild it, commissioning John Webb to undertake the work. The original Tudor palace was demolished and in 1664 work started on the construction of the new palace; the surviving section of Webb's work is to be found in the King Charles Court. The critical date for the development of the site came in 1692 when Queen Mary II, inspired by the sight of wounded sailors returning from the Battle of Le Hogue, ordered the construction of a hospital similar to that built earlier at Chelsea for soldiers. In 1694 Sir Christopher Wren (1632–1723) was commissioned to produce designs; the original scheme was amended in 1699 when it was decided that the Queen's House should

retain a view of the river, a view that would have been lost had Wren's design been completed. Two of the other great Baroque architects of the era were also involved: Nicholas Hawksmoor (c 1661–1736), who was Clerk of Works from 1698 and Deputy Surveyor from 1705, and Sir John Vanbrugh (1664–1726), who sat on the Board from 1702 and became Surveyor in 1716.

The hospital as constructed comprised four main blocks. The first of these was the King Charles Court (the north-west of the quartet). This included the surviving remains of the work undertaken by Webb in the 1660s but also includes the south front designed by James Stuart (1713–88) in 1769 and the west front built to a design of John Yenn (1750–1821) between 1811 and 1814. King William Court (on the south-west), which includes the painted hall with its dramatic ceiling painted by Sir James Thornhill (1675 or 1676–1734), was started in 1698 and completed in 1728 by a west front designed by Vanbrugh. Queen Anne Court (on the north-east) was begun in 1699 and was completed in 1640 by Colen Campbell (1676–1729), author of *Vitruvius Britannicus* and one of the most influential neo-Classical architects of the period, and Thomas Ripley (1682–1758) in 1740. Queen Mary Court (on the south-east), which includes the chapel, was begun in 1699; this building was completed in 1750 under the guidance again of Ripley. The chapel was seriously damaged by fire in 1779, not being reopened until 1798 with the work being undertaken by William Newton (1730–98), the then Clerk of Works.

Also visible in this view taken towards the south are, to the south-west of the main courts, the square two-storeyed Dreadnought Hospital and the single-storey engineering laboratory that dates to the 1840s between

the infirmary and the river. The former was originally the hospital infirmary and was constructed in 1763 and 1764 to a design by James Stuart.

The Royal Hospital for Seamen at Greenwich occupied the site until 1869 and, following conversion, the buildings re-opened as the Royal Naval College in 1873. In 1998, with the Royal Navy's decline in size and as its needs for officers was thus reduced, the decision was taken to close the college. The buildings were transferred to the Greenwich Foundation for the Old Naval College, a charity, under whose auspices much of the site has been leased either to the University of Greenwich or the Trinity College of Music. The Queen's House and its later additions (the two colonnades and accommodation wings designed by Daniel Asher Alexander [1768–1846] that were constructed from 1807 to allow the house to be used as the Royal Hospital School for the sons of seamen) now form part of the National Maritime Museum.

EAW002292

Chatham
2 April 1972

The story of the largely pre-Victorian naval dockyard is narrated on p 261. This view, taken from the north-east, shows the mid-Victorian expansion of the naval dockyard at Chatham and, in particular, the three basins that were constructed between 1865 and 1885. These developments ensured that Chatham was capable of handling the warships of the steam age and accommodating more of the fleet following the closure of the two naval dockyards – Deptford and Woolwich – on the Thames in the 1860s.

The three basins were constructed along the line of St Mary's Creek, which separated the existing dockyard from the marshy area known as St Mary's Island; the latter was effectively drained to provide additional dry land for the expanding naval dockyard. The first of the three basins to be completed was the most westerly – No 1 Basin – which was opened in 1872 along with the first two of the graving docks. Basin No 1 is 1,600ft (488.7m) by 900ft (274.3m) and the first of the graving docks were both 400ft (121.9m) by 100ft (30.5m). This was the repairing basin. Basin No 2, in the centre, was the factory basin and is 1,500ft (457.2m) by 800ft (243.8m). The final basin, No 3, was formally opened in September 1885 and is 1,800ft (548.6m) in length but with an irregular width. This was the fitting out basin and was provided with the two locks visible. Basin No 1 was provided with a tidal caisson for access to the Upnor Reach of the Medway. The additional three graving docks were added subsequently, resulting in four on the south side of Basin No 1, all completed by 1873, and one on the north, built between 1895 and 1903 to accommodate the larger warships then under construction.

By the late 1970s, with the decline of Britain as a world power, the Royal Navy shrank considerably in size and, despite investment at Chatham in the late 1960s (when a facility to refit nuclear submarines was completed), it was announced in June 1981 that the dockyard was to close. Although the Falklands War of 1982 resulted in a number of proposed cuts to the Royal Navy being cancelled, there was to be no reprieve for Chatham and the dockyard closed in 1984. The 18th-century core of the dockyard on the Medway was transferred to the Chatham Historic Dockyard Trust and is now a museum. Basins Nos 1 and 2 have been redeveloped into a marina with residential properties and leisure facilities constructed on the quayside. Basin No 3 was transferred to the Medway Ports Authority and now handles a certain amount of commercial traffic. Current operators, Peel Ports, have plans for the regeneration of the site. The two locks of the eastern side remain operational while much of St Mary's Island, originally part of the naval base, has been redeveloped for housing. The four docks served by No 1 Basin are also still extant. Of the vast number of buildings erected to serve the Victorian dockyard as shown in the 1972 photograph, the majority have been demolished. Among the exceptions are the 1902-built naval barracks – once HMS *Pembroke* – with a number now occupied as the Medway Campus of the University of Greenwich. Apart from this, there are a couple of other survivals from the Victorian-era dockyard. These include the Grade II Dock Pumping Station of 1874 and the No 1 Boiler Ship and the Grade II* No 8 Machine Shop. The latter two buildings were originally erected at Woolwich but transferred to Chatham following the former's closure.

From the mid-19th century onwards, the dockyard at Chatham was active in the construction of warships for the Royal Navy and for the navies of the British Empire and Commonwealth. In later years, this work was largely in the construction of submarines. The last warship to be built at Chatham for the Royal Navy was the 'Oberon'-class submarine HMS *Ocelot*, which was laid down on 17 November 1960 and launched on 5 May 1962; appropriately, this boat is now on display within the historic dockyard. The final construction work at Chatham comprised three 'Oberon'-class submarines for the Canadian navy; the last to be completed was HMCS *Okanagan*, which was laid down on 25 March 1965 and launched on 17 September 1966.

Across Upnor Reach, but not distinguishable in this view, is Upnor Castle; this was built in 1567 to aid the defence of the dockyard. In this, however, it proved less than useful – on the one serious attack against Chatham from the sea (the Dutch raid of June 1667 when Charles II's flagship, the *Royal Charles*, was seized) the enemy fleet simply sailed past it.

EAW223251

Lee-on-Solent
September 1928

During World War I, as air power became more significant, a number of new facilities were constructed around Britain's coastline for the use of seaplanes engaged in anti-submarine warfare and for the training of suitable pilots. Calshot on the Solent was already established as a training base but was inadequate and so further facilities were sought. One of these was Lee-on-Solent across the Solent from Calshot where a temporary base was established in the summer of 1917, formally opening on 30 July 1917 under the command of Squadron Commander Douglas Evill, DSC, RN (1892–1971). Later that year, the decision was made to convert the base into a permanent facility and it is this relatively new site that Aerofilms recorded in 1928.

Work began during November 1917 on the three double-gabled seaplane hangars visible – Buildings 31, 35 and 37 – plus the two larger single-gable hangars further inland with the site now designated as HMS *Daedalus*. On 1 April 1918, the Royal Air Force, successor to the Royal Flying Corps and the Royal Naval Air Service, took over the site known as No 209 Training Station.

Shortly after the date of the photograph, in 1931, the decision was taken to expand the RAF presence at Lee with the construction of an airfield, and work started in September 1932. Through the 1930s the new airfield – transferred from the Royal Air Force to the Fleet Air Arm in May 1939 when the latter was formally established – was developed although it was not until 1942 that the final arrangement of runways was completed. As a military base, Lee-on-Solent was attacked by the Luftwaffe on at least two occasions during the war and the new airfield saw considerable development during the war with new hangars constructed. On D-Day, 6 June 1944, Lee-on-Solent was the busiest of all southern airfields used, flying primarily reconnaissance and gun-spotting operations.

After the war, HMS *Daedalus* – known as HMS *Ariel* between 1959 and October 1965 – was used for a variety of activities; in 1962, the slipway shown in the 1928 view was brought back into use following the creation of the Joint Service Hovercraft Trials Unit. The site was also home of the Naval Air Trial Installation Unit.

As part of the run-down of Britain's defences in the early 1990s, HMS *Daedalus* was formally decommissioned on 29 March 1996. The airfield remains extant and at the time of writing operated commercially as Daedalus Airfield. The original World War I facility remains largely intact with Buildings 31, 35 and 37 – the seaplane sheds with their associated winch houses – now listed as Grade II. These are the two hangars visible in the 1928 photograph on either side of the slipway and that at right angles on the south side of the concreted area. These are believed to be the only examples of Admiralty Type J hangars surviving. Also still standing, but not listed, are the two larger hangars located towards the east of the site. The buildings situated on the north of the site were at the time of writing occupied by the Hovercraft Museum, an appropriate use given the site's role in the development of the hovercraft.

EPW024422

Portland Harbour

3 October 1946

Located to the south of Weymouth and protected by the Isle of Portland, Chesil Beach and the Dorset Coast, Portland is the largest artificial harbour in the United Kingdom with its four breakwaters – totalling 4.57km – enclosing about 520ha of water.

The strategic importance of the area was recognised from the Middle Ages; Henry VIII built two forts protecting the approaches to Weymouth, one of which – Portland Castle – still survives. It was not, however, until the mid-19th century that active steps were taken to provide a sheltered harbour on a stretch of coast notorious for shipwrecks; the resulting dock was to become the largest man-made harbour in the world at the time. Following the work of Royal Commission for Harbours of Refuge, Parliament approved the construction of breakwaters at Portland. The design work was undertaken by James Meadows Rendel (1799–1856) and on 25 July 1849 Prince Albert laid the foundation stone for the Royal Portland Breakwater. The main contractor was John Towlerton Leather (1804–85); following the death of Rendel, the resident engineer became John Coode (1816–92). The two southern breakwaters were completed in 1868 and the harbour was officially opened by the Prince of Wales, the future Edward VII, on 10 August 1872. The final two breakwater arms were completed in 1906; these were designed as a countermeasure against possible attack by torpedo. Ironically, the development of this type of weapon had taken place in Portland harbour at the Whiteheads factory.

Visible in this 1946 view are three of the Royal Navy's major capital ships. On the left is HMS *Nelson*, which, by this date, was active as a training ship. *Nelson* was one of two battleships – the other being HMS *Rodney* – that were built in the early 1920s. *Nelson* was built by Armstrong-Whitworth on the Tyne and launched on 3 September 1925. Commissioned on 15 August 1927, the battleship was to serve in the Atlantic, Mediterranean and Indian Ocean theatres during World War II. Decommissioned in 1948, *Nelson* was scrapped at Inverkeithing, arriving there in March 1949. On the right are two of the 'King George V' battleships; five of the class were built, being commissioned between October 1940 and June 1942. One of the class – HMS *Prince of Wales* – was sunk in the South China Sea on 10 December 1941. The remaining four – *King George* V, *Duke of York*, *Anson* and *Howe* – all survived until being decommissioned in the late 1950s and scrapped from 1957 onwards.

In the background can be seen sections of the Mulberry Harbour caissons; these had originally been constructed as part of the temporary harbours required for the Allied invasion of Normandy in June 1944. After the war, 10 sections were brought back to Portland where they were used to assist the construction of the Queen's Pier. In 1953 eight were removed to the Netherlands to assist in the rebuilding of the dykes following the disastrous flooding (*see* p 285). The two that remained at Portland still survive and were listed as Grade II in 1993 and still offer protection for ships berthing at the Queen's Pier.

Although there was considerable investment by the Royal Navy in Portland, including the construction of two large accommodation blocks in the early 1980s, cuts in the defence budget resulted in the announcement in November 1992 that Portland was to close as a naval base. Royal Navy operations ceased on 21 July 1995 and naval training activity ceased on 29 March 1996 when it was transferred to Devonport. RNAS *Osprey* closed on 31 October 1999, ending the military presence at Portland. In 1996 the harbour was sold to Portland Port Ltd, under whose ownership there has been much development to generate both commercial and leisure trade.

EAW002986

Portsmouth
29 July 1974

With the waters of Portsmouth harbour stretching towards Portchester and Fareham in the distance, the foreground of this image records much of the naval dockyard that dominates much of the eastern side of the harbour. This view records much of the 19th-century expansion of the dockyard, built at a time when the Royal Navy was expanding and when steam was supplanting sail as the navy modernised.

In the foreground is Dock No 1; this was opened in 1801 and remained in use until February 1984. HMS *Victory* (*see* p 165) is berthed in Dock No 2 off Ship Basin No 1; the latter was completed in 1805 and replaced a wet dock that had originally been built during the last decade of the 17th century. The basin and the four docks – Nos 2 to 5 – were declared to be no longer required for operational purposes in 1984. Immediately to the north of Basin No 1 is Dock No 6; this was completed in 1700 and remained in use until 1984; although no longer usable – the western side of the dock area has been rebuilt and now forms Western Way – the dock remains extant.

The first phase of the Victorian expansion of the dockyard occurred in the 1840s. Steam Basin No 2 was opened in 1848 by Queen Victoria. When recorded by the Aerofilms photographer in 1974, the dock still retained its caisson but this has subsequently been removed. Between the new basin and the natural harbour two new linked docks were completed – No 7 on the east and No 10 on the west; these were completed in 1849 and 1858 respectively. The caisson separating the two docks as shown here was added in 1924; this remains in use as part of a base road. The two docks were closed in 1984 (No 7) and 1989 (No 10) and have been infilled and they now form a car park. On the east side of Steam Basin No 2 can be seen the No 1 Shipbuilding (or Ship) Shop;

this dated originally to 1868 with a western extension added during the 1880s. The original building was constructed for the production of armoured plates. On the west side of the basin can be seen the West Factory and the Smithery; the latter was completed in 1852. Both these structures are still extant. To the north of the No 1 Ship Shop is Dock No 11; this was opened in 1865 and remains operational.

The remainder of the 1864 expansion encompasses some 180 acres (73ha). When completed in 1875, the new facility included three new basins – Fitting Basin No 3, Rigging Basin No 4 and Repairing Basin No 5 – with two locks plus a new deep Dock No 9. These were all accessed from the Tidal Basin. Four new docks were served by Basin No 5 – from west to east Nos 15 (1896), 14 (1896), 13 (1876) and 12 (1876); these were all subsequently extended as the size of naval vessels continued to grow. All of these are still operational with Nos 13 and 14 now covered over, with the former surviving as a shipyard, latterly operated by BAE Systems Ltd, until work ceased in 2015. Immediately prior to World War I, two larger locks were added to the north of the existing locks; these were finished in 1913 and 1914. At the same time the three basins were reformed as the single basin as illustrated in the 1974 photograph.

As might be expected Portsmouth suffered significant damage during World War II; post-war, despite the decline in the size of the navy, which has seen bases such as Chatham closed, the dockyard is still a major base for the Royal Navy and will see some work undertaken as the navy's two new aircraft carriers – HMS *Queen Elizabeth* and HMS *Prince of Wales* – enter service.

Although individual ships are not readily identifiable, it is possible to locate HMY *Britannia* (*see* p 173) moored to the north east of the main dock area, while the

preserved HMS *Victory* is located in its dry dock. This view was taken before work on the recovery of the *Mary Rose* had taken place and so the dry dock No 3, which is today occupied by the *Mary Rose* museum, is still fulfilling its original purpose.

EAW280874

Sheerness
17 July 1951

By the mid-17th century the Royal Navy was already established on the Thames – at Deptford and Woolwich – and on the Medway – at Chatham. Following the Restoration in 1660, Anglo-Dutch rivalry was such that, following the outbreak of the Second Anglo-Dutch War, on 4 March 1665, the Navy Board instructed the Commissioner of Chatham Dockyard on 8 August 1665 to undertake the equipping of Sheerness for the maintenance and victualling of Royal Navy ships. This was to be the start of a near 300-year association between the Royal Navy and the harbour.

Although the Thames and Medway Royal Dockyards were to decline in importance during the 18th century as France replaced the Netherlands as England's most conspicuous overseas rival and as the importance of Portsmouth and Plymouth grew, Sheerness continued to develop as a naval dockyard during the period. By the end of the century, Sheerness possessed two dry docks (completed in 1708 and 1720), two slipways and about 30 buildings; these facilities were, however, inadequate and John Rennie (1761–1821) was asked to design a new dockyard. Work started on 23 December 1813 and the new facility was officially reopened by the Duke of Clarence on 5 September 1823.

In the early 1820s, before the completion of the new dockyard, many of the older buildings were destroyed, including the blue houses – built to accommodate the dockyard staff and so named because of the use of naval blue-grey paint on their exteriors – from which the district Bluetown got its name. This view of the dockyard, taken looking towards the east, shows the dockyard as constructed during this period along with additional buildings added during the 19th century. The principle architects for the work during the 19th century were Edward Holl (unknown–1824) and his successor George Ledwell Taylor (1788–1873).

Among the prominent naval buildings seen in this photograph is the boat store; this is the structure with three gable ends located immediately to the south of the two northernmost dry docks. This was designed in 1858 by Col Godfrey T Greene (1807–86), the Admiralty's Director of Engineering and Architectural Work from 1850 to 1864, and constructed in 1859. Four storeys high and more than 61m long, the building is the first multi-storey iron-framed building in the world without any load-bearing walls. It is now listed Grade I. To the south-east of the boat store is the four-storey storehouse constructed around a quadrangle; designed by Holl, this structure was completed in 1829. Unfortunately, this building was demolished in 1980. Further to the south-east, the long terrace is the Archway block; this was completed in 1830, again to the design of Holl. This terrace is still standing as is the perimeter wall of the dockyard. To the north of the two dry docks, Docks No 4 and No 5, is a three-storeyed square block; this is Admiralty House, which was built in 1827 and demolished in 1964. Other survivors include the garrison church, which was designed by Taylor and completed in 1828, and much of the residential property in the officers' quarter again designed by Taylor.

The threat to the future of these buildings, and the other surviving naval structures, was recognised by their inclusion on the Heritage at Risk Register and in 2009 the entire dockyard was added to the World Monument Fund's international watch list of endangered historic sites. In 2011 the Spitalfields Historic Buildings Trust acquired the officers' residential quarter for £1.85 million with the intention of restoring the 10 Grade II and Grade II* listed buildings.

It was announced on 18 February 1958 that the naval dockyard was to close and naval activity ceased in March 1960. The port was then taken over by the Medway Port Authority to be developed for commercial traffic. Today, Sheerness is the port through which the largest number of cars is imported and much of the original naval area, including the dry docks to the south of the 1951 photograph, has been redeveloped.

EAW037832

HMS *Flying Fox*
5 October 1950

For many years the Royal Navy employed redundant vessels in non-naval bases to provide accommodation as training ships or for the Royal Naval Volunteer Reserve. One of these was HMS *Flying Fox*, which was based in Bristol. Bristol Division was one of the five divisions of the RNVR when it was established in 1903. After World War I, when the unit was reformed, the division was provided with a new drill ship in the form of '24-Class' sloop HMS *Flying Fox*.

A total of 24 members of this class of sloop were planned, hence the name, and were ordered between December 1916 and April 1917 for minesweeping duties. Of these, only 10 were completed by November 1918, with a further 12 finished after the war and two were cancelled. The fifth of the type to be completed was HMS *Flying Fox*, which was built on the Tyne by Swan Hunter and launched on 28 March 1918. Unlike most of the type, many of which were either scrapped or sold in the early 1920s, this sloop was transferred to the RNVR on 24 March 1920 and was based in Bristol from 1924.

For the next 50 years, *Flying Fox* served the RNVR; it is pictured here in 1950 berthed alongside Hotwell Road on the north side of Bristol harbour. After World War II the Bristol Division of the RNVR was renamed as the Severn Division and in 1958 the RNVR merged with the original Royal Naval Reserve – which had its origins in Register of Seaman founded in 1835 – to form the new Royal Naval Reserve. HMS *Flying Fox* was to remain with the Severn Division until 1972 when the division moved to a new land-based facility on Winterstoke Road. The redundant sloop was then sold for scrap, being towed across the Bristol Channel on its final voyage to a breaker's yard in Cardiff.

EAW033316

HMS *Victory*
20 July 1995

Views within the Aerofilms collection of the massive naval dockyard at Portsmouth are very limited, but one corner was recorded here when the Aerofilms cameraman photographed HMS *Victory* under repair in 1995. The historic core of the dockyard is now under the care of the National Museum of the Royal Navy and is branded as Portsmouth Historic Dockyard. Apart from the *Victory*, the site also plays host to HMS *Warrior*, the world's first iron-clad armoured warship and the museum devoted to the *Mary Rose*.

The history of Portsmouth as a naval dockyard stretches back to the late 12th century and the world's first dry dock was established here in 1495 by Sir Reginald Bray (*c* 1440–1503) but, until the mid-17th century, the dockyard was overshadowed by those established on the Medway. However, the gradual silting of the Medway ports allied to Britain's growing global ambitions from the mid-17th century onwards, saw Portsmouth's importance grow. The 18th and 19th centuries witnessed considerable expansion with significant new building work undertaken.

This view shows part of a much greater dockyard but three of the dry docks. HMS *Victory* stands in dock No 2, which dated originally to 1802. Next, is dock No 3; this was constructed in 1803. The temporary structure shown housed the remains of the *Mary Rose*; this structure has subsequently been replaced by the permanent museum devoted to Henry VIII's flagship. Beyond this is dock No 4; this dated originally to 1772 and, like the No

3 dock, was extended during 1859 and 1860 as part of the mid-Victorian expansion of the dockyard. No 4 dock ceased to be used from December 1983. Of the buildings visible, the most prominent, with its Classical pediments, is the Victory Building, which is the headquarters of the naval base and was opened on 25 March 1994. To its south, the three-bay building is store No 24; this building, listed at Grade II, was one of a quartet of stores constructed during 1782 and 1783 and was modified just before World War II.

HMS *Victory* was laid down on 23 July 1759 at Chatham and was launched six years later on 7 May 1765 but not formally commissioned until March 1778. A 104-gun first-rate ship, *Victory* is best-known as the flagship of Admiral Lord Nelson at the Battle of Trafalgar on 21 October 1805. Paid off on 7 November 1812, the *Victory* was based in Portsmouth and used for a variety of purposes thereafter but by the early years of the 20th century was in a parlous condition and there was a real threat, not for the first time, that the warship might be scrapped. A public campaign saw the warship moved into No 2 dry dock at Portsmouth and conservation began. It was not, however, until 2005 that the *Victory* was finally restored to her condition at the time of Trafalgar. Still effectively in service, HMS *Victory* is the world's oldest commissioned warship.

EAW648528

HMS *Amethyst*
17 August 1950

For a brief period in 1949 HMS *Amethyst* was perhaps the most famous warship in the world as for three months she was trapped on the River Yangtse in China. *Amethyst* was a Modified 'Black Swan'-class sloop and was built by Alexander Stephen & Sons of Linthouse, Govan, Glasgow. Laid down on 25 March 1942, launched on 7 May 1943 and commissioned on 2 November 1943, the *Amethyst*, with a pennant number of U16, initially served in the Atlantic on convoy and anti-submarine work; during this period she was credited with sinking U-1276 with depth charges on 20 February 1945. Following modification and reclassification – with pennant number F116 – as a frigate, *Amethyst* was transferred to the fleet in the Far East.

On 20 April 1949, the warship was sailing up the Yangtse from Shanghai to Nanking, to replace HMS *Consort* as the guard ship for the British Embassy during the Chinese civil war when the warship came under attack by the guns of the People's Liberation Army. The ship suffered serious damage and a number of the crew were killed and injured. Despite being holed below the waterline, *Amethyst* was kept afloat although an attempted rescue by HMS *Consort* led to further casualties. A second attempt, by HMS *London* and HMS *Black Swan*, also failed, with both ships sustaining damage.

Effectively held prisoner by the PLA, the *Amethyst* was starved of vital supplies. Under the command of Lt-Cdr

John Kerans (1915–85), who had been the Assistant Naval Attaché at the British Embassy before the start of the incident, the *Amethyst* made a break for freedom on 30 July 1949, shadowing the passenger ship *Kiang Lin Liberation* as the warship started its 167km dash for open water. The ships came under attack from the People's Liberation Army's shore batteries and the passenger ship was sunk with a serious loss of life. Early on the morning of 31 July, the *Amethyst* finally escaped and was met by the destroyer HMS *Concord*. There were a number of medals awarded; these included the Dickin Medal – the animal VC – to the ship's cat, Simon, for catching and killing numerous rats despite being severely injured.

This view, with HMS *Amethyst* moored off the breakwater at Plymouth, was taken on 17 August 1950 after the frigate had returned to home waters and after all the damage sustained under the People's Liberation Army's attack had been repaired. In 1957 the warship was used in the making of the film *Yangtse Incident: The Story of HMS* Amethyst, but, by this date, the ship was in poor condition – its engines no longer functioned – and so sister ship HMS *Magpie* was used when the ship was required to move. Having had one final blaze of glory, *Amethyst* was scrapped shortly after filming was completed.

EAW031911

HMS *Loch Dunvegan*
10 November 1955

The 'Loch' class of anti-submarine frigates was a revised version of the earlier 'River' class and was ordered towards the end of World War II. Originally 110 were ordered but as hostilities ceased, only 28 were completed and, of these, nine were transferred: six to New Zealand and three to South Africa. HMS *Loch Dunvegan* was ordered in January 1943 and was laid down on 29 September 1943, being launched on 25 March 1944 and completed on 30 June 1944; the warship was the first of three to be built by Charles Hill & Sons of Bristol. Initial service was with the Arctic convoys and on 24 August 1944 the warship – which had the original pennant number K425, becoming F425 in 1948 – was involved in the action that resulted in the sinking of U-354. On 14 February 1945 the warship was also involved in the sinking of U-989. With the cessation of hostilities in August 1945, HMS *Loch Dunvegan* was transferred to the 1st Anti-Submarine Training Flotilla at Londonderry, from where the warship was paid off into reserve in August 1947.

With the outbreak of the Korean War, F425 was, on 1 May 1950, one of a number of Royal Navy warships reactivated for further service and, along with other members of the 'Loch' class, was allocated to the 2nd Frigate Flotilla in the Mediterranean and based at Malta. After a period in early 1952 as a guard ship at Port Said to protect British interests in the Suez Canal, F425 returned to Devonport later that year and was again decommissioned. The warship then spent the next eight years in reserve, largely at Penarth in South Wales. On 10 November 1955, the Aerofilms cameraman recorded HMS *Loch Dunvegan* in Albion Dock, Bristol. The ship's builders, Charles Hill & Sons, were based at Albion Dock and were to survive in business until 1977. HMS *Loch Dunvegan* made her final journey on 24 August 1960 when she was towed from Penarth to the scrapyard of T W Ward at Briton Ferry.

EAW061875

HMS *Centaur*
4 February 1963

By the date of this photograph (4 February 1963 in Liverpool), the aircraft carrier HMS *Centaur* (pennant number R06) was approaching the end of its operational career. The carrier was the first of a planned class of eight light carriers ordered towards the end of World War II. With the end of hostilities in August 1945, work on the final four was cancelled. *Centaur* was built by Harland & Wolff in Belfast and was laid down on 30 May 1944, being launched on 22 April 1947. Commissioned into service on 1 September 1953, the carrier was modernised between 1956 and 1958 to enable her to carry jet aircraft such as the de Havilland Sea Venom. In 1959 *Centaur* was to feature in the film *Sink the* Bismarck! masquerading as the wartime carriers *Victorious* and *Ark Royal*.

Following a further refit in 1960, *Centaur* was involved in a number of missions overseas. In the summer of 1961, she was sent to the Persian Gulf following a British operation in support of Kuwait against a threat of annexation by Iraq and, in 1964, to East Africa in order to assist in the suppression of a mutiny by the 1st Tanganyika Rifles at barracks close to the capital of the British protectorate's capital of Dar-es-Salaam. Following the cancellation of the ship's proposed conversion to a Commando carrier, HMS *Centaur* was decommissioned in 1965 although retained for use as an accommodation ship until being laid up in 1970; in 1972 the carrier was towed to the Scottish port of Cairnryan where she was scrapped.

The last of the 'Centaur'-class carriers to be completed was HMS *Hermes*; commissioned in 1959, *Hermes* was to achieve fame in 1982 when she led the Royal Navy task force to the South Atlantic following the Argentine invasion and occupation of the Falkland Islands. *Hermes* was sold to the Indian Navy in 1986 and, at the time of writing had just been decommissioned.

EAW108229

HMY *Britannia*
8 May 1959

From the reign of King Charles II onwards there have been 84 ships designated as royal yachts; the most recent was *Britannia*, seen here at Portsmouth on 8 May 1959. Built by John Brown & Co Ltd, Clydebank, the ship was first laid down on 16 June 1952 and launched on 16 April 1953. Commissioned on 11 January 1954, *Britannia* was to serve as the royal yacht for more than 40 years before being decommissioned on 11 December 1997. During the ship's career, *Britannia* made no fewer than 696 foreign trips, with her last official foreign visit being to depart from Hong Kong on 1 July 1997 with the last British governor of the colony, Chris Patten, following the emotional hand-over of the territory to the People's Republic of China.

During her long career *Britannia* was visited by no fewer than four US presidents – Dwight Eisenhower, Gerald Ford, Ronald Reagan and Bill Clinton – and was also used on part of their honeymoon by HRH Prince Charles and Diana, Princess of Wales, following their marriage in 1981. Apart from her role as the royal yacht, *Britannia* was also designated as hospital ship, although she was never actually used for that purpose. Following her decommissioning, *Britannia* was preserved and now forms the centrepiece of the redeveloped harbour at Leith, near Edinburgh, where she is a major tourist attraction.

EAW075124

HMS *Grampus*
27 July 1972

The submarine, as a practical sea-going vessel, only became possible towards the end of the 19th century with the development of the diesel engine. Although there had been earlier experiments using batteries, problems with range and durability meant that the technology was limited. The Royal Navy, as the world's then pre-eminent military force, was one of the pioneers in the adoption of the submarine after overcoming initial resistance to the concept, ordering five 'Holland'-class submarines to be built by Vickers of Barrow-in-Furness under licence from the Holland Torpedo Boat Co. The first submarine, *Holland 1*, which was salvaged in 1982 and is now preserved at the Royal Navy Submarine Museum at Gosport, was launched on 2 October 1901 and commenced sea trials in April 1902.

HMS *Grampus* (S04), pictured here at Portsmouth, was one of eight members of the 'Porpoise' class of diesel-electric submarines that served with the Royal Navy. The boat – the Royal Navy refers to submarines as 'boats' – was laid down at the Cammell Laird shipyard at Birkenhead in 1955 and was launched on 30 May 1957, before being fully commissioned on 19 December 1958.

During the submarine's operational life there were two notable incidents. The first occurred in early 1963 when the boat spent three weeks submerged underneath the Arctic searching for holes in the polar ice cap. The second, and more embarrassing, event was on 11 January 1968 when the French trawler *Formalhaut* caught a slightly larger fish than the crew was expecting; it took three hours for the submarine to be disentangled from the trawler's nets. Used as a harbour training ship between 1976 and 1979, *Grampus* was sunk in Loch Fyne after being been used for target practice on 18 September 1980.

EAW10344

HMS *Broadsword*
11 July 1990

Caught by the Aerofilms photographer off Plymouth, HMS *Broadsword* (F88) was the first of the Royal Navy's Type 22 anti-submarine frigates. By the early 1970s, the navy required work to be undertaken on a replacement for the earlier 'Leander' class of frigate; with resources devoted to the development of the Type 42 anti-aircraft destroyers, initially the RN ordered eight of the privately designed Type 21 frigates. With design work completed on the Type 22s, HMS *Broadsword* was laid down by Yarrow Ltd at Scotstoun, on the River Clyde, on 7 February 1975. Launched on 12 May 1976, the frigate was commissioned on 3 May 1979. Among her first actions was assisting in the rescue operations following the Fastnet disaster of 1979 when a severe storm in August resulted in many of the 306 yachts involved in the race being sunk, damaged or capsized with 18 fatalities.

As with the Type 42 destroyers, the new Type 22 frigates were powered by gas turbines but marked a change in Royal Navy policy in two ways: they were the first Royal Navy warships to be designed using metric – rather than imperial – measurements and they were also the first major warships designed for the Royal Navy that did not have a traditional gun as its primary armament.

In April 1982 Argentina invaded the Falkland Islands in the South Atlantic; HMS *Broadsword*, then en route through the Mediterranean to join a patrol in the Persian Gulf, was diverted to join the Royal Navy task force that was sent south to recover the islands. While serving with the task force, *Broadsword* suffered bomb damage during the Argentinian assault of 25 May 1982 that resulted in the sinking of the Type 42 destroyer HMS *Coventry*. Despite the damage received, *Broadsword* was able to rescue 170 of the Type 42's crew and was to continue to serve in the south Atlantic until the end of the conflict.

Experience in the Falklands War resulted in those Type 22s built after the conflict, and other warships built thereafter, being fitted with traditional guns to improve their capabilities. In all, 14 Type 22 frigates were completed, with the last being commissioned on 4 May 1990. However, the reduction in the size of the Royal Navy resulted in the type having a relatively short career; HMS *Broadsword* was decommissioned on 31 March 1995 and sold to the Brazilian Navy three months later. As the *Greenhalgh*, *Broadsword* remained in service with the Brazilian Navy at the time of writing.

EAW582726

Spithead Review
July 1924

There has been a tradition of holding naval reviews to mark royal anniversaries or other significant events for some 700 years. The first was held in 1415 when King Henry V reviewed the fleet prior to departure on his military campaign that culminated in the great victory at Agincourt. During the 20th century there were 13 royal reviews of the fleet, the last held in 1977 to celebrate the Silver Jubilee of Queen Elizabeth II. No major royal event since then, including the monarch's Golden Jubilee in 2002 and Diamond Jubilee in 2012, has been so marked, ostensibly on grounds of cost (although the massive reduction in the size of the Royal Navy in the years since the Falklands War in 1982 may also have been a factor).

This view records the Spithead Review held on 26 July 1924 when King George V presented new colours to the Royal Navy. The king and the Prince of Wales, the future King Edward VIII, reviewed the fleet from the royal yacht HMY *Victoria and Albert*. In this view the twin-funnelled yacht is seen passing on the starboard side of one of the 'Revenge' class of battleship. The yacht was the third to have carried the name and was launched at Pembroke Dock, which was then a naval dockyard, in 1899. Commissioned on 23 July 1901, the steam-powered *Victoria and Albert* was to remain in service until 1939 when she was decommissioned. Following the royal duties, the ship served as a depot ship during and after World War II, being scrapped in 1954.

In all, some 196 warships were present at the review; these included a significant number that had seen service at the Battle of Jutland. Among the warships present were no fewer than four of the 'Revenge'-class battleships – *Revenge*, *Royal Oak*, *Royal Sovereign* and *Ramillies* – that were all in line astern from west to east

respectively at the eastern end of the review as HMY *Victoria and Albert* sailed towards Southampton. All of the class were laid down between 22 December 1913 and 15 January 1914, launched between 17 November 1914 and 12 June 1916, and commissioned between 1 February 1916 and 1 September 1917. Only two – *Revenge* and *Royal Oak* – were available for service at Jutland and neither was damaged during that engagement.

Of the quartet listed, three survived until after World War II, being scrapped during 1948 and 1949 (*Royal Sovereign* having served with the Russian navy between 1944 and 1949), while *Royal Oak* was sunk by a German U-boat in the harbour at Scapa Flow in October 1939 – the first major casualty suffered by the Royal Navy during World War II. It is suggested that, of the quartet, this view shows HMS *Ramillies*.

Spithead is the eastern channel of the Solent and is situated directly south of the main naval base at Portsmouth. Apart from its use for the reviews, Spithead was also notorious as the scene of a mutiny. This took place between 16 April and 15 May 1797 when the crews of 16 ships took action over the living conditions on board ship and the paucity of naval pay. Unlike the contemporaneous mutiny at the Nore, an anchorage on the River Thames (where the leader and 29 other mutineers were hanged), the mutiny at Spithead was resolved and all received royal pardons and a number of the mutineers' grievances, such as the poor food supplied and the harsh discipline enforced, were acted upon.

EPW011367

SS *Great Britain*
17 April 1973

Designed by the mercurial Isambard Kingdom Brunel (1806–59), undoubtedly one of the greatest British engineers of the 19th century, the SS *Great Britain* was the second of Brunel's three great vessels, coming between the *Great Western* (launched in 1837) and the *Great Eastern* (launched in 1858). Originally conceived as a wooden-hulled paddle steamer, like her earlier sister, the *Great Britain*'s design was modified by Brunel to incorporate an iron hull with screw propulsion. Built in Bristol for the Great Western Steamship Co, the *Great Britain* was launched on 19 July 1843 and, when making her maiden voyage from Liverpool in New York on 26 July 1845, was the largest vessel in service.

The new liner was not a success; design flaws required significant modification following the completion of her second eastbound crossing. In 1846 she returned to service but ran aground on the northern Irish coast on her third eastbound crossing of the year. Refloated in 1847, she returned to Liverpool for repair and further modification; by now she was under different ownership as the travails of the previous years had seen the failure of her original owners.

Refitted, the *Great Britain* made one final transatlantic return journey before again being sold, this time to Antony Gibbs & Sons; the new owners decided to use the ship on the Australian route following the discovery of gold in Victoria in 1852. For the next 30 years she was to operate on the Australian route, conveying vast numbers of emigrants to the rapidly growing British colonies there. In 1882, the *Great Britain* was converted into a sailing ship for the transport of coal but, following a fire in 1886, she was dumped at Port Stanley in the Falkland Islands. Purchased by the Falkland Islands Co, the rusting hulk was used as a warehouse until 1933 when the ship was towed to Sparrow Cove and scuttled. This might have been the end of the story but, in the late 1960s, a campaign was launched to rescue the ship and return her to Bristol for preservation.

The *Great Britain* left the Falkland Islands for the final time on 24 April 1970, finally reaching Bristol on 5 July. Later that month she was moved to the dry dock in the Great Western Dockyard, where she had been built more than a century earlier.

When recorded by the Aerofilms photographer in 1973, she was safely berthed in the now Grade II* listed dockyard, which had been disused since bomb damage during World War II, with restoration work in hand. Initially, the plan was to restore the ship to original condition; subsequently, this was abandoned in favour of conserving as much original material as possible. With work completed, the ship is one of the Bristol's most popular visitor attractions.

EAW250863

Cutty Sark and HMS Worcester
20 May 1939

Two classic vessels from the age of sail stand berthed alongside each other in front of Ingress Abbey, Greenhithe, on the River Thames. Closest to the camera is the clipper *Cutty Sark*. The clippers were among the last sailing ships built for commercial long-distance trade; by the time that the *Cutty Sark* and her sisters were built, steam-powered ships were increasingly dominant and, with the completion of the Suez Canal, steam gained a further commercial advantage. As a result, the clippers spent a relatively short period on the tea run from India and China before being replaced.

The *Cutty Sark* was built by the Dumbarton-based ship builder of Scott & Linton, being launched on 22 November 1869. Owned between 1869 and 1895 by Jock Wilson (1817–99), the *Cutty Sark* was to spend much of her early career bringing wool from Australia to the British market. Sold to Portuguese owners in 1895, the *Cutty Sark* was to return to British ownership in 1922 when she was acquired by Captain Wilfred Harry Dowman (1879–1936) for use as a sail training ship. In 1938, following Dowman's death two years earlier, the ship was sold to the Thames Nautical Training College at Greenhithe where she was used as an auxiliary vessel to the college's HMS *Worcester* for sail training purposes. It is in this condition that she was recorded here. Following damage in the early 1950s, ownership passed to the Cutty Sark Preservation Society, under whose auspices the clipper was preserved in 1953 and was transferred to a new purpose-built dry dock at Greenwich in 1954. The *Cutty Sark*, following a multi-million pound restoration (during which the clipper was seriously damaged by fire), remains on display at Greenwich.

The Thames Nautical Training College – known as HMS *Worcester* – was a ship-based institution designed to train naval officers, funded by London-based shipping interests and supported by the Royal Navy. It gained its name from the first warship – HMS *Worcester* – that the Admiralty loaned the college. This was replaced in October 1876 by HMS *Frederick William* (renamed *Worcester* for the purpose), and this is the warship shown here. The construction of HMS *Frederick William* – an 86-gun first-rate ship of the line – was a long drawn-out affair, as the ship was originally ordered in September 1833 and laid down on 1 July 1841 at Portsmouth but not finally launched until 24 March 1860 and commissioned on 1 July 1864. The primary reason for the delay was that, when originally ordered, the warship was designed to be sail-powered; however, by the mid-19th century steam power was starting to emerge and in early 1857 it was decided to modify the ship's design to include screw propulsion. As a training ship, HMS *Frederick William* had a long life, not being replaced until after World War II. Sold in July 1948, the redundant warship foundered in the Thames the following month. Raised five years later, the wreck was broken up. The college became part of the Merchant Navy College at Greenhithe in 1968.

The building visible on the Kent coast is Ingress Abbey; this was built in 1833 to the design of Charles Moreing (1809–1911) for James Harmer (1777–1853), a lawyer. By the date of the photograph much of the abbey estate had been sold off and the house gradually deteriorated. In the early 21st century, the house, gardens and follies were restored by the developers Crest Nicholson in connection with a redevelopment scheme.

EPW061029

RMS *Mauretania*
April 1933

One of the great Cunard liners of the early 20th century is seen at Southampton towards the end of her career. Built by Swan Hunter on the River Tyne and launched on 20 September 1906, RMS *Mauretania* and her sister ship the *Lusitania* – the latter sunk in controversial circumstances off Ireland by a German U-boat in 1915 – were constructed following a 1903 agreement between the British Government and Cunard to try and counter the increasing German and US dominance of the North Atlantic market through two liners with a contracted maximum speed of 24kt. The original design was for three funnels, but the decision to adopt the then new turbine technology developed by Sir Charles Algernon Parsons (1854–1931) resulted in the fourth funnel being added. The *Mauretania* undertook her maiden voyage on 16 November 1907.

The speed of the two new Cunard liners resulted in both regularly breaking the record for transatlantic crossings; indeed, the *Mauretania* held the record for the fastest eastbound crossing from November 1907 until July 1929, improving her own time on no fewer than seven occasions between those dates, and the fastest westbound crossing from September 1909 until July 1929. It was the German liner *Bremen* that finally managed to break the *Mauretania*'s 20-year record and thus grasp the 'Blue Riband' – the unofficial title bestowed on the ship achieving the fastest westbound crossing.

During World War I the *Mauretania* served as both a troopship and then a hospital ship during the ill-fated Gallipoli campaign of 1915 before acting again as a troopship to bring Canadian and US soldiers across the Atlantic. After the war, the liner reverted to civilian use on the North Atlantic route until 1930 when she became a cruise ship. Following one final transatlantic crossing from New York in September 1934, the *Mauretania* was taken out of service and then laid up at Southampton until the summer of 1935 when, following the sale of her fittings, the hulk was towed to Rosyth, near Edinburgh on the Firth of Forth, for scrap.

EPW041073

RMS *Olympic*
April 1933

Recorded at the same time as the *Mauretania* was another of the classic British liners of the first decades of the 20th century – the RMS *Olympic*. Sister of the *Titanic*, which had sunk with catastrophic loss of life in April 1912 following a collision with an iceberg during her maiden voyage, the *Olympic* was in fact the first of three similar liners built for White Star Line by Harland & Wolff of Belfast. Launched on 20 October 1910, the liner, with a capacity of 2,435 passengers and 950 crew, made her maiden voyage from Southampton – where a specially built dock, known as the White Star Dock, had been constructed – on 14 June 1911, sailing to New York via Cherbourg and Queenstown (Cobh) in Ireland.

On 20 September 1911 while off the Isle of Wight, the *Olympic* was to have the first of a series of collisions that marked her career when she was rammed on the starboard side by HMS *Hawke*. Following the collision, *Olympic* returned to Belfast for repair; however, this work and a further repair in early 1912 delayed the completion of the *Titanic*, the delay resulting in the postponement of the newer ship's maiden voyage and thus, perhaps, contributing to the disaster. The *Olympic* in this view is the result of modifications undertaken following the loss of the *Titanic*, when a lack of lifeboats was identified as one of the causes of the major loss of life. The additional work undertaken in 1913 to improve safety, including revisions to the bulkheads, increased the liner's grt by more than 1,000.

During World War I, following her withdrawal from commercial work, the *Olympic* was initially laid up; however, during her final eastbound crossing in October 1914, she was sailing to the north of Lough Swilly when her crew responded to a distress signal from HMS *Audacious*, which had struck a mine. The White Star liner provided a safe haven for many of the crew from the Royal Navy battleship, although worries about

uncontrolled news of the sinking meant that the liner, along with its passengers and crew, were temporarily detained at Lough Swilly before the passengers were able to disembark at Belfast. As with the *Mauretania*, the *Olympic* served during the Gallipoli campaign and later as a troopship ferrying US and Canadian soldiers. At the end of the war, the *Olympic* re-entered commercial service in 1920 after restoration and the conversion of her boilers from coal to oil burning.

This photograph records the *Olympic* following the completion of a four-month overhaul that saw her restored to her original splendour; it was, however, to prove a final swan-song. The massive decline in transatlantic traffic as a result of the Wall Street Crash of 1929 and subsequent global economic slump, along with the arrival of newer and more efficient liners, meant that, following the merger of White Star with Cunard in 1934 (a deal engineered by the British Government), *Olympic* made its final eastbound crossing in April 1935. Laid up for a brief period, the liner was initially moved to Jarrow, where demolition of her superstructure between 1936 and 1937 provided opportunity for work for that town's unemployed, before the hull was finally dismantled at the Inverkeithing, Fife, yard of T W Ward.

The third of the type was RMS *Britannic*, launched on 26 February 1914 and again incorporating changes to design following the sinking of the *Titanic*. Never destined to have a civilian career, the *Britannic* was requisitioned on 13 November 1915 to serve as a hospital ship. The liner was sunk on 21 November 1916 off the coast of Greece while operating in the Mediterranean; of the 1,065 on board all bar 30 survived.

Also visible in the view is the Canadian Pacific-owned *Empress of Britain*; this had been built by John Brown & Co on the River Clyde and launched on 11 June 1930. Designed for both transatlantic and cruise traffic, the

Empress of Britain was destined to have a relatively short career. With the outbreak of World War II in September 1939 she was requisitioned as a troopship, a role that she carried out until October 1940 when she was attacked and sunk. Although at 42,348grt the *Empress of Britain* was the largest liner to be sunk during the war, casualties were limited.

EPW041070

RMS *Aquitania*
18 April 1949

Launched on 21 April 1913, the Cunard-owned RMS *Aquitania* held the record, until SS *Queen Elizabeth 2*, of being the longest-serving liner on the North Atlantic route. Built by John Brown & Co at Clydebank, the liner was modified during construction to accommodate extra lifeboats following on from the loss of the *Titanic* in April 1912. Built with a grt of 45,647, the *Aquitania* had a capacity, when new, of 3,230 passengers with a crew of 972. The passenger capacity was reduced in the 1920s to 2,200 and the size of the crew was also reduced when, following a refit after World War I, the ship was converted from coal to oil burning.

The *Aquitania*'s maiden voyage to New York started on 30 May 1914, but war clouds were gathering over Europe and the liner made only three return crossings before the outbreak of World War I. Initially requisitioned as an armed merchant cruiser, a role factored into her original design (as with a number of other contemporary British liners), the *Aquitania* was from 1915 to serve as a troopship and then as a hospital ship for the Gallipoli campaign. Latterly, the liner spent the war conveying troops from North America to Europe.

After the war, the *Aquitania* was refitted for civilian use and returned to the transatlantic route until, as with a number of the other great contemporary liners, the Wall Street Crash and subsequent slump resulted in the collapse of the market. Cunard kept *Aquitania* operational, however, generating business through the provision of cruises to the Mediterranean during the 1930s.

With the outbreak of World War II in September 1939, the *Aquitania* was again requisitioned to serve as a troopship. Initially employed to bring Canadian troops to Europe, *Aquitania* was also to be involved in a major convoy transporting Australian and New Zealand troops to Scotland before sailing from Singapore shortly before the Japanese attack on Pearl Harbor. In all, during the war, the *Aquitania* covered some half a million miles and carried more than 400,000 soldiers. Returned to Cunard in 1946, the liner's final years, as recorded in this view in 1949 at the New (Western) Docks in Southampton, were spent transporting war brides and children to North America under charter to the Canadian Government. By this time, however, the ravages of a 35-year career and service in two World Wars – the only major liner to serve in both – had seen the liner's physical condition deteriorate and, following the end of the charter in December 1949, Cunard decided to withdraw the liner. *Aquitania* was scrapped at Faslane, in Scotland, during 1950.

EAW22293

RMS *Queen Mary*
28 June 1946

Just as there had been increasing competition between Britain and Germany prior to World War I militarily, during the late 1920s there was considerable rivalry between the two nations, along with France and the United States, over the transatlantic passenger market. Although ordered on 3 April 1929, it was not until December 1930 that work on construction of the future *Queen Mary* commenced at the John Brown shipyard on the Clyde and, by that date, the world's economy had deteriorated considerably. Work on the liner was suspended in December 1931 as Cunard sought British Government support for her completion; the Government granted a loan on the proviso that Cunard and White Star – great British rivals until this point – merged. The merger was effected in May 1934 and work recommenced on the new liner. Launched on 26 September 1934, when she was officially named *Queen Mary*, the liner undertook her maiden voyage on 27 May 1936 from Southampton to New York; with a grt of 81,237, the *Queen Mary* was at that time the largest liner ever to fly the British flag. She had a capacity of 2,139 passengers with a crew of 1,101.

The new liner was an immediate success, claiming the Blue Riband for the fastest transatlantic crossings in August 1936 and again in August 1938; the pre-war record was not broken until July 1952 when the now-preserved SS *United States* set new record times. With the onset of World War II in September 1939, the *Queen Mary* was initially laid up in New York alongside other famous liners until the decision was taken to convert her into a troopship; the conversion work was undertaken in Australia, with the newly converted troopship's first duty being to transport troops from Australia and New Zealand to Britain.

As part of the conversion work, the *Queen Mary* was repainted in grey and it is in this livery that the liner was recorded by the Aerofilms photographer in 1946. The paint scheme, allied to the liner's reputation for speed, led to her being nicknamed the 'Grey Ghost'. The liner's wartime career was not without incident; in October 1942 she rammed HMS *Curacoa*, causing the naval vessel to sink with the loss of 239 lives, and two months later, while carrying just over 16,000 US soldiers, the liner was almost capsized by a freak wave in stormy conditions.

The *Queen Mary* in June 1946 was approaching the end of her military career; refitted between September 1946 and July 1947, the liner returned to its peacetime work on the transatlantic route for a further 20 years. However, by the 1960s, the economics of the business meant that Cunard was losing money and the decision was taken to decommission the *Queen Mary*. The liner made her final commercial crossing from New York to Southampton in September 1967. Her final voyage, from Southampton to Long Beach in California, started on 31 October 1967. Since 1967 the liner has been a tourist attraction in California, although she is now shorn of much of her mechanical equipment and her financial position has not always been secure. In 1993 she was added to the US National Register of Historic Places.

EAW001368

RMS *Queen Elizabeth*
18 April 1949

The second of the two great liners to be built for Cunard White Star following the 1934 agreement with the British Government, RMS *Queen Elizabeth* was again built by John Brown & Co on the River Clyde and was launched on 27 September 1938. The newer vessel featured several significant changes from her sister; most obvious was the reduction in the number of boilers – from 24 to 12 – which permitted the use of two rather than three funnels, allowing greater cargo and passenger space, with the result that the *Queen Elizabeth* could carry 2,283 passengers.

In September 1939 World War II broke out before the new liner could be completed and so her maiden voyage, from the Clyde to – theoretically – Southampton in March 1940, was completed in some secrecy in order to avoid the attention of German U-boats, given that there were only two spring tides high enough to permit her safe passage down the Clyde. In the event, the liner sailed directly from Glasgow to New York with the Southampton harbour pilot having an unexpected trip across the Atlantic. In November 1940 *Queen Elizabeth* sailed to Singapore for conversion into a troop ship – she had already been painted grey before departure from John Brown & Co – and, from February 1941, she was initially employed bringing troops from Australia and New Zealand to North Africa and Asia before transferring to the North Atlantic to convey US and Canadian troops to Europe.

After the war, the *Queen Elizabeth* returned to John Brown & Co for refitting and for her formal sea trials – not completed in 1940 – to be undertaken. She plied the transatlantic route for some two decades and is pictured here viewed from the south-west on her approach to Southampton. However, the economics of the traditional passenger market were rapidly deteriorating and, despite an attempt to use the liner for the Caribbean cruise market in the winter months (for which the liner was slightly modified in 1965), the decision was taken to decommission the *Queen Elizabeth*. The liner departed New York for the final time in October 1968.

Sold to a group intending to convert her into a hotel at Port Everglades, the *Queen Elizabeth* was briefly based in Florida before a further sale saw her sold to the Hong Kong-based C Y Tung, who intended to convert her into a floating university. However, on 9 January 1972, fire broke out on board the liner in Hong Kong harbour and the *Queen Elizabeth* foundered. The wreck, deemed to be a hazard to shipping, was largely scrapped in the mid-1970s but not before she had one final moment of glory – an appearance in the James Bond film *The Man with the Golden Gun* as a secret Far Eastern base for MI6.

EAW022298

RMS *Mauretania*
18 April 1949

Photographed on the same occasion as RMS *Aquitania* on p 189, this was the second Cunard liner to bear the name *Mauretania*. Built by Cammell Laird in Birkenhead, the *Mauretania* was the first new liner to be ordered by the newly merged Cunard White Star Line and was launched on 28 July 1938. Constructed with a capacity of 1,360 passengers with a crew of 802, the liner was designed to operate alongside the new *Queen Elizabeth* and *Queen Mary* on the transatlantic route. The liner's maiden voyage was on 17 June 1939 when she sailed from Liverpool to New York but her initial civilian life was short-lived as, following the outbreak of World War II in September 1939, she was requisitioned for military service. Fitted initially with two six-inch guns, the liner was employed as a troopship, seeing service in the Pacific, Indian and Atlantic oceans and covering more than half a million miles and transporting more than 340,000 soldiers. Between the end of the war and 2 September 1946, when the requisition ceased, the *Mauretania* carried soldiers being repatriated.

Fully refurbished at Cammell Laird, the *Mauretania* re-entered civilian service with a crossing to New York on 26 April 1947; based initially at Liverpool, by the date of this photograph she had been transferred to Southampton again to act alongside the two 'Queens'. During this phase of the liner's career, the *Mauretania* operated on the transatlantic route in the summer months and as a cruise ship in the West Indies in the winter sailing from New York. In 1962 the liner underwent modification, leading to a reduced passenger capacity of 1,127, to operate a transatlantic service from New York to Naples that was launched on 28 March 1963. The new service was not successful, however, and, following a final cruise from New York to the Mediterranean that started on 15 September 1965, the *Mauretania* was taken out of service and on 20 November 1965 started her final voyage to the scrapyard of T W Ward at Inverkeithing.

EAW022294

SS *Queen Elizabeth 2*
1 February 1969

Like her illustrious sisters, the *Queen Elizabeth 2* – or *QE2* as she was more popularly known – was built in the yard once owned by John Brown & Co on the Clyde, although by the date of the liner's construction the yard was owned by Upper Clyde Shipbuilders. Launched on 20 September 1967, the *QE2* is, perhaps, the last great passenger liner to be built in a British yard; economics and other factors have dictated that more recent liners to have flown the Red Ensign, such as the *Queen Victoria* and *Queen Mary*, have been constructed elsewhere.

Following completion, the new liner's maiden voyage, from Southampton to New York, started on 2 May 1969, some three months after the Aerofilms photographer recorded the then brand-new liner in Southampton for final preparations for service. Reflecting the fact that the new liner would spend part of the year on transatlantic work and the rest on cruise work, the *QE2* was smaller than the earlier 'Queens' in order to permit her passage through the Panama Canal.

In May 1982, following the Argentinian invasion of the Falkland Islands, the *QE2* found herself pressed into military service, conveying some 3,000 troops of the British 5th Infantry Brigade to the South Atlantic. An inevitable target for Argentine forces while deployed, the *QE2* returned to home waters in June 1982 and was restored for civilian service.

For the next 20 years, the *QE2* remained in service, with periodic modernisation (including a highly controversial refurbishment in Hamburg in 1994). In 2004 the liner was withdrawn from the transatlantic route, in favour of the new *Queen Mary 2*, to concentrate thereafter on cruise work until late 2008. On 11 November 2008 the *QE2* departed from Southampton for the final time; her destination was Dubai where it was intended that the liner would be converted into a hotel. However, the financial meltdown of 2008 resulted in this venture not progressing and the long-term future of the *QE2* remained in some doubt at the time of writing.

EAW191249

Dover Hoverport
1 June 1969

One of the most significant transport innovations perfected in Britain after World War II was the hovercraft; although there had been earlier experiments, it was the work of Christopher Cockerell (1910–99), who was later knighted for his services to engineering, that led to the development of hovercraft as a practical form of transport.

The potential of the hovercraft to offer faster channel crossings was exploited by two companies: Seaspeed, a subsidiary of British Rail, based at Dover, and the Swedish operation Hoverlloyd, based at Ramsgate. Seaspeed also operated services across the Solent linking Portsmouth with Ryde and Cowes. In order to operate the services, special facilities were provided and this is a view of the first hoverport to serve Dover when it was relatively new.

The terminal, which was situated in Dover Eastern Docks adjacent to the ferry terminal, was opened in August 1968 and was used initially by two British-built SR.N4 (Saunders-Roe Nautical 4) hovercrafts. Named *The Princess Anne* and *The Princess Margaret*, the two craft were the largest hovercraft that had been built by that date and could carry up to 254 passengers and up to 30 cars. The crossing time was about 35 minutes, much faster than the conventional ferries of the time although the journey could be unpleasant in rough conditions. The original hoverport remained in use until July 1978 when it was replaced by a larger facility located in the Western Docks; this was designed to accommodate the extended SR.N4s – they were increased in length by just over 17m, which increased capacity to some 418 passengers and 60 cars – as well as the introduction of a third, French-built, craft to the service. Following the transfer of services to the new terminal, the original port shown here was redeveloped as part of the expansion of Dover Eastern Docks as a ferry terminal.

The cross-channel hovercraft service saw the merger of Hoverlloyd and Seaspeed in 1981 to create Hoverspeed but the opening of the Channel Tunnel in 1994 resulted in a significant loss of business and the use of hovercraft from Dover ceased on 1 October 2000. The two ex-Seapeed hovercraft were preserved, although their future was in some doubt at the time of writing; those inherited from Hoverlloyd, which had not been stretched, were less fortunate, being scrapped between 1983 and 2005.

EAW193516

Dover Eastern Docks
10 September 1971

Bounded on the west by the Hoverport and on the east by the Camber, this view records Dover Eastern Docks following the initial land reclamation scheme of the late 1960s and the completion of the new terminal in 1970.

The origins of the facility at the Eastern Docks were outlined on p 145; here the view portrays more detail of the actual Camber. On the north-east side can be seen the oil terminal; this had originally been built for the Admiralty when the Camber was in use by the Royal Navy. After World War II the depot was sold, with part passing to BP and part to Shell. Although much of the traffic through the docks was ferry-based, there was still some limited freight traffic. In 1918 the Admiralty authorised the construction of a railway along the Promenade to link the Prince of Wales Pier, in the Western Docks, with the Eastern Arm. After World War I the line was used for commercial traffic before reverting to military use during World War II. The growth of the roll-on/roll-off ferry business resulted in the line's closure in the mid-1960s, and by the date of this photograph all traces of the line had been eliminated.

Three ferries are visible in the view, two of which were owned by British Railways and operated as part of the Sealink fleet; in the foreground can be seen the *Normannia*; this ferry had originally been built by William Denny & Brothers at Dumbarton and completed in 1952 for service on the Southampton to Le Havre route. Rebuilt on the River Tyne, the *Normannia* re-entered service in 1964 as a roll-on/roll-off car ferry with a capacity of 111 cars. The ferry had a varied career, being operated from Holyhead and Weymouth as well as Dover, before being withdrawn in May 1978 and scrapped. In the centre is *Maid of Kent*; this was also built by William Denny & Brothers but was completed in 1959. With a capacity of 190 cars, the *Maid of Kent* operated from Dover primarily on the service to Boulogne; the ferry was scrapped in Spain in 1982. The third ferry is the SNCF-owned *Chantilly*; this was built by Dubigeon-Normandie of Nantes and completed in 1966. Used primarily on the service from Dover to Calais, the ferry was sold in 1987 and has since been in operation in the Mediterranean, the Baltic and the Red Sea.

EAW215109

Dover Western Docks
28 June 1947

This view, taken shortly after the end of World War II, is dominated in the foreground by the train ferry terminal. In the background are Granville Basin and to its north, Wellington Dock.

The Dover Harbour Commission was established in 1606 (replaced by the Dover Harbour Board in 1861), but the facilities seen in this 1947 view reflect modernisation undertaken during the 19th century when the original docks were enlarged to cope with the increasing size of steamships.

Work commenced on the enlargement of the existing Inner Basin in the late 1830s and the new Wellington Dock was formally opened by the Duke of Wellington on 13 November 1846. The access to the dock at the southern end was widened in 1888 to accommodate ever larger vessels and the bridge across, visible in this scene, was replaced in 1904. Wellington Dock was increased in size in 1928. In 1847 work started on Admiralty Pier, which was considerably extended in 1909 with the creation of Dover Eastern Docks. Granville Dock, also a reconstruction of an earlier facility, was formally opened on 6 July 1874 by the 2nd Earl of Granville, the Lord Warden of the Cinque Ports, after whom it was named.

Visible in Granville Dock are two ferries: to the north TSS *Canterbury* (built by William Denny & Brothers and completed in 1929) and to the south TSS *Dinard* (also by William Denny & Brothers but completed in 1924). The former was built specially for the 'Golden Arrow' service from London to Paris; after wartime use, the ferry was refitted and re-entered service in April 1946. It survived until September 1964. The TSS *Dinard* had been converted into a car ferry immediately after the war, entering service in June 1947. The *Dinard* served as a ferry until sale to Viking Line in 1958 and final withdrawal in 1970.

A train ferry terminal at Dover was constructed following the rejection of earlier plans for a fixed link and a decision that Dover was more suitable than Richborough. Contracts for the work were let in the summer of 1933 to Edmund Nuttall, Sons & Co Ltd and John Mowlem & Co Ltd; the contract specified a dock of 415ft (126.5m) long by 72ft (21.9m) wide to be situated between the original Admiralty Pier and South Pier. Work was completed in 1936 and the new facility was first used by the SS *Hampton Ferry* on 28 September 1936. Services operated to Dunkirk until May 1940 when they were suspended due to the war; they were not resumed until after May 1945. Used by both passenger – most notably the 'Night Ferry' until 31 October 1980 when the service ceased – and freight stock, the facility was last used for the maintenance of the MS *Nord Pas-de-Calais* between 28 and 30 December 1988.

The ferry in the train ferry terminal is one of the three 2,839grt ferries – SS *Hampton Ferry* (launched 30 July 1934), SS *Shepperton Ferry* (launched 23 October 1934) and SS *Twickenham Ferry* (launched 15 March 1934) – that were constructed for use on the Dover to Dunkirk route by Swan Hunter & Wigham Richardson Ltd of Walker-on-Tyne for the Southern Railway. All three were requisitioned by the Admiralty in 1939 and used initially as minelayers or minesweepers. In the build-up to D-Day, the three were modified with a heavy gantry crane – as seen in this 1947 view – to lift steam locomotives for shipment to France. The trio continued in service, carrying both passenger and freight stock, until the early 1970s; they were broken up in Spain in 1972 (*Shepperton Ferry*), 1973 (*Hampton Ferry*) and 1974 (*Twickenham Ferry*).

To the left of the ferry terminal are the railway lines leading to Dover Marine station – which saw initial use for military personnel on 2 February 1915 and first public services on 18 January 1919. Timetabled services continued until 25 September 1994 and the station finally closed on 19 November 1994; the Grade II listed building is now used as a cruise terminal. Beyond the railway lines can be seen part of Lord Warden House; this Grade II listed structure was designed by Samuel Beazley (1786–1851) as a hotel for the South Eastern Railway and was named in honour of the then Warden of the Cinque Ports, the Duke of Wellington, when it opened on 7 September 1853. The building was requisitioned by the military during World War II, and is now used for offices.

Following the closure of the train ferry and the infilling of the dock, it was used by Brett Hall Aggregates as a terminal; the site now forms part of the Dover Western Docks Revival project. This was announced during the summer of 2015 with plans for a new £120 million cargo terminal to be completed in 2017. Virtually all the buildings associated with the train ferry terminal have been demolished; still extant and visible on the quay alongside the train ferry is the former Customs Watch House. This 1909 Arts and Crafts building, designed by Arthur Beresford Pite (1861–1934) is now listed Grade II. The area of the Inner Harbour between North and Prince of Wales piers was reclaimed during the 1960s and was used as the landing stage for cross-Channel hovercraft services from 1968 until the early 21st century. The innermost three docks visible in the 1947 view are now used as marinas.

EAW007615

Folkestone Pier with cross-Channel steamer
February 1920

Ferry services started from the original harbour at Folkestone on 1 August 1843. These were promoted by the South Eastern Railway but for legal reasons the vessels used were sub-chartered from the New Commercial Steam Packet Co. The steeply graded Folkestone Harbour railway branch was promoted by the railway and the first passenger station opened on 1 January 1849; this was to be relocated slightly seven years later. The success of the ferry service resulted in the use of larger vessels but these highlighted problems with the existing facilities at Folkestone, with the result that a new pier, with a 9m-high lighthouse, was completed in September 1861. The railway line was extended from the re-sited station, which was situated slightly to the north of the view shown here, in the late 1870s. The New Pier, as seen here, was widened and extended in 1904.

Folkestone continued to be served by ferry services to Europe until services to Calais were transferred to Ostend in March 1985 and those to Dover in June 1985; the final cross-Channel connection, the service to Boulogne, operated until September 1999 when a combination of the Channel Tunnel and the abolition of the Duty Free allowance made the ferry service uneconomic. The pier, now shorn of its railway lines (the branch – officially closed from 31 December 2014 after a decade of limited use – was cut back to the passenger station after freight services over the branch were withdrawn in 1968), is now the subject of a planned major redevelopment linked into the regeneration of the whole harbour area.

Pictured at the quay is one of the cross-Channel steamers owned by the Dutch shipping line Stoomvaart Maatschappij Zeeland (Zeeland Steamship Co), a company that operated a steamer service between Folkestone and Vlissingen (Flushing). This was introduced in 1911 and survived, although suspended during World War I (between 1916 and 23 June 1919), until December 1926 when the service was transferred to Harwich. The ship illustrated is the SS *Oranje Nassau*; this ferry was built by the Fairfield Shipbuilding & Engineering Co Ltd on the Clyde – Yard No 462 – and was launched on 5 July 1919. With a grt of 2,885, the steamer could carry 356 passengers. The *Oranje Nassau* managed to evade the Germans following the invasion of the Low Countries in May 1940 and spent much of the war based at Holyhead as an accommodation ship for members of the Royal Netherlands Navy. Restored for use as a passenger steamer after the war, the *Oranje Nassau* was eventually withdrawn from service in August 1953 and scrapped the following year.

EPW000089

Trinity Pier and the train ferry berth, Harwich
4 June 1952

Until World War I no train ferry had operated from British waters; however, military necessity resulted in the establishment by the army of a service from Richborough to ports in France towards the end of the war. In 1922 the Great Eastern Railway, in conjunction with the government of Belgium, acquired the equipment and three ferries in order to introduce a train ferry service between Harwich and Zeebrugge. Following the relocation of one of the pontoons with lifting gantry to Harwich, services were launched on 24 April 1924 under the auspices of Great Eastern Train Ferries Ltd by HRH Prince George (later Duke of Kent). In 1932 the company failed financially and the operation was taken over by the LNER. The service was operated by three ferries; two of these were, however, lost during World War II and, in 1947, a new vessel – *Suffolk Ferry* – was introduced and it is this ferry that is seen berthed at the pontoon.

The *Suffolk Ferry* was built by John Brown & Co Ltd, Clydebank, as Yard No 638. Launched on 7 May 1947, the ferry was completed in August 1947 with a grt of 3,134 and a carrying capacity of 35 railway wagons. In January 1948, ownership passed to the BTC following the nationalisation of the railway industry. The *Suffolk Ferry* had an operational life of more than 30 years, not being scrapped until 1981. The train ferry service from Harwich continued until 29 January 1987 when the final crossing was made, with all surviving train ferry traffic diverted to Dover.

Also visible in this view is the Continental Pier; this had been constructed in 1866 and was used by the passenger ships of the Great Eastern Railway until the completion of the new terminal at Parkeston Quay in 1883. The wooden pier was replaced during the 1950s by Trinity Pier, which is now used by Trinity House (an organisation that has its operational headquarters for England and Wales in the town) for the berthing of lighthouse tender ships. Heading into the harbour is a small vessel; this is believed to be the MV *Brightlingsea*, which was a small passenger-only ferry that provided a link across the River Orwell between Harwich and Felixstowe. The service was launched in 1912 and the *Brightlingsea*, built by the Rowhedge Ironworks of Colchester with a grt of 51 and a capacity of 152 passengers, was introduced in 1925. Inherited by the BTC in 1948, the ferry and service passed to the Orwell & Harwich Navigation Co in May 1964. The service continued until the mid-1990s when ongoing redevelopment at Felixstowe meant that the ferry's berth was no longer available. *Brightlingsea* still survives and is now used for harbour cruises around Harwich.

EAW043677

Heysham Harbour
30 August 1934

Originally the Midland Railway (MR) attempted to serve the Irish Sea market with a port at Poulton-le-Sands (Morecambe) and then through Piel in conjunction with the Furness Railway, but neither was satisfactory. As a result, in 1891, the railway appointed the consulting engineers James Abernethy & Son to examine the potential for an enclosed harbour, with locks, at Heysham. This scheme, however, did not progress but a revised plan was produced, again with James Abernethy & Son as consulting engineer, for the port. Parliamentary sanction was gained in 1896 and in July 1897 the contract for the work was let. Following purchase of the land, the MR's contractors, Price & Wills, commenced work in July 1897 with a workforce that soon numbered 2,000.

Originally it was intended that two docks would be completed; in the event only the wet dock, as shown here, with a basin some 800m long by 200m wide was completed. The first ship to dock at the newly completed harbour was the *Antrim* on 31 May 1904; this was one of a quartet of vessels built for the MR for the new service and delivered in 1904. A sister vessel, the *Londonderry*, was the first passenger sailing from the port when she undertook a day trip to Douglas on 13 August 1904.

Seen adjacent to the ferry terminal are two of the three ferries introduced by the LMS in 1928 to replace the original MR vessels. The trio – the *Duke of Argyll*, the *Duke of Lancaster* and the *Duke of Rothesay* – were all larger, at 3,600grt, than their predecessors and were all built at Dumbarton by William Denny & Brothers. The three ferries were to survive until 1956 when they were replaced by three larger ferries with the same names.

The last of these survived until the withdrawal of the ferry service to Belfast in April 1975.

In order to serve its new harbour, the MR opened Heysham Harbour station on 11 July 1904; four years later, the route from Morecambe and Heysham to Lancaster (Green Eyre) was electrified as one of the country's pioneering overhead AC installations. Services between Morecambe and Heysham commenced on 13 April 1908. Evidence of the electrified services can be seen clearly in this view. The power station to supply the line was also located at Heysham, slightly to the east of the scene pictured. Modernised in the early 1950s, electric services between Morecambe, Heysham and Lancaster ceased on 1 January 1966. The station at Heysham was slightly relocated on 4 May 1970 and the substantial station seen here demolished. Following the withdrawal of the Belfast service, passenger services to the new station were withdrawn on 6 October 1975. Occasionally used for boat train passengers thereafter, the station formally reopened on 11 May 1987; the station is now known as Heysham Port.

In May 2001 the port of Heysham was taken over by the Mersey Docks & Harbour Co; this was itself acquired in 2005 by Peel Ports. At the time of writing, Heysham continued to provide a base for ferry services, with the Isle of Man Steam Packet Co, the world's oldest continuously operating shipping company (dating from 1830), providing a link to Douglas, and with Stena Line providing a link to Belfast and Seatruck Ferries providing freight links to Dublin and Warrenpoint.

EPR000293

Paddle steamer moored at Victoria Pier, Hull
August 1931

Until the opening of the Humber Bridge on 24 June 1981, a railway-owned ferry service linked Victoria Pier with New Holland in Lincolnshire. This dated originally to 1 March 1848 when the Manchester, Sheffield & Lincolnshire Railway (MS&LR), which later formed part of the Great Central Railway and (from January 1923) the LNER, opened its line from Grimsby to New Holland Pier and replaced an earlier ferry service linking Hull with New Holland that dated back to c 1825. The pier, known originally as Corporation Pier, was renamed after Queen Victoria following a royal visit on 13 and 14 October 1854 to Hull when the queen sailed from the pier to Grimsby on the morning of the 14th. The pier was completed in the form seen in this view in 1877 with the addition of a floating pontoon.

Visible on the landward side of the pier is the building on Nelson Street that once housed the booking offices for the ferry. The MS&LR acquired the site in May 1849 and the current building was the result of rebuilding in 1880. This building still survives, having now been rebuilt as apartments following a period of disuse after the withdrawal of the ferry service. Also visible on Nelson Street are the Pier Hotel to the east of the ferry station and the offices of the United Towing Co Ltd to the west. This company had been established in 1920 through the merger of seven existing Hull-based tug companies.

Alongside the pier are two vessels. The larger of the two is the PS *Frodingham*, one of the paddle steamers owned by the LNER that operated the service at the time. This steamer had originally been built for the North British Railway, another constituent of the LNER, by the Glasgow shipbuilder A & J Inglis in 1893 as the PS *Dandie Dinmont* for use on the River Clyde. Originally 195ft (59.4m) in length, the steamer was lengthened and reboilered in 1912. Again reboilered in 1918, the steamer was transferred to the Humber in 1928 and renamed the *Frodingham*. The steamer survived until January 1936 when she was sold for scrap. The second vessel is a pilot cutter. From the mid-1930s the ferry service was operated by a new generation of paddle steamers as, with their shallow draft, these vessels were ideal for operating across an estuary with shifting sandbanks.

EPW036413

Hull
31 May 2002

The early history of the development of King George Dock in Hull was narrated on p 15; this view, one of the most recent in the book, shows the dramatic changes wrought at the dock over 50 years as the ferry terminal expanded. One of the most significant changes was the extension to the wet dock at the south-eastern corner; this was officially opened by HM Queen Elizabeth II in August 1969 and is known as the Queen Elizabeth Dock. The expansion of roll-on/roll-off ferry services has seen the construction of a number of dedicated berths; the first were opened in 1965 and by 2010 there was a total of 10.

Visible in this view are three ferries owned by P&O Ferries and in use on the service from Hull to Rotterdam. Berthed at the riverside quay is the MS *Pride of Hull.* This was built in Italy by Fincantieri and launched on 11 April 2001, entering service on 2 December the same year. Thus, when recorded in this view, the ferry was just over six months old. The ferry has a grt of 59,925 with a capacity for 1,360 passengers.

In the centre can be seen the freight-only roll-on/roll-off ferry the MS *Norcape*. This ferry was built by the Mitsui Engineering & Shipbuilding Co of Tamano in Japan and launched in 1979. Owned initially by the British & Irish Steam Packet Co (known as B&I Line)

from new when, as the MS *Tipperary*, the ferry operated from Liverpool to Dublin. Sold to P&O in 1979, renamed and transferred to the Hull-Rotterdam/Zeebrugge service, the *Norcape* had a grt of 14,087. From 2002 until 2010, the *Norcape* also operated for P&O across the Irish Sea and was sent to Troon in Scotland for a refit at the end of that period. However, the ferry grounded while at Troon and was subsequently sold for scrap to a Turkish breaker.

Furthest from the camera is the MS *Norsun*. This ferry was also built in Japan, by the Yokohama-based Nippon Kokan KK, and was launched in August 1986. Originally owned by the Nedlloyd company for operation by Noordzee Veerdienste/North Sea Ferries (a joint venture owned by Nedlloyd and P&O), the *Norsun* entered service in 1987. The ferry passed, with Nedlloyd's share in North Sea Ferries, to P&O in 1996. With a grt of 31,598 and a capacity of 930 passengers, the *Norsun* was originally used on the Hull to Rotterdam service but, following the arrival of the larger *Pride of Hull* and *Pride of Rotterdam*, was transferred to the Hull to Zeebrugge route. Known as the *Pride of Bruges* since 2003, the ferry remains in service.

EAW693178

Hythe Flying Boat Maintenance Base and Depot
8 December 1948

In the years before World War II Imperial Airways launched a number of services using flying boats based at Southampton to provide links between Britain and the Empire, following agreement with the government for the creation of the Empire Air Mail Scheme. In March 1937 services were launched to the Middle East, in June 1937 to East and South Africa and, on 8 July 1937, the first transatlantic services flew to North America. In order to service the aircraft used, Imperial Airways took over an existing facility at Hythe, to the south-west of Southampton, and it is this site that Aerofilms recorded in December 1948. In 1940, Imperial Airways became part of BOAC.

The main structure illustrated here is the hangar built during the latter part of World War I for the construction of flying boats for the Royal Air Force. The hangar was designed by Sir Frank Baines (1877–1933) for the Office of Works and was constructed by John Mowlem & Sons. The site as initially completed included the hangar, concrete apron and slipway. Management of the site was taken over by May, Harden & May, a company that continued to manufacture flying boats at Hythe, most notably the *Felixstowe*. In September 1925 the Hythe site was taken over by Supermarine, the company that would become famous as the manufacturer of the Spitfire, with the hangar refurbished for the manufacture of the company's range of flying boats. Supermarine was taken over by Vickers in 1928 and production ceased until 1935 with construction of the Supermarine Stranraer. In 1937 Imperial Airways took over part of the Hythe site for aircraft maintenance and, following the transfer of all aircraft production from Hythe to Woolston, occupied the entire site in 1939. The Empire Air Mail Scheme services were transferred to Poole Harbour early in World War II, although maintenance continued at Hythe.

Among the aircraft visible in front of the main building are G-AKCO, a Short S.25 Sandringham 7 that was ex-RAF JM719 (which was preserved in France following a period of operation and preservation in Australia), G-AKCP, also a Short S.25 Sandringham 7, and G-AHIY, which was a Short S.45 Solent. The Sandringham flying boats were all conversions from the Short Sunderland military flying boats, the majority of which had served with the RAF Coastal Command. The first conversions took place in late 1942. The Short S.45 Solent was a post-war civilian development, which first flew on 11 November 1946.

BOAC's operation of flying boats was approaching its end when Aerofilms recorded the Hythe site in December 1948 as the airline's strategy post-war was largely based around the acquisition and use of aircraft such as the Lockheed Constellation, which used conventional runways. Hythe ceased to be used for aircraft maintenance at the end of 1949. In 1953 the site was taken over by the Royal Navy and it remained with the navy until 1963. Following the French withdrawal from the NATO alliance in 1966, the site was offered to the US army. As RAF Hythe the site was used by the US Field Army Support Brigade/Combat equipment Battalion between 1967 and 2006. Since the withdrawal of the US army, much of the site has been redeveloped but the original hangar, now listed as Grade II, and the pier survive.

EAW020642

Liverpool Pier Head
25 July 1977

Pictured at the Pier Head at Liverpool is one of the Isle of Man Steam Packet Co's ferries that provided a link between the city and the Isle of Man. MV *Mona's Queen* was built for the company by the Ailsa Shipbuilding Co of Troon in Scotland and was launched on 22 December 1971, entering service six months later. The ferry's maiden voyage was on 9 June 1972; this was a day later than originally planned (something of a trait for this particular vessel as her launch had also been 24 hours late as a result of gale-force winds on 21 December 1971). *Mona's Queen* was the third of four ferries completed by the Ailsa Shipbuilding Co for the Isle of Man Steam Packet Co but was the first ferry owned by the company to be fitted with diesel engines.

With a capacity of around 100 vehicles and 1,600 passengers along with a crew of 55, the ferry was a regular feature of the Liverpool–Douglas service and also provided the first car ferry on the service from Douglas to Dublin in 1974 and from Fleetwood to Douglas two years later.

Following the merger of the Steam Packet Co with Manx Line in 1985, *Mona's Queen* was effectively surplus to requirements and used mainly on charter or during the holiday season. In September 1989 *Mona's Queen* was used on services between Cherbourg and Portsmouth or Weymouth while on charter to Sealink. By this date the ferry was coming to the end of its life in UK waters; withdrawn on 3 September 1990 she spent some five years in store at Birkenhead before being sold to the Philippines. For almost a decade the ferry, now renamed *Mary the Queen*, sailed between Manila and Boracay. This second career came to an end on 9 February 2004 when the ferry caught fire. The ferry's final voyage, ending on 1 September 2008 on a beach in India, was to the breakers.

The ferry is seen docked at one of the floating landing stages at Liverpool Pier Head. The Pier Head itself, on which the three famous buildings stands (*see* p 19), was constructed over the infilled George's Dock.

EAW366628

Newhaven Harbour and Harbour Station, Newhaven
August 1933

Situated at the mouth of the River Ouse in East Sussex, the harbour at Newhaven was largely developed by the London, Brighton & South Coast Railway (LB&SCR). Prior to the arrival of the railway Newhaven was a small fishing village with a harbour that had been provided with piers on both banks of the river from 1630 onwards. However, on 8 December 1847, the branch line from Lewes to Newhaven was opened and the LB&SCR started to redevelop the harbour to replace its existing facilities at Brighton for cross-Channel services. The railway branch was extended to Seaford on 1 June 1864 and major work upgrading the harbour was undertaken after that date under the auspices of the LB&SCR's chief engineer, Frederick Banister (1823–97). However, work was suspended in 1867 due to financial problems and did not resume until the 1870s. The work undertaken included the construction of an 800yd (731.5m)-long concrete breakwater, new entrance piers and lighthouses, new sea walls and additional quays. Facilities were further improved on 17 May 1886 by the opening of Newhaven Harbour (Boat Station) – later Newhaven Marine – which was situated at the end of a short branch off the line between Newhaven and Seaford. This station still survived at the time of writing, although no services used it because of the poor condition of its roof.

The LB&SCR started its ferry service to Dieppe in 1847; one of the earliest passengers was King Louis Philippe of France who, with his queen, fled through Dieppe to Newhaven following the revolution of 1848. The ferry service, along with the railway and harbour, passed to the Southern Railway in 1923 and to the BTC at nationalisation in 1948. Through much of its history the ferry service was jointly controlled by the railways in England and France; in the latter case this was SNCF from 1936. In 1985, following privatisation of Sealink (which had taken over BR's responsibility for the route in 1979), SNCF assumed total responsibility for the Newhaven-Dieppe service; following various changes of operator, at the time of writing the service was operated by DFDS Seaways France, which is majority owned by the Danish shipping company DFDS.

EPW042949

Poole Harbour
3 October 1946

Poole Harbour in Dorset is the largest natural harbour in Europe with an area of some 36sq km. There is archaeological evidence of its use for more than 2,000 years and the harbour was one of the routes that the Romans used during their invasion of Britain. Poole was to develop from the mid-15th century as a major port for the export of wool, with trading links to much of Europe and, once trade was established with North America, Poole was, by the 18th century, England's principal port for transatlantic traffic.

By the mid-20th century its sheltered waters made it an ideal location for the use of flying boats during the era when these aircraft offered the preferred means of long-distance air travel. The aircraft featured in this view was one of three Short S.26 flying boats constructed in late 1939/early 1940. Built for Imperial Airways, the three aircraft were designed to be able to fly across the Atlantic without refuelling and were a development of the same company's C-class Empire flying boats.

Part funded by the Air Ministry, the intention was that, in the event of war, the three aircraft could be converted to military use. The first two were initially delivered to the airline, but they were requisitioned for military use by the RAF before they could enter service and the third was delivered direct to the RAF. One of the trio was lost in June 1941 but the remaining two were returned to civilian use in December 1941, being handed to BOAC as successor to Imperial Airways (it had been formed in November 1939 through a merger of Imperial with British Airways Ltd). A second aircraft was lost at Lisbon in January 1943, leaving this one example – G-AFCI – in service. This had been the first of the trio to be built at Short's Rochester factory, being first flown on 21 July 1939 and is seen here prior to a trip to Cairo. In military service, a tail gun turret had been fitted; when returned to civilian use this feature was removed. By the date of this photograph, flying boat operations were in decline; G-AFCI was taken out of service in 1947 and then stored at Rochester Harbour until 1954. Following damage it was scrapped.

BOAC had a significant presence at Poole harbour until flying boat operations ceased there in 1948. There was a terminal on the east side of the harbour and up to 24 flying boats were based at the harbour at the peak of the traffic. Some 60 members of the airline's staff were employed on 12 launches used to ferry passengers and crew to and from the aircraft and a further 14 launches were operated by the Ministry of Civil Aviation for water control purposes (for marking the five runways used by the flying boats and checking that they were free from obstructions).

EAW002991

Portsmouth
14 March 1968

Although owing its pre-eminence to the great naval dockyard situated slightly upstream from the view recorded here, Portsmouth is also an important port for ferry services to Ryde on the Isle of Wight and across the estuary to Gosport.

When the railways first reached the area, Portsmouth itself was served by a ferry that linked to the railway at Gosport that had opened on 29 November 1841. Following the developments of the early 1840s, the London, Brighton & South Coast and London & South Western railways jointly promoted a line from the Chichester–Southampton line through Hilsea to Portsmouth. However, when this opened on 14 June 1847, the station known today as Portsmouth & Southsea, was some distance from the ferry terminal. As a result, an extension with a new harbour station was proposed; this opened on 2 October 1876 and is seen to good effect in this 1968 photograph being approached by MV *Shanklin*, one of three vessels employed at the time on the Portsmouth–Ryde service.

The *Shanklin* was built by William Denny & Bros on the Clyde in 1951 and was to operate over the link until 1980. Sold for charter work and renamed *Prince Ivanhoe*, the ferry was to founder on 3 August 1981 in Port Eynon Bay, South Wales. Harbour station remains open and Portsmouth's role as a ferry port has expanded with services to France, Spain and Belgium operating from a separate ferry terminal sited to the north of the naval dockyard.

Although this view focuses on the harbour station, it is impossible to miss the presence of the Royal Navy with three of the 'Ton'-class minesweepers evident to the south. Clearly identifiable are HMS *Dufton* (M1145), one of two moored at the bottom right of the scene, and HMS *Quainton* (M1175) moored at Gunwharf Quay. The 'Ton' class, largely designed by John I Thornycroft & Co Ltd, numbered 119 ships built during the early 1950s that saw service with the Royal Navy as well as the navies of certain Commonwealth countries, either new or second-hand, and with the navies of Argentina and the Republic of Ireland, again when sold for further service. M1145 was built by the Goole Shipbuilding & Repair Co Ltd and launched in November 1954; it was to be scrapped at Sittingbourne in June 1977. M1175 was built by Richards Ironworks of Lowestoft and launched on 10 October 1957; spending much of its time attached to the Tyne Division of the Royal Naval Reserve and named *Northumbria*, M1175 was paid off in 1972 and scrapped seven years later. Sister ship HMS *Bronington* (M1115) was commanded by HRH Prince Charles during his naval career and was preserved in 1989. The minesweeper was, at the time of writing, laid up in a very poor condition in Vittorio Dock, Birkenhead.

Gunwharf Quay was first established on this site in the late 17th century. Until 1855, all of the ordnance on board Royal Navy warships belonged not to the Admiralty but to a separate Board of Ordnance, and Gunwharf Quay in Portsmouth was one of a number of ordnance yards owned by the latter. Between 1855 and 1888 the role of the Board of Ordnance was taken on by the War Office; in 1888 the ordnance yards were divided between the Army and the Royal Navy with the site at Portsmouth being split. It was not until World War I that the Royal Navy gained sole control of the facility. As naval needs changed, Gunwharf Quay became a store establishment named HMS *Vernon* in 1923, becoming part of HMS *Nelson* in 1986. Naval use of the site ceased in 1995 and the quay was sold for redevelopment. It was opened as the Gunwharf Quays development in 2001. The harbour area between Harbour station and Gunwharf Quay has been infilled and the western end of the wharf is now dominated by Spinaker Tower. Of the naval buildings seen in this 1968 view, only one building survives. Now known as the Old Custom House, this is the two-storey pedimented building visible to the east of the stern of HMS *Quainton*. This redbrick structure was constructed as an administration building in the late 18th century and is the oldest surviving building on the Gunwharf site.

EAW178152

Studland Ferry
24 September 1947

Although Poole harbour is a large but relatively shallow body of water, its entrance – between the Sandbanks and Studland peninsulas – is narrow (no more than 350m). The road journey from Poole through Wareham to the Isle of Purbeck is, however, quite long – 30km from Poole to Swanage but only seven as the crow flies – and tortuous and, thus, the idea of establishing a ferry between the two peninsulas developed.

In July 1923 powers were granted by an Act of Parliament for the Bournemouth–Swanage Motor Road & Ferry Co to establish the ferry and build the necessary roads. The leading proponents of the scheme were Frank Gerard Aman (1857–1938) and his sons Gerard (1897–1949) and Arthur (1899–1977). The Aman family connection was to survive until 1961. Operation of the Sandbanks Ferry commenced on 15 July 1926 with the first vessel, built by the Isle of Wight-based J Samuel White & Co, being steam operated with an initial capacity of 15 cars. Although only recently introduced, the ferry might have had a relatively short life as the company decided to seek powers in 1926 for the construction of a high-level bridge to replace it. This was, however, never progressed although the concept did resurface in the 1950s, only to be rejected as a result of local opposition.

The service operated until the outbreak of war in September 1939 and, thereafter, a restricted service operated until 1943 when the military took over. Much of the Studland area was required by the military for training prior to the Allied invasion of Europe in June 1944. Although returned to civilian use after the war, the ferry required significant refurbishment and the road on the Studland peninsula also needed repairs as a result of damage and modifications following the military occupation.

Services were restored in 1947 and so this view, taken looking towards the eastern slipway at Poole with the Haven Hotel dominating the shoreline to the south, records the ferry's second post-war summer season. The ferry is still the original vessel acquired in 1926 although, by this date, it had been modified to take 18 vehicles. The original ferry – supplemented by a smaller second vessel acquired after the war to act as a locum when the first ferry required maintenance – remained in service until 1959 when it was replaced by a second – larger – vessel. The new ferry remained operational until 1994 when it was replaced by the ferry – the *Bramble Bush Bay* (the first of the quartet actually to carry a name) – that remained in service at the time of writing.

The ferry operates through having two parallel chains laid across the harbour mouth that guide the powered ferry across the channel. The Sandbanks Ferry is one of a number of such ferries that operate in the British Isles; other notable examples include the King Harry Ferry across the Fal in Cornwall and the ferry across Windermere.

EAW010961

Tilbury Riverside
May 1934

When recorded in May 1934, the scene pictured here represented virtually the latest in travel for those wishing to make the long journey from London to Australia. Pictured berthed at Tilbury Riverside is one of P&O's five-strong 'Strath' class of turbo-electric liners; these, the first owned by the company to be finished with white hulls, were nicknamed 'The White Sisters', and two – RMS *Strathnaver* and RMS *Strathaird* – were registered at Tilbury for use on services to the antipodes. Both were constructed by Vickers Armstrong at Barrow with the *Strathnaver* making her maiden voyage on 2 October 1931 and the *Strathaird* on 12 February 1932. They were requisitioned during World War II as troopships before returning to their traditional route to Brisbane via the Suez Canal after hostilities ceased. They survived until the early 1960s, before sailing for scrap to a Hong Kong breaker on 17 June 1961 (*Strathaird*) and 1 March 1962 (*Strathnaver*).

The berth at which the liner is moored was also a relatively new feature when photographed in May 1934. There had been a station providing an interchange between the London, Tilbury & Southend Railway and the steamer/ferry traffic at Tilbury from 13 April 1854, but the station shown here was the result of investment by the Port of London Authority (PLA) and the London, Midland & Scottish Railway. The new station was opened in May 1930 by Prime Minister Ramsay MacDonald. The new facility replaced berths within the dock complex that the PLA had first provided in 1916. The station was renamed Tilbury Riverside in 1936.

To the north-west of the liner is the port of Tilbury itself. This was authorised by an Act of Parliament of 3 July 1882 that empowered the East & West India Dock Co to build a new facility. The new dock was first used on 17 April 1886; initially access was achieved by the locks seen in the 1934 photograph but, four years earlier, a new lock was added slightly upstream. When completed the dock possessed the three branches visible in the photograph and two dry docks (the third was added subsequently); in 1963, work started on a fourth branch, nearly one mile in length, to the west of the existing three. This extension was completed in 1966.

Between the liner and the tidal basin can be seen the Tilbury Hotel; this was completed in 1882 by the East & West India Dock Co as part of its development of the dock. The hotel survived until 4 February 1944 when it was destroyed by fire following a German attack using incendiary devices; one person was killed in the raid.

Tilbury Riverside lost its passenger services on 30 November 1992 as passenger traffic using the ferry connections across to Gravesend declined. Although the main building remained at the time of writing and formed the London Cruise Terminal (so-named at reopening in 1995), the platforms and platform canopies have been demolished and much of the land is now used for car parking in connection with the cruise terminal. Railway track still extends towards the terminus but this is now used solely for container traffic generated by the port of Tilbury. Of the wet dock itself, the locks seen in this view have been abandoned and the two westernmost ones have been filled in. The northern section of the third remains, accessed from the wet dock as a second – but smaller – graving dock; the original graving dock as shown here was completed in 1929. The tidal basin between the locks and the Thames has been reclaimed and now provides some warehousing but is primarily used for the storage of cars, one of the major types of trade to pass through the port.

Tilbury, until its privatisation in 1992, represented the last wet dock still operated by the PLA; at the time of writing, the Port of Tilbury is owned by the Edinburgh-based Forth Ports Ltd.

EPW044227

Weymouth
24 September 1947

With evidence of coastal defence from two centuries, this view shows the approach to the estuary of the River Wey and the ferry terminal at Weymouth shortly after World War II looking towards the west. On the south side of the estuary is Nothe Fort; this was constructed between 1860 and 1872 in order to improve the defence of Portland (*see* p 157), which was becoming an increasingly important Royal Navy base and was located just south of Weymouth. At the time of the photograph the fort was still in military use; it was abandoned in 1956 and purchased five years later by the council. Now converted into a museum, much of the site is now listed Grade II*. During World War II, with Portland Harbour's increased importance, coastal artillery, anti-aircraft guns and searchlights were installed in and around the 19th-century fort.

On the Nothe Fort side of the estuary, the stone pier was constructed to act as a breakwater. Across the estuary, the first record of what became the Pleasure Pier dates it to 1812; this structure was, however, replaced in 1840 and then rebuilt during 1859 and 1860. In 1865 the Weymouth harbour branch was opened by the Great Western Railway; initially this was purely a freight line servicing harbour-side businesses. The pier was then extended in 1877 to include a cargo area. During 1888 and 1889 a new landing stage to handle the GWR's ferry services to the Channel Islands was added and a passenger terminus was built at the end of the harbour branch; this was originally known as Weymouth Landing Stage and opened on 4 August 1889. The Pavilion Theatre, visible on the pier, opened in 1908. The pier was rebuilt in concrete and extended from 600ft (182.9m) to 1,300ft (396.2m) in the early 1930s; the new structure was officially opened by the Prince of Wales, later King Edward VIII, on 13 July 1933.

In this 1947 view, the paddle steamer moored to the landing stage is believed to be the *Victoria*; this was owned by the Weymouth-based company Cosens & Co Ltd, which owned a fleet of paddle steamers that operated excursions and cross-channel trips from the town. By the date of this photograph, Cosens & Co Ltd had been acquired by its Southampton rival Red Funnel. The PS *Victoria* had been built in the Netherlands by J & K Smit Kindedijk of Rotterdam in 1884; it survived in service until 1952 and was scrapped the following year.

The stone pier and ferry terminal remain, as does much of the Pleasure Pier, although the Pavilion Theatre shown on it was destroyed by fire in 1954 and replaced by a new theatre, which was completed in 1961. This was itself damaged by fire in 1993 and repaired. More significant, there has been much land reclamation to the north of the Pleasure Pier to provide parking and facilities for the cross-channel ferries; this work was completed in 1980. Cross-channel ferry services continue to operate from the landing stage although early 2015 witnessed the transfer of certain services to Poole. The harbour branch, however, is no more; regular passenger services were withdrawn on 26 September 1987 and the last known special to use the line ran on 30 May 1999. The track of the branch remains largely intact and there is some debate as to what, if any, future it might have.

EAW010936

Brixham
25 June 1947

With the natural protection afforded by Berry Head and Torbay, Brixham was the largest fishing harbour in the south-west during the Middle Ages and it was at Brixham that William of Orange landed on 5 November 1688 as a precursor to the Glorious Revolution, which saw King James II forced from the throne.

The development of the harbour saw the completion of King's Quay in the late 17th century; this was followed by the Eastern Quay in 1760 and, pursuant to the Piers Haven & Market Improvement Act of 1799, the first – short – breakwater was constructed on the western side of the harbour along with a new fish market. These improvements were both completed in 1804.

By the mid-19th century the existing breakwater protecting Brixham harbour was no longer adequate as the number of vessels and their size increased. As a result, a new breakwater, designed by James Meadows Rendel (1799–1856) prior to a bill being presented to parliament on 25 February 1837, was constructed by the end of 1843 when the funds dried up. At this stage the new breakwater was some 1,400ft (426.7m) in length. It was not until the late 19th century, when the new Brixham Urban District Council took over, that there was any impetus for the breakwater's extension. In 1909 it was extended by 600ft (182.9m) and between 1912 and 1916 a further 1,000ft (304.8m) was added.

By the 1890s the harbour was home to some 300 fishing vessels; the vast majority were wooden deep-sea trawlers of a design – the 60–80ft (18.3–24.4m)-long Brixham trawler – that was pioneered by the shipbuilders of the town. Marked by their sails, which were coated with red ochre for protection, the Brixham trawlers were fast and capable of sailing considerable distances. Trawlers based upon the Brixham design were also to be widely used from the North Sea fishing harbours of Great Yarmouth, Grimsby, Hull and Lowestoft. A handful of these colourful vessels remain seaworthy.

Today Brixham remains an important fishing port; since the photograph was taken in 1947, the shipyard of J W & A Upham, visible on the eastern side of the harbour, which dated originally to the early 19th century with a small dry dock completed just before the outbreak of World War II, has closed. The site has subsequently been redeveloped for housing. The railway line, a factor that aided Brixham's development when it opened in February 1868, lost its passenger and freight services on 13 May 1963. The south-eastern corner of the harbour protected by the 1843 breakwater is now a marina. The facilities for the fishing industry, which was worth about £30 million per annum at the time of writing, have been improved by the construction of new fish quays in 1971 and 1991 and a new southern quay also in 1991.

EAW007577

Fleetwood Docks

25 May 1949

The town of Fleetwood owes its origins to the Preston & Wyre Railway, which founded it in 1836 when work began on both the town and the railway to Preston. The town, where the architect Decimus Burton (1800–81) was employed in the design of the principal buildings, is located to the north of this view of the dock complex. The principal reason for the construction of the railway was to provide a connection to a location for a steamer port for services linking Lancashire with Scotland and Ireland. An iron wharf located on the River Wyre was completed in 1841; a wooden pier was added in 1845 and a stone wharf to the south the following year.

The major development of the dock at Fleetwood began following the passage of the Fleetwood Docks Act of 1864; this permitted the construction of the northern of the two enclosed docks in this view. Work started in 1869 but was suspended soon afterwards; following a second Act of 1871 work recommenced under the auspices of the Lancashire & Yorkshire Railway in 1873. The contractor was John Aird & Sons under the control of the railway's Chief Engineer, Sir John Hawkshaw (1811–91). Work on the Wyre Dock was completed in 1879. To the south of the Wyre Dock was a timber pond; this was relocated in the early 20th century when construction began on the southern of the two enclosed docks – the Fish Dock – which was opened in 1909. The previous decade had witnessed a considerable growth in the importance of Fleetwood as a fishing port following the arrival of the first steam-powered trawler in 1891; it was the only major fishing port on the west coast – Hull, Grimsby and Aberdeen all faced east – and fish offered an attractive business to the port at a time when its general cargo traffic was in decline.

Today Fleetwood remains a fishing port, with its inshore fleet still based in the traditional Fish Dock. However, the trawlers that once dominated the scene have largely disappeared as a result of the overall decline in the fishing industry in Britain. The port is, like many of the other erstwhile railway-owned facilities, a subsidiary of Associated British Ports Holdings Ltd. With the decline in fishing and more general traffic, Wyre Dock has been converted into a marina with many of the dock buildings demolished.

EAW023417

Great Yarmouth
19 November 1953

The town of Great Yarmouth, situated on the estuary of the River Yare in Norfolk, expanded considerably from the mid-18th century as its role as a seaside resort developed. Its origins, however, date back to the 10th century and the rise of the fishing industry. The port as seen here, had its origins in the mid-16th century and followed from earlier quays built from the mid-14th century onwards that had suffered from the silting up of the river estuary. In 1670, the town obtained its first Haven Act; this permitted commissioners to raise duties on all cargoes, except fish, to support the maintenance of the quays. Such was the status of Great Yarmouth in the early 18th century that Daniel Defoe could claim that the South Quay was 'the finest quay in England, if not Europe' in 1724 in his *A Tour through the Whole Island of Great Britain*. From the early 19th century, there was also a Royal Navy presence in the town; this included a naval hospital (now converted into flats) built in 1800 and an arsenal completed in 1806.

This view, taken looking towards the north-west, shows Breydon Water in the distance, beyond the railway swing bridge (which was opened in 1903 as part of the line from Yarmouth Beach to Lowestoft), with quays on both the east and west banks of the River Yare heading southwards. Prominent on the west bank is the timber yard of Jewson; this company, established in 1836 and based in Norwich, was the largest timber merchant in much of eastern England. With its access to the North Sea, Great Yarmouth was an ideal port for the importation of Scandinavian timber.

The east bank is dominated by the town's fishing fleet; it was said that the quayside railways carried nothing but salt and coal in and loose fish out. The fishing industry, based largely around herring, developed during the Middle Ages. Based initially around an annual herring fair, the trade expanded. In 1334 Yarmouth raised more in tax than any other provincial town other than York, Bristol and Newcastle. Until the late 13th century, the annual fair was controlled by the Cinque Ports but in 1277 King Edward I gave the town joint authority over it; despite this, rivalry continued, to such an extent that ships from Yarmouth engaged ships from the Cinque Ports in battle off the coast of Belgium in 1297. It was not until 1662, however, that representatives of the Cinque Ports ceased to be involved in the annual fair. The fishing industry continued to grow until the late 19th century, aided by the arrival of railways, which enabled the fish to be moved to markets in London and elsewhere. However, the herring industry peaked just before World War I and was, by the date of this photograph, in almost terminal decline. Alongside the fishing fleet itself, industries grew up to process the catch; it was at the local Birds Eye frozen fish factory that the 'fish finger' was first developed in the 1950s.

Historically, the old centre of Great Yarmouth had been formed by 145 narrow streets – the Rows – built within the mediaeval town walls; constructed in the 13th and 14th centuries, these were largely to survive until World War II when much of this unique streetscape was destroyed by enemy action, with Great Yarmouth suffering severely. After the war, most of the surviving Rows were demolished as a result of slum clearance. The dereliction and vacant land visible in the view show this process underway.

The potential importance of Great Yarmouth as a port has increased since the start of the new Millennium as a result of the construction of the Outer Harbour. Work on this site, which is situated at the mouth of the river, commenced in June 2007 with construction being handled by Van Oord UK Ltd and Edmund Nuttall Ltd. The new facility included two breakwaters, with a total length of 1.4km, and was completed in January 2010. Some 1,000m of new quay have been provided at EastPort UK, as the new docks is called, although two massive gantry cranes, installed in 2009, were soon removed. The new dock is close to the East Anglian Array wind farm; as a result, its developers hope that manufacturing and construction of such equipment will be drawn to the adjacent quay space.

Of the traditional harbour viewed in the 1953 some 36 quays survive although the scene today is very different. The quayside tramway prominent running from North Quay to the fish market was progressively run down and finally closed completely in January 1976. The track has been largely removed although it is still possible to find traces of the route. The Jewson timber yard is no longer extant and the once vast numbers of trawlers that once graced the port are now much diminished. This trade was replaced in part by the rise of the oil and gas industry. The 1903 swing bridge is also no more; it and the line that it once served it have been replaced by the new A12, opened in 1985, that now bypasses Great Yarmouth centre.

EAW052975

No 1 Fish Dock, Grimsby
6 May 1925

Grimsby was, and remains, one of the key fishing ports in Britain. This view taken towards the east shows the No 1 Fish Dock in the foreground with the 300ft (91.4m)-high Dock Tower dominating the background alongside the Royal Dock.

The port at Grimsby developed from the use of a small inlet, which became known as the Haven, as a shelter for ships in the Humber following work to construct the town's first dock by John Rennie (1761–1821) between 1798 and 1800. The growth of the dock started, promoted by Ayscoghe Boucherett (1755–1815) and George Tennyson (1750–1835), with an Act of 1796 that permitted the construction of new quays, but it was not until the middle of the 19th century that the construction of the enclosed docks commenced. The first to be completed in March 1852, the Royal Dock, was named after Queen Victoria following a royal visit in 1854. Two locks connected the dock to the Humber; the lock gates were hydraulically operated and this resulted in the construction of the Dock Tower to provide a head of water. This was completed on 27 March 1852 to a design of James William Wild (1814–92) and was based upon the style of the Palazzo Pubblico in Siena, Italy. The most significant facet of the installation at Grimsby is that, for the first time, hydraulic power was used as an independent system for the transmission of power to a variety of machines and for a variety of purposes. The hydraulic machinery used was designed by Sir William Armstrong (1810–1900), the Newcastle engineer who would build Cragside for his home. The original intention was that the tower would also act as a lighthouse but it has never fulfilled this function.

Following on from the Royal Dock, the facilities at Grimsby were expanded by the opening of the first fish dock (seen here) in 1856, by No 2 Fish Dock in 1877 and the opening of the Union and Alexandra docks in 1879. The final expansion came in 1934 with the completion of the No 3 Fish Dock.

One of the major requirements of Grimsby's growing fishing industry was ice and the Grimsby Ice Factory was constructed between 1900 and 1903 to supply this trade. At its peak it produced some 1,200 tonnes of ice per day. However, declining demand led to the factory's closure in 1990 and the building has been on the Heritage at Risk Register since 2008. Around the Ice Factory grew up an area of commercial activity – shops and other industries – that became known as the Kasbah. This is the area between the Royal and No 1 Fish docks. At the time of writing, there was considerable controversy over plans by Associated British Ports to demolish a number of the surviving late Victorian buildings in the Kasbah. The importance of Grimsby to the British fishing industry can be gauged by the fact that some one-third of fish by revenue was landed at the port in 1965 when 250 trawlers were based there. Much of the industry, however, was based around deep-sea fishing well away from British territorial waters and was to be severely affected by the second (September 1972–November 1973) and third (November 1975–June 1976) cod wars with Iceland. More recently, the Common Fisheries Policy of the EU has resulted in measures to reduce the overfishing of the North Sea and efforts to replenish fish stocks. Despite this, Grimsby remains an important fish port with a new £14 million fish market being completed in 1996.

EPW012666

Lowestoft Harbour

15 May 1958

Although the town of Lowestoft has ancient roots, its development as a port – one of the key fishing ports of East Anglia – was very much a 19th-century phenomenon. Its genesis can be seen in the early 19th century when Norwich-based merchants, fed up with dealing with the harbour at Great Yarmouth, promoted a cut between the rivers Yare and Waveney thus bypassing Great Yarmouth.

Despite opposition from Yarmouth, the Norwich & Lowest Navigation Co received parliamentary approval on 28 May 1827 for the construction of the New (or Haddiscoe) Cut. The principal engineer was William Cubitt (1785–1861) with the actual construction being undertaken by Thomas Townshend of Birmingham (c 1770–1846). The cut opened on 30 September 1833 and linked into the new harbour at Lowestoft, which had been completed two years earlier based around Lake Lothing (which was opened up to the sea for the purpose); this area is now known as the Inner Harbour.

The pivotal figure in the expansion of Lowestoft was Sir Samuel Morton Peto (1809–89), who had bought Somerleyton Hall, to the west of the town, in 1844. Peto acquired the financially weak existing harbour and, following the incorporation by Act of Parliament dated 30 June 1845 of the Lowestoft Railway & Harbour Co, invested heavily in its development. The 17.5km route of the railway from a junction on the line from Norwich to Great Yarmouth at Reedham opened to freight traffic on 3 May 1847 and to passenger services on the following 1 July. With the improved harbour also opening in 1847, the growth in trade resulted in the railway line being extended to the new fish market. Peto was also involved in the development of railways in the then Danish-ruled Duchy of Schleswig and this resulted in a significant trade in cattle and other goods developing between Lowestoft and Denmark.

It was, however, the fishing industry that resulted in the further growth of the dock facilities. Famous as a herring port, when vast numbers of itinerant Scottish fisherwomen would descend on the town as they followed the herring shoals southwards, Lowestoft also hosted trawlers that sought out cod, plaice and other white fish. It was the fishing industry that brought the famous novelist Joseph Conrad (1857–1924) to the town; it was in Lowestoft that the Polish-born writer first landed in Britain in 1878 and he spent a brief period working on trawlers from the port.

This view from the east shows the Inner Harbour with the new cut stretching to the west, the trawler basin constructed by Morton Peto between 1846 and 1848 and Waveney Dock. The latter, with its fish market, was completed in 1883 and was designed to accommodate drift-net trawlers. This was not the final expansion of the port; in 1906 Hamilton Dock, to the north of Waveney Dock, was completed.

During both World Wars, Lowestoft accommodated elements of the Royal Navy, which resulted in the town coming under enemy attack in both conflicts. On 24 April 1916, for example, the town came under bombardment from the German navy and the Luftwaffe attacked the town during World War II.

The fortunes of Lowestoft as a port have fluctuated. The herring industry largely disappeared by the mid-1960s although some fishing activity remains and the fish market, located on the western side of Waveney Dock, is still used (albeit under threat as the port's commercial activity alters). Being railway-owned, the port was nationalised in 1948 and now forms part of Associated British Ports. As the fishing industry declined, so a new industry – that of North Sea oil and gas – arrived, providing new business for the port. The commercial traffic is now largely concentrated in Waveney Dock; Hamilton Dock, out of sight to the north in this view, has been converted into a marina.

EAR032727

Mevagissey
11 August 1953

Fishing ports are highly reliant upon their staple catch and, when that catch declines (for whatever reason), the economy of the fishing village will inevitably suffer. For much of Cornwall, including Mevagissey, pilchard fishing was the staple catch but, from the late 19th century, this type of fish largely disappeared from Cornish waters. During the 20th century the town's fortunes have ebbed and flowed with the availability of fish stocks – herring, mackerel and, more recently, a revival in pilchard fishing.

The town's origins date back to the first recorded mention in 1313 and a medieval quay existed serving the settlement. In 1774 an Act of Parliament was passed allowing the construction of the East and West quays. This created an inner harbour. The next phase of the harbour's development came with the completion of the outer harbour with its two piers in 1888; these were, however, seriously damaged in a storm in 1891 and not fully repaired until 1897. Situated in the outer harbour and visible in the left of the photograph is the concrete structure used to house the RNLI lifeboat that served Mevagissey between 1896 and 1930. Originally there was a lifeboat at Port Mellon but this was relocated to Mevagissey in 1868 and initially the boat was stationed in the harbour. Modernisation at neighbouring Fowey rendered the lifeboat at Mevagissey redundant. The old lifeboat station at Mevagissey remains extant.

Despite the exigencies of the fishing trade, Mevagissey remains a buoyant fishing harbour with local industries to support it. In addition, the harbour is also now used for leisure activities, with tourism being an increasingly important contributor to the town's economy. The harbour trust, which owns the harbour, became a registered charity in 1988.

EAW051337

Newlyn
August 1932

The importance of Newlyn as a fishing harbour stretches back to the 15th century; it was in 1435 that the Bishop of Exeter noted that Newlyn had 'repairing and maintaining of a certain quay or jetty for forty boats'. This is the first known reference to the fishing industry at Newlyn. As with Mevagissey, the fish that initially created the town's wealth was the pilchard; the pilchards were caught using a fleet of sailing ships – the Cornish luggers – and a drift net. From the mid-19th century the fishermen at Newlyn started to catch mackerel, exploiting the arrival of the railways to reach the London market. The mackerel fishermen used slightly larger vessels, known as mackerel drivers, which used a different method of catching the fish.

Reflecting the growth in the fishing industry in the mid- to late 19th century, the area of the old harbour was extended through the construction of new South and North piers in 1887 and 1888 respectively. As a result, Newlyn could be accessed at any stage of the tide and was one of the safest man-made harbours of the South West. It was not just fish that brought fame to the town; from the late 19th century the Newlyn School of artists, led by Samuel John 'Lamorna' Birch (1869–1955), Henry Scott Tuke (1858–1929) and Stanhope Forbes (1857–1947), resulted in artists coming to the town to study and to paint.

The caught pilchards were salted and stored in wooden barrels for transport; one of the key markets for the pilchard catch was Italy. However, this trade was effectively to end when, following the Italian invasion of Abyssinia in 1935, trade sanctions were imposed on Italy. During World War II the harbour was used for air–sea rescue craft patrolling the south-west approaches; as such it became a target for the Luftwaffe and a beached collier, the *Greenhithe*, was hit during one raid.

Fishing remains a vitally important industry in Newlyn and considerable investment has gone into it over recent years. In 1980 a new pier, the Mary Williams Pier, was officially opened by HM Queen Elizabeth II; this was followed by a new fish market in 1988. However, as with so many other ports, much income is derived from the leisure industry and new pontoons for small boats were erected in 2006. Since 1906, when they were established by Act of Parliament, Newlyn Pier and Harbour Commissioners have had control of the port. Today Newlyn is one of the premier fishing ports of Britain.

EPW039842

North Shields
18 June 1973

Situated on the north bank of the River Tyne as it approaches its estuary, North Shields has been a port used in the fishing industry since the early 13th century. It was in 1225 that Prior Germanus from Tynemouth Priory first established a small settlement of 'shielings' (huts or grazing pastures, from which the town's name derives) slightly to the east of this view. The original Fish Quay was established at the mouth of the Pow Burn. The area became known as Low Lights and the town of North Shields, despite opposition from Newcastle (which had rights over the export of coal mined along the Tyne), developed around the quay. Again slightly out of view to the east, in 1672 Clifford's Fort was constructed; this was built as part of the coastal defences against any possible Dutch invasion; this was once on the Buildings at Risk Register but has been converted for new uses, including a heritage centre. The creation of the Tyne Improvement Commission in 1850 led to improvements in the navigability of the river.

The Fish Quay as seen in this view was built in 1866 on the site of Dodgin's Shipyard; it was extended in the late 19th century. In order to provide some protection for the moored fishing boats from the tidal race a jetty was constructed at the same time; the first fish market sheds were erected in 1871. Alongside the quay were originally a large number of smokehouses for the production of kippers – North Shields was the largest kipper producing town in Britain – but the decline in the herring catch had seen this trade reduced to a single smokehouse at the time of writing, although other smokehouses survive, having been converted into alternative uses.

One of the features of the harbour was the two lighthouses: High and Low lights. The latter is situated out of the frame on the quay and the former can be seen at a higher level immediately above the quay. Both are now listed. The new High Light and house are Grade II and comprise two structures: the lighthouse itself, which dates to 1808, and the associated house that dates to 1860. The architect of the lighthouse was the Newcastle-based John Stokoe (c 1756–1836) on behalf of Trinity House. The juxtaposition of the two lighthouses at differing levels was to aid mariners heading into the Tyne; by aligning the two lights, it was possible to use them as a guide to the river's estuary thus avoiding the dangerous rocks known as the Black Middens on which many unsuspecting ships had foundered. The early 19th-century lighthouses replaced two earlier structures; one of these is also visible in the 1973 view immediately to the west of the 1808 lighthouse at the road junction. This was one of two lighthouses built in the early 18th century that replaced the two original structures authorised by Henry VIII in 1536. This building, completed in 1727, was converted to almshouses when the new lighthouse was completed and is now a private residence; it is also listed as Grade II.

Today there is still a commercial fish quay at North Shields, with the port's proximity to Dogger Bank attracting a number of fishing vessels from other ports to relocate there. There are still extant traders who handle fresh fish and crustaceans from fishing vessels that have unloaded their catch at the quay.

EAW259632

Porthleven Harbour
29 April 1948

Porthleven in Cornwall is the most southerly harbour in England. Although fishing from the area can be dated to the Middle Ages, it was not until the early 19th century that the harbour itself was constructed, largely as a refuge for ships in storms facing the treacherous waters of Mounts Bay and after a number of notable disasters.

Prior to the establishment of Porthleven, the River Cover to Helston was navigable but silting and the creation of the notorious Loe Bar sandbank resulted in the river no longer being navigable during the 12th century. This led to a small fishing settlement being established at Porthleven that grew over the succeeding centuries with the rise of local industry. The plentiful supplies of pilchard and mackerel in Mounts Bay ensured a steady catch for the local fishermen and, surrounding the harbour, were the traditional trades – such as net and rope making – that supported the fishing trade. The spur, however, to the construction of the harbour came following the wrecking of HMS *Anson*, a 64-gun third-rate ship, on Loe Bar on 29 December 1807. The actual number of fatalities is uncertain – with estimates ranging from 60 to 190 – but the disaster led to an Act of Parliament of 1811 'for constructing a harbour, in Mounts Bay in the County of Cornwall'.

Work commenced immediately, initially using French prisoners of war, but the complexity of the task meant that it was not until 1825 that the quay and the granite pier were completed. Thirty years later, in 1855, the harbour was acquired by the Hayle-based company Harvey & Co and the new owners employed the engineer William Husband (1822–87) to construct the inner harbour; this work was completed in 1858 and resulted in the harbour recorded in this view taken after World War II.

The date of the image is significant as there remains evidence of the defences built during World War II to protect the harbour, with a pillbox located on the west side of the harbour entrance and an anti-tank wall across the road. One other reminder of World War II can be found on the town's war memorial, where the name of Wing Commander Guy Gibson, commander of No 617 Squadron during the Dambuster Raid, is inscribed as his maternal grandmother came from the town.

Today, the harbour at Porthleven continues to function with seafood – most notably crab, crayfish and lobster – being landed and yachts being accommodated. The harbour is controlled by the Porthleven Harbour & Dock Co Ltd, which was established in 1869 and which is accommodated in a Grade II-listed warehouse, built in 1814, which is situated on the western side of the inner harbour but is not visible in this picture as it is obscured by the higher ground to the west.

EAW015146

Situated on a promontory on the north coast of Cornwall, St Ives was one of the most important fishing ports in the county but, as this trade declined, it gained a new importance as a holiday resort. From the early 20th century, the town also became very popular with artists, rivalling Newlyn on the south coast, with artists such as Barbara Hepworth (1903–75) and her husband Ben Nicholson (1894–1982) settling there after World War II. Reflecting the importance of the town's artistic heritage, the Tate St Ives gallery was opened in 1993. The gallery was constructed on the site of the town's erstwhile gasworks, out of view in this scene.

St Ives's role in the fishing industry dated back to the Middle Ages, but it was during the mid-18th century that the harbour as seen here began to be developed. Prior to this work, there had been a small pier but none of this original structure remains. The engineer of the new pier was John Smeaton (1724–92); the structure was constructed between 1767 and 1770 and was originally 360ft (91.4m) in length, costing some £9,480 to build. The actual construction was handled by Thomas Richardson (fl 1756–77), who had also worked with Smeaton on the Eddystone Lighthouse. At the original end of Smeaton's pier, an octagonal look-out was constructed, again to Smeaton's design; this also acted as a lighthouse. This structure still stands and, at the time of writing, had been converted into apartments.

In 1886, by an Order in Council, the harbour and quay were transferred to the ownership of the corporation. The new owners were empowered to borrow £32,000 to improve the facilities at the harbour. The major work was the extension of Smeaton's pier and the construction of a new lighthouse; this work, which added 300ft (91.4m) to the pier's length, was undertaken between 1888 and 1890. Also built, and completed in 1894, was the short West Pier that can be seen at the bottom right of the photograph. This cost some £8,000 and was designed to prevent the tidal scouring of the sand in the harbour that was occurring as a result of the modified pier.

Although the harbour was constructed primarily for the fishing industry, other traffic – such as stone and locally mined tin – was also shipped through it. It was during the 19th century that the fishing industry at St Ives reached its apogee; the main catch was the pilchard and the peak year for that trade was 1868. During these years, the bulk of the catch was exported to Italy. By the early 20th century, however, the once plentiful pilchard shoals deserted St Ives Bay and the fishing industry declined. Traditionally, the fishermen of St Ives practised the method of fishing using nets that hung vertically in the water, being held down by weights and up by floats – a process known as seining. However, this largely disappeared during the 1920s.

While the fishing industry has declined considerably over the past century, there is still some limited activity through St Ives although the harbour is today more heavily used by leisure craft. The complex of Smeaton's original pier plus the 19th-century extension and the two lighthouses is now listed as Grade II*.

EAW257342

Scarborough Harbour
23 June 1948

When recorded by the Aerofilms photographer in June 1948, the harbour at Scarborough was benefiting from the brief post-war boom in the herring industry. During both world wars herring stocks had made a recovery as a result of the inability of the fishing industry to exploit the once plentiful fish. Annually the herring shoals, which could measure 10km in length by 6km in width, traversed the North Sea and pursuing them from north to south came the fishermen. Trawlers from Scotland and further afield would make their way down, using harbours like Scarborough to land their catch before ending up at Lowestoft. Along the route, fisherwomen also migrated to gut and cure the fish; despite dwindling stocks, Scottish fisherwomen still made the trip until the 1960s. However, changing methods of trawling, which made the catch all the more efficient, effectively ensured the demise of the herring fishing industry.

Located to the south of Scarborough Castle, there has been a harbour here since the 13th century. In July 1252, King Henry III granted by a Patent-roll certain duties to fund the construction of a new port with a timber and stone pier. This was followed by a further Act of 1546 that required a duty to repair the pier; further Acts of 1564 and 1605 imposed similar duties. The latter Act referred to the fishing trade as 'verie muche decaied'. The Old Pier, as renovated in 1565, was 800ft (243.8m) in length with a width of 20ft (6.1m); over the next two centuries this pier, which can be seen in the image dividing the old and east harbours, was modified until, in 1732, a further Act was passed to permit the extension of the pier; this was completed by 1746 and was named Vincent's Pier after the engineer William Vincent (fl 1734–54). In 1752 work started on the new East Pier, again initiated by Vincent, but not completed until the mid-19th century. In 1822 the West Pier, designed by William Chapman (1749–1832), was completed; this was subsequently extended. Corporation Wharf (or North Pier) was added to the harbour in 1928 and a short extension to Vincent's Pier, the Chicken Walk Jetty, was also added.

When Vincent's Pier was completed, there was no lighthouse; work started on the construction of one during the first decade of the 19th century. This structure was modified during the 19th century but was to suffer severe damage on 16 December 1914 when the East Coast of England came under bombardment by the German warships *Derfflinger* and *Von der Tann* (the abbey at Whitby also suffered damage during this attack). The lighthouse was finally restored in 1931 with the lantern being reconstructed in the 1980s.

Today the east harbour is used exclusively for leisure activities; the old harbour has a marina at its northern end with all commercial activity, of which fishing remains a part, based on the West Pier. Immediately to the south of the West Pier is the RNLI station; in August 1801 Scarborough was the third place in the UK to have a lifeboat station – following on from Montrose and Sunderland, both of which opened the previous year. Work started in 2015 on the construction of a new lifeboat station on the site.

EAW016690

Whitby Harbour
July 1932

Situated at the estuary of the River Esk on a natural fault line, Whitby was one of the most significant whaling ports in Britain, a fact recognised in the arch formed by the jaw bones of a whale situated on the West Cliff, which still stands (having been replaced most recently in 2002). It was in 657 that the famous abbey was first established and seven years later the Synod of Whitby helped determine the future of Christianity in Britain by resolving the date of Easter between the Celtic and Catholic churches.

Whitby's importance grew from the early 17th century; long a haven for ships in stormy weather (it was designated a 'harbour of refuge' in 1702), a harbour developed initially in the Middle Ages under the patronage of the abbey. Shipbuilding commenced during the reign of King James I and, by the early 1790s, the town was the third most important shipbuilding area after London and Newcastle. Among the ships built here was HMS *Endeavour*, on which Captain James Cook, who moved to the town in 1746 at the age of 18 to learn seamanship, undertook his exploration of the Pacific Ocean. The trade continued through to the 19th century when iron replaced wood and Whitby was no longer able to compete. Much of the early maritime wealth in the town came from its role in the shipping of coal from north-east England to London; indeed, HMS *Endeavour* was originally constructed for this trade.

The port was one of the main centres of the whaling industry; the Whitby Whaling Co was first established in 1753 and between then and 1833, when the trade from the town ceased, some 55 whalers operated out of Whitby, returning to port with an estimated 2,751 whales. In order to process the blubber into oil, great boiler houses were constructed on the harbour.

Following the demise of the whaling industry, fishing became increasingly important, particularly of herring, and this activity continues in a more restricted form into the 21st century. Inshore fishing for crustaceans and line fishing are the mainstays, with a seasonal harvest of salmon as the fish make their way through the estuary to spawn upstream. A fish market is still held on the quay when required.

The view taken here records the scene in the early 1930s before considerable work was undertaken in the removal of much of the earlier residential property, particularly the flying tenements that once clung to the hillsides. The entrance to the harbour is guarded by the Grade II listed East and West piers with their lighthouses; these were constructed in 1855 and 1831, respectively. The swing bridge that divides the upper and lower harbours is the result of a replacement constructed during 1908 and 1909 but the earliest record of a bridge on the site is 1351 when permission was granted to levy a toll on the river crossing. Today the upper harbour is largely used as a marina with commercial traffic in the lower harbour.

EPW038925

Blackpool Victoria Pier
July 1920

The third of the piers to be completed at Blackpool, following on from North and Central, was Victoria Pier. The structure was renamed South Pier in 1930.

Registered in November 1890, the Blackpool South Shore Pier & Pavilion Co started work on the pier in 1892. The structure was designed by the locally based architect T P Worthington with a pavilion designed by John Dent Harker (1860–1933), and was completed in 1893. At 429ft (130.8m) long (albeit subsequently lengthened slightly), Victoria Pier is the shortest of the three Blackpool piers and is one of only two piers in Britain built upon cast-iron jetted piles. These were installed at the impressive rate of one every 20 minutes by the sub-contractor Robert Finnegan.

Seen operating along the coastal tramway in the background are a number of Blackpool Corporation trams; these include two of the 18 'Dreadnought' type, which were new in 1900 and 1902 and unique to Blackpool; these possessed twin stairs at either end suitable for dealing with the crowds on the promenade allied to an open top-deck. There are also two single-deck 'toastrack' cars; these were also designed to permit those travelling along the promenade route to make the most of the British summer.

The scene as recorded here was shortly to be dramatically altered as, in 1923, an enormous open-air swimming pool – the Southshore Coliseum – was completed in an impressive neo-Classical style immediately to the south of the pier. This was to survive until 1981 when it was closed and subsequently demolished and replaced in 1986 by the Sandcastle Waterpark.

The pier as recorded in the 1920 view is very different today; two fires – in 1958 and 1964 – saw the destruction of the Grand Pavilion. The building was replaced by a new theatre; this was to survive until December 1997 when it was demolished and replaced by a further ride. Another fire, in 1964, destroyed an amusement arcade and shops. The Regal Theatre at the pier's entrance was converted into an amusement arcade. Today, the pier is largely a platform to provide accommodation for a range of rides and other types of entertainment.

EPW002075

Brighton West Pier
21 May 1952

Widely regarded as perhaps the finest of all of Britain's seaside piers, the West Pier at Brighton was designed by Eugenius Birch (1818–84), an engineer who spent time in India and who was responsible for the design of a significant number of seaside piers between 1856 and his death. Apart from Brighton West Pier, he also designed the North Pier at Blackpool, the Royal Pier at Aberystwyth and that at Eastbourne among many others. He pioneered an improved means of driving the piles, using screw blades on his iron piles, that resulted in deeper and thus more resilient support to the pier structures.

Work started on the pier's construction in 1863 and it was formally opened three years later, on 6 October 1866. As built it was 1,115ft (339.9m) long and, at its seaward end, was 310ft (84.5m) wide. The ironwork for the superstructure was supplied by the Glasgow foundry, Barrowfield Iron Works, of Robert Laidlaw, and the pier was initially completed with six small ornamental houses, two toll houses and glass screens to protect visitors at the seaward end. The pier was modified by the addition of a central bandstand in 1875 and, during the following decade, landing stages for steamers were added, with the pavilion at the seaward end being completed in 1893; this was converted from a concert hall to a theatre during the first decade of the 20th century. The pier was also widened, had shelters fitted and the pier-head enlarged. The view taken in 1952 shows further changes. In 1916 the central bandstand was replaced by a new concert hall, while in 1932 a new top deck and entrance were built.

Subsequent to the photograph, the pier appeared in the classic 1969 film *Oh! What a Lovely War* after having undergone some refurbishment earlier in the decade. However, it was closed as a result of high maintenance costs in 1975, being acquired by a trust in 1984. The trust had hoped to secure the pier's future but its condition deteriorated and the early years of the 21st century saw much of the structure destroyed following on from earlier damage, such as that incurred during a storm in 1987. There was a partial collapse on 29 December 2002 and on 20 January 2003 the concert hall in the middle of the pier partially collapsed; on 28 March 2003, the pavilion at the seaward end was destroyed by fire. The remains of the concert hall were also destroyed by fire on 11 and 12 May 2003. Further destruction was wrought on 23 June 2004 when high winds caused the middle of the pier to collapse. Although listed at Grade II, the condition of the pier was such that English Heritage recognised in December 2004 that restoration was no longer possible. At the time of writing further demolition had resulted in the removal of more of the structure and the remains that survive are a sad reminder of the vulnerability of seaside piers. The West Pier Trust, however, was hopeful that the i360 project may result, eventually, in the rebuilding of the pier.

EAW043167

Brownsea Island
April 1933

The largest of the islands situated in Poole is Brownsea, which is now owned by the National Trust, and it is this that forms the backdrop to Montague Grahame-White's (1877–1961) steam yacht *Alacrity*. Grahame-White's business interests included ship broking and the hire of yachts like the *Alacrity* to wealthy individuals. In an era when paid holidays were restricted, leisure sailing was very much the preserve of the rich; the marinas that are such a feature of the modern harbour were virtually unknown until the growth in individual wealth in the late 20th century.

Lt-Cdr Montague Grahame-White RNVR came from a moneyed background; his brother Claude was a pioneer in the British aviation industry; Montague himself was well-known as a pioneering racing driver in the early 20th century while also acting as yacht and aircraft broker. He wrote an autobiography – *At the Wheel, Ashore and Afloat* – a copy of which he presented to King George V in 1935 and which remains in the royal collection – and the National Portrait Gallery holds a portrait of him.

Visible on Brownsea Island is the now Grade II listed castle; this dated back originally to a blockhouse and gun emplacement built in 1548 on the orders of King Henry VIII for the protection of Poole. The building was extended during the 1760s and again in the early and mid–19th century. However, the building was gutted by fire in 1896 and the structure that remains is largely the result of work undertaken thereafter by the Southampton-based architect Philip Brown. Between the castle and the settlement is the gatehouse; this is also listed Grade II and was built in the early 1850s, following the acquisition of the island and castle by Colonel William Petrie Waugh (1812–80) in 1852. It was also following Waugh's acquisition that the Grade II* listed church of St Mary, visible to the north of the castle, was completed in 1854. A number of the other properties visible in front of the gatehouse, such as the Boat House, the Warden's House and the Quay Cottages are also listed.

Apart from the architectural history of the island, Brownsea also has an importance in the history of the Boy Scout movement; it was on Brownsea Island that Robert (late Lord) Baden-Powell (1857–1941) held his first ever scout camp in August 1907 prior to the publication of his hugely influential *Scouting for Boys* the following year.

The *Alacrity* had an interesting career. Originally built by the Greenock-based shipbuilder Scotts and launched on 30 April 1900, the 1,830grt yacht was originally named *Margarita* and ordered by an American customer. In 1913 she was sold to a Russian and renamed the *Semiramis*. Following the Russian Revolution in 1917 and the British military action in support of the White – anti-communist – forces, the yacht, which had been used in the Arctic by the Russian navy during the war and renamed *Mlada* in January 1917, was seized by the Royal Navy in the Far East. Initially known as HMS *Mlada*, the yacht was renamed HMS *Alacrity* in August 1919 when she became the Commander-in-Chief China's yacht based in Hong Kong. Paid off in July 1922, the yacht again passed, briefly, to Russian ownership before being acquired by Grahame-White in 1926. The new owner had the yacht overhauled in the Isle of Wight yard of John Samuel White & Co before using it on private charter work. Among work undertaken was a world cruise that had to be foreshortened in 1927 in Burma as a result of ill-health. Retaining the name *Alacrity*, the yacht continued to undertake charter work until the late 1930s; she was scrapped in July 1939

EPW041058

Chatham
6 July 1993

As the Royal Navy contracted in the late 20th century, the number of bases that it required declined. This potentially could have led to the loss of much of the country's naval architectural heritage. One of the bases that succumbed was the dockyard at Chatham. As one of the country's oldest naval bases, Chatham had been a home to the fleet since the reign of Henry VIII and had grown significantly in the 17th century when the country's main threat was perceived to be the Netherlands.

The importance of Chatham – or Jillyingham Water as it was known originally – as a naval dockyard grew from the mid-16th century, with the first reference to shore facilities dating to 1547. Strategically, as Britain's imperial ambitions grew in the 18th and early 19th centuries, Chatham became overshadowed by both Portsmouth and Plymouth but, as outlined on p 153, it continued to develop through the 19th and early 20th centuries. However, as the Royal Navy shrank in the late 20th century, the dockyard became the victim of rationalisation and was to close in 1984.

This view, taken looking towards the north, shows that, a decade after closure, much of the site of the later dockyard development had already been cleared but, along the west, the buildings that formed the pre-Victorian dockyard remained. Recognising that the historic core represented, arguably, the most complete naval dockyard from the age of sail, some 80 acres (32ha) were transferred to a charity – the Chatham Historic Dockyard – at closure and a maritime museum was established.

Visible from the south can be seen three long buildings constructed alongside Anchor Wharf. On the quayside are two: at the southern end, the No 3 Storehouse, and at the northern, the Fitting Rigging House. These are now both listed Grade I and were completed in 1785 and 1805, respectively; these were, at some 700ft (213.4m) in length, the longest warehouses ever constructed for the Royal Navy. Alongside to the east is the long ropery. This Grade I listed structure was constructed between 1785 and 1791 with an engine house, containing a Boulton and Watt beam engine, added in the mid-1830s. The interior includes forming machines and winches supplied by Henry Maudslay (1771–1831) that mechanised the process of rope making. Although Plymouth and Portsmouth still have ropeyards, Chatham is the only one of the four ropeyards in naval dockyards that is still functioning. Immediately to the east of the ropery at its north end is the Grade II* Hemp House; originally built in 1729 as a single-storey structure and enlarged between 1743 and 1747. A first floor was added in 1812.

To the east of the Hemp House the square Royal Dockyard Church can be seen. This was designed by Edward Holl (unknown–1824), architect to the Navy Board, and completed between 1808 and 1811 in a Classical style. The church possesses a three-sided galley supported on cast-iron pillars. Slightly to the south of the church, the original entrance to the dockyard can be identified; this is now a scheduled Ancient Monument and dates originally to 1722. To the north of the church can be seen the Officers' Terrace; this Grade I listed row of 12 houses was constructed between 1722 and 1831. To the north-west of the terrace, covered slips Nos 3 to 7 can be identified; these are all now listed Grade I. Covered slips were developed from the 1720s as a means of protecting wooden warships during construction. The southernmost – No 3 – was constructed in wood with a corrugated sheet roof in 1838; it was probably designed by Sir Robert Seppings (1767–1840). Nos 4, 5 and 6 were constructed in wrought and cast iron by Messrs George Baker & Sons between 1845 and 1847. No 7 was added between 1852 and 1855 and was designed by Colonel Godfrey T Greene (1807–86), who was the Admiralty's Director of Engineering and Architectural Works between 1850 and 1864. It was built by Grissell & Peto. To the east of the covered slips, one final structure is clearly evident; this is the North Mast pond. Now a scheduled Ancient Monument, the pond dates to 1702 and was the second to be constructed at the dockyard. The Southern Mast Pond, immediately to the south, dated originally to 1696 but has been infilled.

As well as the historic buildings, including those described above, the dockyard is also home to a number of ex-Royal Navy vessels: HMS *Gannet* (1878) and the World War II destroyer HMS *Cavalier* (of 1944) and the submarine HMS *Ocelot* (of 1962). The first chairman of the trust was Sir Steuart Pringle (1928–2013) who commented on his appointment that the trust was also the owner of the world's largest collection of 18th-century ordnance. When asked where it was, he identified the large number of bollards around the site that had been formed by upturning redundant canons.

EAW622364

Hartlepool
9 May 2003

The story of the development of the docks in Hartlepool is covered earlier (*see* p 11), but the decline of the town's once extensive network of wet docks saw a number of the facilities filled in and the land opened up for possible redevelopment. Three of the southernmost docks – Coal, Jackson and Union – were retained, however, as was the Victoria Dock to the north. The Coal and Union docks became the Hartlepool Marina but Jackson Dock, which was opened originally on 1 June 1852, was developed by the Teesside Development as a visitor attraction. The basic concept is a re-creation of an 18th-century naval dockyard and includes a range of replica buildings that are designed to provide visitors with the feel of a dockyard of that period. Originally opened in July 1994 and known as Hartlepool Historic Quay, the site has been known as Hartlepool's Maritime Experience since 2005.

One of the major attractions at the dock is the preserved 19th-century warship HMS *Trincomalee*. This is a Royal Navy 'Leda'-class frigate that was originally built – out of teak rather than the more usual oak – at Bombay, where the ship was launched on 12 October 1817. The frigate had a long career with the navy, seeing service off the coast of Canada and in the Caribbean, the Pacific and during the Crimean War before being paid off in 1857. Between 1860 and 1897 the frigate was used as a training ship in Sunderland and West Hartlepool. Sold for dismantling in 1897, the *Trincomalee* was purchased by Geoffrey Wheatley Cobb (1859–1931) to replace HMS *Foudrayant*, which had recently been lost at sea. Renamed TS *Foudrayant*, the frigate was subsequently used for the training of teenagers in basic nautical skills. During World War II, when based at Portsmouth, the frigate was used as a store and as an accommodation vessel, before reverting to its training role after the war ended. In 1987, having spent the last 30 years moored at Haslar Creek, Portsmouth, and with its training role having ended the previous year, *Trincomalee* was moved to Hartlepool for restoration. The 11-year programme was completed in 2001.

The Jackson Dock site also includes the Museum of Hartlepool. The museum is home for the preserved PS *Wingfield Castle*, one of the trio of paddle steamers that once used to ply their trade on ferry services from Hull to New Holland (*see* p 211). This ferry was built, appropriately, by the Hartlepool-based William Gray & Co, being commissioned on 24 September 1934. The 550grt ferry operated on the Humber until 1974, when she was withdrawn and preserved. Sister ferry PS *Tattershall Castle* is now moored, in a much modified form, as a floating restaurant and bar on the River Thames in London, while the third of the trio, the Glasgow-built PS *Lincoln Castle*, was scrapped in controversial circumstances in 2010.

EAW695745

Morecambe

June 1933

The Lancashire resort of Morecambe was, until the opening of Heysham in 1904, one of the harbours from which passengers could board steamers to the Isle of Man or Ireland. The town became a popular holiday destination, with strong connections to the industrial West Riding of Yorkshire and during the 19th century two piers were constructed for the benefit of holidaymakers and day-trippers.

The foreground of this view is dominated by the town's Central Pier. Construction of this began in 1868 and it opened on 25 March 1869. Extended early in the following decade, the pier eventually extended for 912ft (278m) and was provided with a large pier head that was regularly used by pleasure steamers until the outbreak of World War I. The impressive pavilion on the pier head was added during 1897 and 1898 but the date of this view is significant – on 1 July 1933 the pavilion was destroyed by fire and replaced by a new 2,000-seat structure two years later. Central Pier was closed in 1986 after part of its decking collapsed; further damage occurred in February 1987 when fire damaged the amusement arcade at the shoreward end. Sold in 1990, work began on repairing the structure but a further fire, at Easter 1991, which destroyed the replacement pavilion, led to the pier's demolition the following year. West Pier, which was sited further west and out of this view, has also been demolished.

The two jetties visible to the west of Central Pier were both constructed by the North Western (later Midland) Railway. The earlier of the two was the wooden pier; this was built on behalf of the railway by John Watson (c 1816–90) and was completed in 1850. Work started on the stone jetty in the early 1850s under the supervision of Richard Smallman (1816–73) who had succeeded Watson as the railway's engineer in 1851. Both piers were railway served and a stone-built station was erected on the stone pier; this opened in c 1856 and remained open until 1 September 1904 when services were transferred to Heysham. The building survives as a café. The wooden pier saw passenger trains until the completion of the stone pier.

At the landward end of the two piers can be seen one of the town's most important buildings: the Midland Hotel. This Grade II* listed structure was designed by Oliver Hill (1887–1968) for the London, Midland & Scottish Railway and opened in July 1933 – shortly after the date of this photograph. Built in an Art Deco style, the building featured sculptures by Eric Gill (1882–1940) and murals – now lost – by Eric Ravilious (1903–42). In 1948 ownership of the hotel passed, on nationalisation of the railways, to the British Transport Commission and it was sold in 1952. Run down for many years, a comprehensive programme of restoration and refurbishment, undertaken by architectural renovators Urban Splash, began in 2006 and the hotel reopened in 2008.

Today, part of the bay to the east of the original pier has been reclaimed and a leisure park established on it. The stone pier itself survives – although the wooden one has disappeared – but in a much modified form and now forms part of the sea defences that protect the town from storm damage. The pier itself was damaged during a storm in 1988.

EPW042128

St Katharine's Docks, London
13 July 1993

By the date of this photograph, St Katharine's Dock – the furthest upstream of London's wet docks – had been closed to commercial traffic for more than two decades and was part way through the regeneration project that would see the historic dock converted into a marina with associated residential and mixed-use property surrounding it.

Named after the medieval hospital of St Katharine's (founded in 1148) and the 14th-century church of the same name that had both stood on the site until its redevelopment, the St Katharine's Dock Co obtained an Act in June 1825 to permit the construction of the new dock. The docks were designed by Thomas Telford (1757–1834) and represented his only work in London; he worked with the architect Philip Hardwick (1792–1870) with construction work starting in May 1826. Apart from the hospital and church being demolished, more than 11,300 individuals were also evicted to enable work to be completed on the site.

The West Dock with entrance basin opened on 25 October 1828 and the East Dock in October 1829. In order to ensure a constant supply of water to the entrance lock two Watt steam engines were installed in an engine house on the east side of the lock. Hardwick's original six-storey warehouses were planned in such a way as to minimise the transhipment time from ship to warehouse as the docks were designed to handle high value goods – such as spices and tea – in such a way as to reduce, in Telford's words, 'lighterage and pilferage'. Six brick warehouse blocks were completed by 1852; over the working life of the docks, these warehouses were modified and replaced.

As with the rest of London's dock area, St Katharine's suffered severe damage during World War II. The Victorian warehouses designed by Hardwick and George Aitchison (1825–1910) were hit and much demolition was undertaken of those structures deemed beyond economic repair. In particular, those structures around the East Dock suffered and much of the land they occupied was left derelict until the rebuilding of the 1990s.

The relatively small size of St Katharine's Docks meant that, as ships grew larger and with increased containerisation, the facilities were increasingly inadequate. As a result the docks closed in 1968 and the entire complex was sold to the Greater London Council. In 1969 a lease was granted to Taylor Woodrow for the redevelopment of the site; this was to be the first post-war dock redevelopment in Britain. Work started in 1970; while much of the surviving warehousing was deemed uncommercial and demolished, Warehouse No 1 – now called Ivory House – designed by Aitchison in 1860 was retained along with Dockmaster's House of 1828. The surviving historic structures are now listed Grade II. The first phase covered the West Dock; the East Dock was completed between 1995 and 1997, after this photograph was taken. Still extant when the photograph was taken was the wrought iron footbridge designed by Thomas Rhodes (1789–1868) and built in October 1829 that was located between the East Dock and the entrance basin. This was to survive *in situ* until 1993 when it was relocated and conserved. Originally designed to retract to permit ships to enter the East Dock, this facility is no longer operational in its new site. The growth of leisure sailing has given a number of docks and ports such as St Katharine's a future use and has ensured their survival.

EAW622105

Sandown Pier
August 1933

The use of seaside piers as landing stages for pleasure cruises was a feature of many traditional seaside resorts. This view sees the PS *Southsea* at Sandown on the Isle of Wight in 1933.

Although the construction of a pier was first considered in the 1860s, it was not until 1874 that the Sandown Pier Co Ltd was granted powers under the Pier & Harbour Order to construct a pier of 640ft (195.1m) in length. Designed by W Binns and built by London-based contractors Jukes & Coulson, the new pier was opened on 29 May 1878. However, the structure was only 360ft (109.7m) when opened as a result of the owner's financial problems. In 1884 an Act was obtained to extend the pier, but the Sandown Pier Co was unable to raise the finance and the company was wound up following a decision made in October 1885. Ownership of the pier passed to the Sandown Pier Extension Co Ltd the following year. The new owners obtained powers to extend the pier to 875ft (266.7m) in 1893 and work, designed by Theodore Ridley Saunders (1850–1929) and undertaken by the Southampton-based contractors Roe & Grace, commenced the next year. The pier extension, along with the landing stage and pier head pavilion as seen in this 1933 view, were all opened amidst much celebration on 17 September 1895.

The PS *Southsea* was one of two paddle steamers built for the Southern Railway by the Govan-based Fairfield Shipping & Engineering Co Ltd and completed in 1930. The *Southsea* was Yard No 641 and was launched on 2 April 1930; sister vessel, the PS *Whippingham*, was Yard No 642. The two vessels were designed primarily for use on the Portsmouth to Ryde ferry service. With a grt of 825, the two were claimed to be the 'largest and most luxurious excursion steamers on the South Coast'.

As shown in the photograph, alongside their regular duties, both were used regularly for excursion trips. The two paddle steamers were both requisitioned for military service in World War II and were both involved in the evacuation of British and allied troops from Dunkirk in June 1940. The *Southsea* was sunk by a mine and lost with all hands on 16 February 1941 when undertaking minesweeping duties in the mouth of the River Tyne. The *Whippingham* was to survive the war, having also served at D-Day in June 1944, and was finally scrapped in Antwerp in May 1963.

The pier at Sandown remains, although today it is radically different to the scene presented in the 1933 image. Shortly after the date of the photograph, a new pavilion at the shore end of the pier was constructed; this was opened by Lord Jellicoe on 23 October 1934. Used primarily for much of its life as a theatre, the building was severely damaged by fire in 1989. Reopened in June 1990, the theatre finally closed in 1997. The rebuilt structure survives, however, providing a range of leisure activities.

During World War II the pier was requisitioned by the military and suffered damage. Compensation for the damage eventually was paid and between 1950 and 1954 a new concrete landing stage was constructed. In 1970, following the condemnation of the pier beyond the theatre as unsafe two years earlier, work began on its restoration. The pier head pavilion illustrated in the 1933 view was, however, to be demolished in 1971 as a result of a fire, with the actual pier being reopened officially on 22 July 1973. The pier remains open for its entire 875ft (266.7m) length and the landing stage still sees occasional use.

EPW043023

Southend Pier

6 July 1948

With a length of 7,080ft (2,158m), Southend Pier is the longest in the world and despite threats of closure and damage from fires and collapse remains today a popular destination for those enjoying the Essex coast.

The first pier at Southend was a wooden structure built following the passage of an Act of Parliament on 14 May 1829. The first, 600ft (182.9m), section was opened by June 1830; it was tripled in length for the 1833 season to permit its use by vessels at low tide and extended further, to 7,000ft (2,133.6m; making it the longest in Europe) in 1846. In 1873 the pier was sold to the local authority and in 1887 the new owners decided to replace the pier with an iron structure. The engineers for the new pier, on which work started during 1887, were James William Brunlees (1816–92) and John Wolfe Barry (1836–1918) and the contractors were Arrol Brothers of Glasgow. The pier, although opened in part in 1887, was not completed until 1889. Such was the pier's popularity that an extension was proposed, the work being completed in November 1897 by the contractors Murdock & Cameron. In 1908 an upper deck was added to the then pier head before, in 1927, a further concrete extension was constructed by Peter Lind & Co Ltd. The new pier head, with its three levels, also incorporates an RNLI station. This is known as the Prince George Extension after Prince George, Duke of Kent, who formally opened it on 8 July 1929. Visible running between the shore and the original pier head is the famous pier railway; the original wooden pier had employed a horse tramway but during 1890 and 1891 the new iron pier was supplied with an electric railway. The rolling stock seen in this view was replaced in 1949.

Moored to the pier head is PS *Queen of Thanet*. This 792grt vessel had originally been built in 1916 by W Hamilton & Co of Port Glasgow as a minesweeper for the Royal Navy. Serving as HMS *Melton,* the ship was laid up after World War I before being sold for scrap in 1927; sold by the breakers to the New Medway Steam Packet Co two years later and renamed the *Queen of Thanet*, the steamer was operated along the Thames estuary. Requisitioned for minesweeping duties in 1939, the vessel, based at Dover, made four return crossings to Dunkirk during Operation Dynamo of May/June 1940. At the cessation of hostilities, the ship was returned to her pre-war owners and is seen here during her last summer serving passengers on the Thames. Sold to the Southampton, Isle of Wight & South of England Royal Mail Steam Packet Co – better known as Red Funnel – and renamed PS *Solent Queen*, the ship made her maiden voyage for her new owners on 5 June 1949, Whit Sunday. Unfortunately, *Solent Queen* was seriously damaged by fire on 22 June 1951 and was sold for scrap, making her final voyage to a shipbreaker at Dover in October the same year.

Although the pier survives, it has changed significantly since the 1948 view. In 1959 a fire destroyed the pavilion at the shore end; this was replaced by a bowling alley three years later. This itself was damaged by fire in 1977; this followed a fire in 1976 that seriously damaged the pier head. The decline in the traditional British seaside holiday led to the threat of closure in 1980, but this was averted and funding was secured. With restoration largely completed, the pier faced a new challenge in June 1986 with a 70ft (21.3m) section being demolished when a small tanker, the MV *Kingsabbey*, collided with the structure. In 1995 a further fire destroyed the bowling alley and in 2005 the original pier head was also destroyed by fire. The 1929 pier head was redeveloped in 2000 and in 2012 a new pavilion – Culture Centre – was added, designed by Sprunt Architects and with the Kier Group as main contractors.

The tradition of paddle steamers operating summer season tours remains, with the *Waverley*, promoted as being the last sea-going paddle steamer, still offering coastal cruises. Although based in Glasgow, the *Waverley* makes regular calls to ports and harbours in England.

EAW017029

Eddystone Lighthouse
29 April 1948

The approaches to Plymouth from the south-west were notoriously treacherous, dominated by the Eddystone rocks, a reef lying some 18km from land. The threat that these rocks posed, particularly as the port of Plymouth became increasingly important during the late 17th century, resulted in the construction of a lighthouse.

The lighthouse shown here was the fourth to be built on the site. The first was that designed by Henry Winstanley (1644–1703), which was started in 1696 and first lit on 14 November 1698. Constructed originally in wood, the structure was largely encased in stone during 1699. This structure was swept away, however, during the Great Storm of 27 November 1703, killing its staff of five along with Winstanley himself, who was present to supervise more improvements.

The second lighthouse, commissioned by Captain John Lovett (who had been granted a 99-year lease in 1705 and who was allowed by an Act of Parliament to charge passing ships a toll), was designed by John Rudyard (1650–c 1718). The new light was first lit in 1708 and the new structure, built with a core of stone and concrete encased in wood, was completed the following year. The second lighthouse was to survive until 2 December 1755 when fire engulfed the lantern.

The third lighthouse, the foundations of which are visible in this 1948 view, was designed by John Smeaton (1724–92). Work commenced in 1756 under resident engineer Josiah Jessop (1710–60) and the new light was first lit on 16 October 1759. Smeaton's design, based upon his observations of an oak tree, and construction were pioneering. The granite blocks used were carefully cut and trial fitted at the yard at Millbay, in Plymouth, before being shipped to the reef. The design was to ensure a low centre of gravity and also to see the waves deflected from the building in heavy seas. The mortar used, based around lime and pozzolana, was developed by Smeaton to set in water.

Smeaton's lighthouse was built on the same section of reef as the two earlier structures; however, erosion of the rock beneath the lighthouse resulted in the structure becoming unstable, despite efforts to secure it, and the decision was made in the late 1870s to replace it with the fourth lighthouse – the structure that is shown here.

The new building was designed by Sir James Nicholas Douglass (1826–98), who was Trinity House's Engineer-in-Chief between 1863 and 1892. Douglass's lighthouse was almost three times the height – 161ft (49m) as opposed to 59ft (18m) – of Smeaton's but the method of construction – the testing of the granite blocks onshore before actual placement – was similar. The then Duke of Edinburgh laid a ceremonial stone on 19 August 1879 and the building was topped out on 1 June 1881. The new lantern came into use on 18 May 1882.

Following the completion of the new lighthouse, the bulk of Smeaton's building was dismantled and re-erected on Plymouth Hoe; the lower levels, however, were found to be too strong for demolition and were left *in situ*. When recorded in 1948, the lighthouse was still fully staffed. In 1982 the light was automated – the first of Trinity House's offshore lighthouses to be so treated – and remains operational. The only significant change to the structure as seen here is the addition of a helicopter pad above the lantern to facilitate access by maintenance crews. No longer do Trinity House vessels make the hazardous crossing to deliver supplies – a feature that was regularly shown on the BBC children's programme *Blue Peter* in the 1960s and 1970s.

EAW015156

Needles Lighthouse
17 April 1949

The western approaches to the Isle of Wight are marked by a line of three stacks of chalk known as the Needles; the feature is named after a fourth stack, located between the two more northerly existing stacks, that was nicknamed Lot's wife, after the Biblical story in which the wife of Lot was turned into a pillar of salt as she looked back on the destruction of Sodom. Pillar-like, this fourth chalk stack collapsed following a storm in 1764.

Just to the south-west of the Needles is a bank of shifting shingle known as the Pebbles; this was a hazard to shipping and the first lighthouse to protect the coast at this point was one erected on the cliff overhanging Scratchell's Bay on the Isle of Wight itself, which was first used on 29 September 1786. The original lighthouse was designed by the architect Richard Jupp (1728–99), surveyor of the East India Company, following pressure from merchants on Trinity House.

The first lighthouse, however, being some 144m above sea level, was prone to be obscured when there was sea mist or low cloud and so, in the mid-19th century, the decision was taken to construct a replacement. The Scottish engineer James Walker (1781–1862) was employed to undertake the work; he had had previous experience working with lighthouses, being involved with Start Point in Devon in 1836, Wolf Rock between 1840 and 1862, and Bishop Rock Lighthouse in 1858. The work at the Needles occupied him between 1856 and 1859.

The structure as seen here was unlike many other lighthouses built in exposed positions, such as that at Eddystone, in that the new lighthouse at the Needles was not tapered but constructed in granite to a constant 21ft (6.4m) diameter. The foundations, which are sunk four feet into the chalk on a platform created on the chalk by dynamite, are constructed of concrete and faced by stone; the walls of the structure are 3ft 6in (1.1m) thick at the base tapering to 2ft 0in (0.6m) at the top. The balcony is some 23ft (7m) in diameter and the lantern is about 80ft (24.4m) above the high tide level. The new lighthouse, which cost £20,000, was first lit in 1859.

The Needles lighthouse is still operational; since the view was taken in 1949, however, there have been some changes. It was one of the final three lighthouses to be fully manned with the last permanent staff leaving on 8 December 1994. Prior to that date, a helipad was installed above the lantern in 1987 and the glass lantern was replaced seven years later when mains electricity was provided. More significantly, from June to August 2010, a project to underpin the structure was undertaken by the contractors Nuttall John Martin. The work involved the construction of a trench around the existing structure and the insertion of concrete to counter the threat posed by the erosion of the chalk.

EAW022202

HMS *Warspite*
1947

Towards the end of the 19th century and into the first decade of the 20th, Britain and Germany became engaged in a race for naval supremacy. During this period the size, armaments and speed of warships all increased dramatically. Britain led the way with the completion of HMS *Dreadnought* in 1906; this new warship's radical design led to its imitation by other navies although Britain attempted to maintain its position through its policy of ensuring that the Royal Navy retained a strength equal to that of the next two most powerful navies combined. As part of this policy, six 'Queen Elizabeth'-class battleships were planned, of which five were completed. These were the first battleships in the world to be fitted with 15in guns.

HMS *Warspite* (pennant number 03) was the second of the class to be constructed, being laid down at Devonport on 31 October 1912 and launched on 26 November 1913. Commissioned on 8 March 1915, *Warspite* was to see service at the Battle of Jutland on 31 May 1916 in which the battleship sustained serious damage, which required two months of repair subsequently in Rosyth. *Warspite* underwent considerable reconstruction at Portsmouth between 1934 and 1937, during which time a hangar and crane to enable the battleship to carry up to four aircraft were fitted.

During World War II *Warspite* saw service on the British landing at Narvik, on Arctic convoys, and in the Mediterranean, where she was involved in the battles of Calabria, Taranto and Matapan before suffering serious damage during the defence of Crete. Repaired in the USA, *Warspite* then spent time in the Indian Ocean and the Mediterranean again, before returning to home waters where, after further repair, she was the first warship to start the shelling of Hitler's Atlantic Wall on the morning of 6 June 1944. Her final action was on 1 November 1944 when she shelled targets on Walcheren Island.

Although there were proposals for her preservation, in July 1946 the decision was made to scrap the battleship and she sailed to Portsmouth for her guns and other equipment to be removed. On 19 April 1947 she sailed, under tow, from Portsmouth on her final journey to Faslane for scrap; unfortunately, four days later, in a storm, with no power and with the tow ropes having failed, *Warspite* was forced to drop anchor. This failed to hold, and *Warspite* was driven on to the coast. Initially refloated, the battleship was again to ground a short distance further on in Prussia Cove, to the east of Marazion in Cornwall. This is the scene that the Aerofilms photographer has captured shortly after the incident. Work started to dismantle the wreck *in situ* and, by 1957, the warship had largely disappeared.

EAW005977

Wreck on the Duddon Sands
15 October 1948

The SS *Anastasia* ran aground of Walney Island on 25 December 1946 while en route from Barrow-in-Furness to Kilkeel in Northern Ireland. The coaster had only recently changed hands and had been renamed after her new owner, S Anastasi of Barry in South Wales. The 283grt coaster is believed to have broken down off St Bees Head before drifting onto the sand at Walney Island; there was no loss of life among the crew but efforts to refloat the ship failed and she was thus declared a total loss.

By the date of her beaching, the coaster was almost 40 years old, having been constructed in the Clyde shipyard of Scott & Sons in 1909 as Yard No 213. Owned originally by John S Monks and named SS *J & J Monks*, the coaster was 130ft (39.6m) in length, 23ft (7m) in breadth and was fitted with a two-cylinder coal-fired compound engine. It had been used for the shipment of manganese ore from Porth Ysgo in Wales.

Recorded by the Aerofilms photographer less than two years after her beaching, the sea was already starting to take its toll on the rusting hulk; more than 65 years on, however, the remains of the *Anastasia* can still be seen at low water.

EAW019741

Wreck on the Goodwin Sands
9 November 1948

The Goodwin Sands, a 16km-long sandbank situated some 9km off the Kent coast to the east of Deal, represents one of the most significant hazards to shipping in the English Channel. Although protected historically by two lighthouses on the mainland, of which only the northern one is still operational, and by a lightship today on the easternmost extremity, over the centuries the Goodwin Sands have claimed in excess of 2,000 ships. This scene is believed to record one of these lost ships: the SS *Luray Victory*, which came to grief during the evening of 30 January 1946 with all 49 of the crew being rescued by the Walmer lifeboat *Charles Dibdin* under her coxswain Freddie Upton.

The *Luray Victory* was one of the 'Liberty' ships, freighters that were mass produced in American shipyards during World War II to replace the vast amount of merchant shipping sunk by the U-Boats during the Battle of the Atlantic and to facilitate the vast movement of food, raw materials and military equipment required. This particular ship had been built by the California

Shipbuilding Corporation at the company's yard in Los Angeles, being completed in 1944. She was some 455ft (138.7m) in length with a beam of 62ft (18.9m) and had a grt of 7,612. By the date of her foundering, she was owned by the Black Diamond Steamship Co and was en route from Baltimore, on the eastern seaboard of the USA, to Bremerhaven in Germany. One of the contributory factors to her running aground was the lack of a pilot; according to the American War Shipping Administration there was no need to take a pilot on board as the Channel was deemed relatively free of dangers. Unfortunately, the weather conditions that evening caused the *Luray Victory* to miss the deep water channel and thus end up running aground.

As with the *Anastasi*, the wreck of the *Luray Victory* could still be seen at the time of writing, although how much is visible is dependent upon the shifting sands for which the Goodwin Sands are notorious.

EAW020497

Dunwich
4 July 1949

The impact of coastal erosion can be far-reaching and perhaps no community has suffered as dramatically as Dunwich on the Suffolk coast. Believed to have been the capital of the kingdom of East Anglia and, in the period up to the end of the 13th century, an international port to rival London, today the village of Dunwich has a population of fewer than 1,000 and much of the once large settlement is now under the waves.

A significant urban centre at the time of the Domesday Book of 1086, Dunwich had a harbour at the estuary of the Dunwich River; however, a shift in the river saw the estuary shift northwards to Walberswick and Southwold leading to a decline in the harbour. As the harbour declined, so too did the town and its sea defences were consequently allowed to deteriorate. From the late 13th century a number of tidal surges ravaged the Suffolk coast and caused the loss of much of the town. The first of these occurred on 1 January 1286 with two more in February and December the following year. Three storms in the 14th century – in 1328, 1347 and, finally, in 1362 – saw the bulk of the medieval town, including eight churches, destroyed. The process of erosion continued thereafter with the church of All Saints disappearing under the waves during the period from 1904 to 1919.

The view, taken shortly after the end of World War II, shows the wartime coastal defences constructed to prevent any possible German invasion. In the distance can be seen a radar tower while in the foreground can be seen a pillbox and a line of concrete blocks installed to prevent the easy egress of tanks from the beach.

Slightly inland can be seen the site of a six-pound gun emplacement.

In the years since the photograph of Dunwich was taken in 1949, much effort has gone into the protection of the coastline south of Southwold. The consequence is that the coastline at Dunwich has not retreated as much as elsewhere and much of the scene illustrated in this 1949 photograph, including the remains of the 13th century Greyfriars Priory situated to the south of the surviving settlement, is still standing.

The threat of erosion, however, remains significant along many stretches of the coast as a consequence both of rising sea levels and of stormier weather. While sea defences, as at Dunwich, may well result in erosion being reduced, elsewhere the encroaching sea – as on the north Norfolk coast around Happisburgh or on the North Yorkshire coastline around Whitby – can lead to significant losses. In reality, the entire coastline cannot be defended and, in certain areas, 'managed retreat' and the re-creation of traditional salt marshes will see a very different landscape in the future. One of the consequences of this will be the disappearance of historic structures and sites of archaeological interest; the process that saw many of Dunwich's medieval structures washed away will be a feature of the evolution of the English coastline in the future. Just as it was the presence of the sea that was a critical point in the establishment of settlements, so too it will be the sea that will see their destruction.

EAW024304

Felixstowe
9 February 1953

On the night of 31 January and morning of 1 February 1953, Britain was struck by one of the most destructive floods of recent centuries. A combination of a high spring tide and a severe gale resulted in a storm surge heading southwards through the North Sea with, in places, the water level up to more than 18ft (5.5m) above the mean sea level. Coastal defences in Britain and in Western Europe were overwhelmed with some 2,551 people killed, the majority in the Netherlands. The trail of destruction started between Scotland and Northern Ireland with the sinking of the ferry MV *Princess Victoria* sailing from Stranraer to Larne with the loss of 133 lives.

In an age before most houses had telephones and when other means of communication were much more restricted, there were few means of warning coastal communities of the threat that the storm surge posed with the result that the storm moved inexorably and fatally southwards. Among the places most severely affected was Felixstowe on the Suffolk coast, where 38 people died when the prefabricated wooden houses in the town's west were inundated. The Aerofilms photographer has recorded the site of this destruction more than a week after the actual event.

In all, 1,600km of the UK's coastline suffered damage, with over 960sq km of low-lying land flooded. Some 24,000 properties were damaged and 30,000 evacuated. Worst hit was Canvey Island where 58 were killed, and 37 died at Jaywick on the Essex coast. Flooding also affected the East End of London and the threat posed to the capital by a storm surge was one of the factors that lay behind the construction of the Thames Barrier.

EAW048298

Fiddlers Reach, River Thames
8 November 1964

The River Thames, with its myriad docks and wharves, was one of the busiest rivers in the world; serious accidents, however, were relatively uncommon although not unknown as evinced by the sinking of the *Marchioness*, a pleasure steamer, that sank on 19 August 1989 with the loss of 51 lives following a collision with the dredger *Bowbelle*. An earlier collision, described at the time by the Port of London Authority as the worst since World War II occurred at 1.52am on 27 October 1964 when the East German cargo vessel the MV *Magdeburg*, built in 1958, collided with the Japanese-owned *Yamashiro Maru* near the Grays side of the river at Broadness Point.

The *Magdeburg* was loaded with a batch of 42 buses that had been built by Leyland and were destined, theoretically, for Havana in Cuba. The East German vessel was sailing downstream from Dagenham with the Japanese vessel heading upstream towards the Royal Docks when the collision occurred, with the *Magdeburg* holed below the waterline. The crew of 54, including three stewardesses, as well as two passengers were all recovered safely from the stricken vessel, although the buses were all written off as a result of the salt water. The buses were part of a contract to supply 400 45-seat buses to Cuba for $10 million plus over $1 million of spare parts signed by Leyland in January 1964. However, this deal flew in the face of the US government's desire to impose trade sanctions on Fidel Castro's Cuba. Leyland's decision to employ an East German freighter for the shipment was symptomatic of the problems that the company had in trying to get a Western shipping line to breach the US sanctions.

The Aerofilms photographer recorded the site just over a week after the sinking of the 6,629-grt *Magdeburg*. The salvage of the freighter proved to be complex, with the first attempt in March 1965 failing. The freighter was eventually salvaged at the second attempt in July 1965 and was repaired at Tilbury. However, the repaired freighter was not to survive much longer; it sank in the Atlantic shortly after being repaired.

Although not queried at the time, there was evidence that emerged from the East German archives that suggested that all was not quite as accidental as the collision appeared. This seemed to suggest that the sinking was part of a CIA plot to scupper any trade that might breach the US-imposed boycott of Cuba. Whether this is correct or not is uncertain; it's certainly the case, however, that the US authorities took a dim view of the Leyland contract.

EAW143996

Wreck at Fox Cove, Cornwall
25 September 1969

With its rocky coves and treacherous seas and currents, the Cornish coast represents one of the most dangerous areas for shipping in the British Isles – and that's even when the crew know fully where they are. On 12 May 1969 an elderly British tanker – the *Hemsley I* – was to come to grief at Fox Cove, Porthcothan, about six nautical miles south-west of Padstow and it is the wreck of this vessel that the Aerofilms cameraman caught some six months later.

At the time of the tanker's sinking, the vessel was on its way from Liverpool to Antwerp for scrapping. The weather conditions were poor, with a heavy fog, and it was reported at the time, and subsequently confirmed in the Board of Trade wreck report, that the crew of the *Helmsley I* had lost its way, believing the vessel to be south of the Lizard rather than off the north Cornish coast. When the distress call was issued, this stated that the ship had foundered on the Lizard and initially all the rescue efforts were concentrated on the south coast; it was only after the search area was extended that the stricken ship was found and the crew saved. Fortunately, there were no casualties but both the captain and first mate were to be blamed by the wreck report.

The *Hemsley I* had had an interesting career. Built originally by the Tyne Iron Shipbuilding Co of Willington on Quay, Howdon, Northumberland and launched on 23 June 1916, the ship had originally been built as a harbour oiler to the Royal Navy as RFA *Scotol*. This was one of 18 members of the 'Creosol' '1,000-ton' class of tanker built for the Royal Navy's new RFA service during World War I. Steam powered, the *Scotol* remained with the Royal Navy until July 1947 when the tanker was transferred for disposal. Acquired by Hemsley Bell Ltd of Southampton and renamed, the tanker spent the next 20 years on a variety of work in and around British waters.

Following the tanker's foundering, there were initially hopes that the ship could be salvaged; these, however, proved over-optimistic, although some of the wreck was salvaged *in situ* with a temporary road created for recovery vehicles on the cliff top. More than 40 years after the *Hemsley I* foundered, there remained at the time of writing traces of the wreck at Fox Cove.

EAW200562

Woolwich
1992

The 1953 floods highlighted the risk to the East Coast of a tidal surge through the North Sea and the vulnerability of the low-lying land around the Thames estuary to flooding. With rising sea levels, a consequence of global warming, allied to the gradual sinking of southern England, the potential threat of flooding to the tidal stretch of the river has increased considerably since the end of World War II. The Thames is tidal as far as Tedington Lock, to the west of London, and so this threat of flooding affects the whole of central London.

From the late 1950s onwards plans were developed for the construction of some form of barrier to protect London. Although initial plans were rejected, in 1969 a scheme to construct a barrier at Woolwich Reach was agreed upon. Based upon a concept by Charles Draper, who had been experimenting with rotating cylinders since the 1950s, the detailed design work was undertaken by Rendel, Palmer & Tritton with construction starting in 1974. The barrier was built by a consortium of Tarmac Construction, Costain and Hollandsche Beton Maatschappij, with the actual gates being produced on the River Tees by Cleveland Bridge UK Ltd.

Construction work was completed in October 1982 at a cost of £535 million, with a further £100 million spent further downstream on additional flood defences. The Thames Barrier was officially opened by HM Queen Elizabeth II on 8 May 1984 and protects some 125sq km of central London. The finished barrier stretches across a 570-yard (520m) stretch of the river and comprises nine concrete piers with 10 gates. There are six channels for navigation and four that are non-navigable. The piers are founded on steel cofferdams built into solid chalk some 15m below river level. The four central rising sector plates weigh 3,300 tonnes each and span 61.5m; the two flanking sector plates span 31.5m each.

When originally conceived, it was anticipated that the Thames Barrier would be required to operate two or three times per annum; by the middle of the second decade of the 21st century use was running at three times that annually on average (excluding the regular monthly closure for testing). Originally expected to have a design life that would see it in use until about 2030, it is now expected to see operation through until 2070, although, with the rise in sea levels expected, its effectiveness will decline from 2030 onwards unless remedial action is taken. For the future, there is the possibility of a second barrier being constructed further downstream as part of the Thames Hub project.

EAW572435

Finale – Ramsgate
11 September 2003

We started this survey of England's maritime heritage with a view of Ramsgate harbour in 1920; it seems appropriate to conclude with a view taken more than 80 years later that shows how dramatic the changes wrought during the 20th century have been.

The early history of the development of Ramsgate is narrated on p xv; here the old harbour is now dominated by the Royal Harbour Marina. This was developed from 1976 and now offers some 700 berths. The ferry terminal is built on reclaimed land but, at the time of writing was unused following the bankruptcy of TransEuropa Ferries in April 2013.

Seen at the ferry terminal is the MV *Larkspur*, one of the ferries employed by TransEuropa Ferries before the company's demise, on the route from Ramsgate to Ostend in Belgium. The *Larkspur* was originally built in Bremerhaven, Germany, and was completed in 1976 for operation between Gedser in Denmark and Travemunde in Germany when the ferry was named *Gedser*. After passing through a number of hands (and with its name changing with each new owner), the ferry was acquired by TransEuropa Ferries in 1999. The *Larkspur* had previously operated between Ramsgate and Dunkirk between 1988 and 1999 when operated by Sally Line. Sold after the collapse of TransEuropa Ferries, and renamed initially *Larks* and then *Luck Star,* the ferry was at the time of writing laid up out of use at Piaraeus in Greece.

The growth of leisure sailing, as evinced by the scale of the marina here, is one of the great changes in the use of traditional docks and harbours over the past 50 years. Leisure, in another guise (that of the greater number of people who travel abroad for holidays), has also been evident since the end of World War II. The facilities that these travellers require – particularly now that most will be travelling by car rather than by train as would have been the case 60 years ago – has resulted in massive investment in ferry terminals despite the opening in the mid-1990s of the Channel Tunnel.

EAW696658

Bibliography

Ashmore, Owen 1982 *Industrial Archaeology of North-west England*. Manchester: Manchester University Press

Associated British Ports 2009 *Port of Southampton: Master Plan 2009–2030*. Southampton: Associated British Ports

Atkins, Tony 2014 *Great Western Docks & Marine*. Manchester: Noodle Books

Awdry, Christopher 1990 *Encyclopaedia of British Railway Companies*. Wellingborough: Patrick Stephens Ltd

Carradice, Phil 2009 *Nautical Training Ships: An Illustrated History*. Stroud: Amberley Publishing

Clegg, W Paul 1987 *Docks and Ports: 2 London*. London: Ian Allan Ltd

Coad, Jonathan 1982 *Historic Architecture of Chatham Dockyard, 1700–1850*. London: National Maritime Museum

Conway-Jones, Hugh 2009 *Gloucester Docks: An Historical Guide*. Lydney: Black Dwarf Publications

Cossons, Neil and Jenkins, Martin 2011 *Liverpool Seaport City*. Hersham: Ian Allan Publishing

Course, Captain A G 1964 *Docks and Harbours of Britain*. London: Ian Allan Ltd

Curl, James Stevens 2006 *A Dictionary of Architecture and Landscape*, 2 edn. Oxford: Oxford University Press

Danielson, Richard 1996 *So Strong and So Fair*. Liskeard: Maritime Publications

Drummond, Ian 2013 *Southern Rails on Southampton Docks*. Leeds: Holne Publishing

Easdown, Martin and Sage, Linda 2011 *Piers of Hampshire & the Isle of Wight*. Stroud: Amberley Publishing

Fleming, Robin 2011 *Britain after Rome: The Fall and Rise 400–1070*. London: Penguin

Foyle, Andrew 2009 *Pevsner Architectural Guides: Bristol*, rev reprint. London: Yale University Press

Greenway, Ambrose 1981 *A Century of Cross-Channel Passenger Ferries*. London: Ian Allan Ltd

Greenway, Ambrose 1986 *A Century of North Sea Passenger Steamers*. London: Ian Allan Ltd

Hadfield, Charles 1959 *British Canals: An Illustrated History*, 3 edn. London: Phoenix House

Jarvis, Adrian 1988 *Docks of the Mersey*. London: Ian Allan Ltd

Kurlansky, Mark 1999 *Cod: A biography of the fish that changed the world*. London: Vintage

Lenton, H T and Colledge, J J 1973 *Warships of World War II*, 2 edn. London: Ian Allan Ltd

MacDougall, Philip 1983 *Chatham Built Warships since 1860*. Liskeard: Maritime Books

Marden, Dave 2012 *London's Dock Railways Part 1: The Isle of Dogs and Tilbury*. Southampton: Kestrel Railway Books

Marden, Dave 2013 *London's Dock Railways Part 2: The Royal Docks, North Woolwich and Silvertown*. Southampton: Kestrel Railway Books

Marriott, Leo 1983 *Royal Navy Frigates 1945–1983*. London: Ian Allan Ltd

Marshall, John 1969–1972 *The Lancashire & Yorkshire Railway*, 3 volumes. Newton Abbot: David & Charles

Pevsner, Sir Nikolaus, *et al* 1951 onwards 'Buildings of England' series. London: Penguin and Yale University Press

Port of Bristol Authority 1947 *Port of Bristol: Official Handbook of the Port of Bristol Authority*. Bristol: F G Warne Ltd

Quick, Michael 2009 *Railway Passenger Stations in Great Britain: A Chronology*, 3 edn. Oxford: Railway & Canal Historical Society

Ritchie, L A (ed) 1992 *The Shipbuilding Industry: A Guide to Historical Records*. Manchester: Manchester University Press

Sharples, Joseph 2004 *Pevsner Architectural Guides: Liverpool*. London: Yale University Press

Tomlinson, William Weaver with introduction by Hoole, Ken 1987 *Tomlinson's North Eastern Railway*, 3 edn. Newton Abbot: David & Charles

Vincent, Mike 1983 *Reflections on the Portishead Branch*. Poole: Oxford Publishing Co

Williams, David L 1983 *Docks and Ports: Southampton*. London: Ian Allan Ltd

Worth, Jack 1984 *British Warships since 1845: Part 4 Minesweepers*. Liskeard: Maritime Books

Location index